Reagan Jackson is the most important writer you might not have read yet. If a cat has nine lives, Jackson's living ten. She's in a Veracruz hotel room watching the Ferguson protests unfold on CNN. She's in Seattle's CHOP district in the summer of 2020 leading a Black healing event. If she's not starting up a study abroad program for students of color or summing up with stunning clarity the epic drain of a "well intended white person" (see page 65!), she's learning to box, dance burlesque, and surf. And whatever country Jackson travels to or whatever theatre, comedy show, or lecture she attends, she listens, introducing us to voices we don't often hear who speak of oppression, liberation, and hope. Reagan Jackson's stories in *Still True: The Evolution of an Unexpected Journalist* drop us right onto the fault lines where plates are converging, where our culture—our very world— is being forged into something new. And with brilliant insight, candor, and vulnerability, Jackson shares the moments with us. We are there— right there—with her, as she shows us with precision and grace who we are and who we have yet to become. ~Theo Pauline Nestor, author of *Writing Is My Drink*

The great Robin Kelley calls *Still True* "an abolitionist take on space and power—a desire to make the space we call earth habitable and bountiful for all life," a beautiful description that rings 100% true. The intensely local pieces uplifted me, depressed me, but I add an enthusiastic thank you to Reagan Jackson for reminding us of the value—for People of Color, especially for Black Americans—of knowing the world beyond the USA. Jackson's take on the world is lifesaving, one of the many gifts of this fine book's authentic journalism. ~Nell Irvin Painter, author of *Old in Art School: A Memoir of Starting Over* and Edwards Professor of American History, Emerita, Princeton University

In *Still True: The Evolution of an Unexpected Journalist*, Reagan Jackson bears powerful witness to a city she aims to shape into a truer and more human reflection of its peoples. Her essays provide necessary testimony that shores up our collective resolve in perilous times. ~Kristen Millares Young, author of *Subduction*

In a world desperate for the space/time to respond to change and to reflect on deep continuities, Reagan Jackson's *Still True* offers a glimpse of new and renewed forms of connection. Like a mixtape she weaves an emotional and intellectual mosaic out of the fragments of though-in-the-moment. Formally innovative, aware of the ancestral resonances, and just plain smart, this is a book that testifies to a mind and spirit helping us think our way to something beyond the mess we're in. ~Craig Werner, Author of *A Change Is Gonna Come: Music, Race & the Soul of America*

Never was there a better time than right now to read Reagan Jackson's masterful body of work in *Still True: The Evolution of an Unexpected Journalist*. What you read in her collection of articles is what happens when a Black journalist does not compromise their identity to do their job. Jackson is a reluctant journalist but we should all be grateful for her contribution to the industry. Her commitment to tell the stories of communities with them and not about them is everything that is missing in our ecosystem today. The book is an examination of life in the Pacific Northwest for BIPOC. Jackson opens the curtain to reveal the impacts of gentrification, economic inequality and the struggle for #BlackLivesMatter in a region where allyship means making room for white people in all spaces. Jackson also masterfully writes about the Black experience abroad and why it's necessary for Black people to become globally engaged. Finally, Jackson excavates her own truths about her body, her beauty and healing from trauma as resistance. Jackson is a talented and gifted writer whose words are moving, challenging, and needed. ~Sonya Nichole Green, journalist

This book is evidence of how Reagan Jackson is changing journalism for the better. In this book Reagan Jackson is showing journalism what its future needs to look like. You're welcome. Every journalist should read this book. Reading this book affirmed so many of the feelings I've had about the rules of "good journalism:" the myth of objectivity, the bias against first person. Good journalism for who? This book is not only an innovative form of autobiography that tracks Jackson's life through her coverage of Seattle news, but it's a welcomed foray into what is possible for the field of journalism. ~Virgie Tovar, author and activist

Still True: The Evolution of an Unexpected Journalist is a vibrantly, herstorical, rageful ritual of essays. Each ritual a gift "…for Black people to come together in the privacy of our own communities to laugh, and cry, to dance and love and enjoy." It will be difficult for readers to choose their favorite experiential track from Jackson's mixtape of essays but it won't be hard for readers to perform each ritual, hands holding hearts first, and profusely nodding along. ~Anastacia-Reneé, Writer, Educator and Archivist

Reagan Jackson's mixtape of articles passionately personifies black culture and values, providing intimate experiences of racism, inequity and the self. Reagan takes us across the world, delving into political injustices and complicated cultural experiences; and into her neighborhood, the gentrification encroaching, the resistance on her lawn, and the powerful voices of the undervalued community that she is a part. There is a rawness, an openness to Reagan's words that draw forth compassion, making one feel the humanity and connection she is so fervently trying to foster. Reagan Jackson's *Still True: The Unexpected Evolution of a Journalist* creates an understanding not only of the systemic issues that plague us but of the compassion that is needed to change the tides that be and to heal the psyche that endures. Reagan compels us to be better, to do better. ~Jini Palmer, musician, filmmaker, and creator of Seattle Town Hall's *In the Moment* podcast.

When Reagan Jackson writes, be prepared for straight talk. She does not hold back when talking about race, black lives, gender, white privilege, police accountability, the kind of hot button issues that make people uncomfortable. Like it or not, that's a good thing. Reagan lives and works in Seattle's south end, where people of color are struggling to live because of gentrification, rising property taxes along with dual pandemics of racism and now, Covid-19 that has revealed even more the racial disparities in America today. Our nation is being pushed like never before to see its original sin of inequality as the coronavirus devastates communities of color. As you read her stories, you will see a changing Seattle, a majority white city where people of color are still struggling to have a voice, and where a new kind of multi-media journalist and writer like Reagan Jackson are not just covering a community but living there to fully understand the changes underway. What you will find in Reagan's collection is powerful, and at times, humorous writing about everyday herself, life, human foibles, complicated issues, race, justice, injustice, and hope for a better Seattle and world. Keep on kicking ass, Reagan! ~Enrique Cerna, broadcast journalist

In dark and confusing times, Reagan Jackson's writing is a compass pointing toward liberation. ~Alex Stonehill, Co-Founder of the *Seattle Globalist*, Head of Creative Strategy for the UW Comm Lead Program

Katrina,
I'm looking forward to reading
Rough Trade. Hope you
enjoy my work.
:) Reagan

STILL TRUE

The Evolution of an Unexpected Journalist

essays by

Reagan E. J. Jackson

Foreword by Robin D. G. Kelley

Hinton

print: 978-1-60944-154-8

ebook: 978-1-60944-155-5

Published in the United States by
Hinton Publishing
Seattle, WA

marcus@hintonpublishing.com
hintonpublishing.com

Hinton is an imprint of Vertvolta Press
vertvoltapress.com

Please contact the publisher for Library of Congress Catalog Data

To the late great Barbara James for the gift of memoir.
To Rainier Beach for the gift of home.
To the writers and storytellers who tell the truth-never stop.

Foreword

by Robin D. G. Kelley

"Do I have equity?"

~Reagan Jackson

Seattle's Town Hall was one of the stops on my tour to launch the 20th anniversary edition of my book, *Freedom Dreams: The Black Radical Imagination.* I half-jokingly called it my "trauma tour" since I spent the early to mid-1970s, the worst period of my childhood, in Seattle. The hell we endured inside our apartment under a violent and dictatorial patriarch was nearly matched by the hell we confronted outside in the so-called liberal city on seven hills. Those were the days when the Central District was Black and poor, Rainier Beach had a large Asian-Pacific population, suburbs like Ballard were white and racist, and busing designed to rescue ghetto kids from bad, underfunded schools merely put us in harm's way. We lived in neighborhoods where property values determined the value of our education, which was exceedingly low. The solution, mandatory busing, was never about addressing economic inequality or desegregating Seattle but a concession to families struggling to educate their kids--families who saw education as cultural capital, their ticket out of the ghetto.

I arrived on the morning of the event (September 21, 2022) so I would have time to revisit my old haunts in the CD—the Central Area Youth Association (CAYA), Garfield High School, Medgar Evers pool, our old apartment. Gentrification left the city unrecognizable. I was not surprised. Similar to busing, gentrification is not a strategy of desegregation but a modern-day form of settler colonialism. With settlers come new restaurants, shops, rising property values, and improved schools. The old neighborhood had been erased but the memories linger like ghosts.

The organizers of the Town Hall event paired me with Reagan Jackson, a writer, activist, and resident of the south side who not only made the "new" Seattle legible but provided the kind of incisive, critical analysis to which I could relate. In preparation for our conversation on stage, I picked up a copy of *Still True* and devoured it in one day. I felt an immediate bond. In eloquent and uncluttered prose, Jackson writes about racism, gentrification, reparations, abolition, the everyday, and the spectacular at the scale of

the local, the global, and the body. She penetrates Seattle's liberal veneer—
its hipsters, chill cannabis vendors, sympathetic gentrifiers planting kale,
rainbow flags, and Black Lives Matters signs on their property—and
exposes the contradictions, hypocrisies, and genuine missteps endemic to
a deeply unequal multiracial city governed by capitalism over cooperation.
Our bond deepened when I learned that she is the daughter of Dr. Stanlie
James, a renowned Black feminist scholar whose work and example I've followed and admired for three decades.

Therefore, when Reagan Jackson asked me to write a foreword to the
new, expanded edition of *Still True*, it took all of three seconds to say yes.
Jackson is emerging as one of the great writers of her generation. A master of
the personal essay, she works in the tradition of James Baldwin, Joan Didion,
Joyce Carole Oates, Patricia Williams, Zadie Smith, Claudia Rankine, and
others capable of plumbing their own experiences and encounters in order
to make sense of the world. She deftly employs personal stories to examine
what it means to live Black and female in the 21st century, navigating a sea
of whiteness, fighting the fires of patriarchy and racism, and the bursting
through the strictures of heteronormativity. From her unique perspective as
a cosmopolitan Black woman who has lived on the precipice of economic
precarity, Jackson shows us how to love, fight, make community, find joy,
survive, and write the truth in a so-called post-truth era. She models what it
means to be a journalist in 2024 and write about racism, gender, and sexuality when states are trying to ban discussions of racism, gender, and sexuality.

The public lynching of George Floyd by a Minneapolis law officer and
the international rebellion that followed in its wake has certainly shaped
the new edition of *Still True*. But more remarkable are the ways in which
the first edition *anticipates* the massive spring and summer protests of
2020. Jackson's keen observations of the #blacklivesmatter protests over
the years remind us that "Black Spring" of 2020 was preceded by an eight-
year winter of persistent state-sanctioned killings, protests, and struggles
just to hold space for black healing without being labeled a segregationist.
She documents the trauma and frustration of fighting a city whose empa-
thetic posture masks its intransigence and organizing white liberals who
don't have a clue. She reminds us of how hard and long the fight has been;
Jackson and her comrades were already exhausted by the time Floyd was
murdered.

Ultimately, *Still True* is what I would call an abolitionist take on space
and power—a desire to make the space we call earth habitable and bountiful for all life. Gentrification stands in stark opposition to Jackson's vision

of how the world can and should be. Having lived through and resisted its consequences, she understands that gentrification is not just about property values. It is as much about political power and human value—or, more precisely, how humans are differentially valued. Her story about how the white-owned Uncle Ike's cannabis store was allowed by the city to continually flout the law by operating near predominantly Black youth centers is a case in point. Despite community demands that Uncle Ike's comply with the law by moving its operations, the protests fell on deaf ears because the protesters were Black and politically powerless. The story's significance extends far beyond Seattle. First, most municipal governments have historically zoned "red light" districts in Black communities, even when activities that fall under the category of "vice" are legal. Why? Because these are often the most vulnerable and politically disfranchised communities. Second, the legalization of cannabis is a euphemism for whitening the industry. Jackson's essay forces us to reflect on all of the young Black people who would have been candidates for the Joshua Generation Teen Center and the Mount Calvary Christian Center but are locked up for selling weed before legalization. Uncle Ike's not only enjoyed the protection of the law but could skirt legality because of its corporate power. White profits trumped Black safety.

For Jackson, holding or occupying space is inseparable from safety. Although she does not use the language of abolition, it seems evident to me that *Still True* promotes an abolitionist vision of public safety drawn directly from her own experience as a victim of gun violence and a resident committed to humane policies toward unhoused people. "It is time," she writes, "to reimagine safety in a way that is radically inclusive. We've started the conversation about defunding the police, but what about defunding gun lobbies? What about teaching meditation in schools and shifting punitive practices to restorative ones? What can we be doing to cultivate a culture of connection and accountability that can lead to safety? We owe it to ourselves and to the next generation to create a framework where all communities can truly be called beautiful and safe." This is the world we desperately need if we expect to *remain* here, on this planet, alive and well. Reagan Jackson's unexpected journey, with its many twists and turns, routes and revelations, may turn out to be our salvation.

The Beginning

won't you celebrate with me
what i have shaped into
a kind of life? i had no model.
born in babylon
both nonwhite and woman
what did I see to be except myself?
i made it up
here on this bridge between
starshine and clay,
my one hand holding tight
my other hand; come celebrate
with me that everyday
something had tried to kill me
and has failed.

~Lucille Clifton

I have long felt the crushing weight of the strange paradox of being both invisible and hyper visible as a Black woman in America. The need to process my experiences has kept me coming back to writing. Though I have been a writer for the majority of my life, I didn't see a place for myself in journalism. Life had to show me.

This book is part time capsule, part existential musing, a collection of essays and articles written between 2013-2023 that cover a range of topics from a distinct perspective—mine. Through the work you'll learn as much about me as you do the people I interview and the issues I cover. As vulnerable as that feels at times, I stand by my approach because how I see the story and how I tell it is shaped by who I am and what I've lived through and to not acknowledge that is a lie of omission.

Authentic journalism is a quest to tell the truth. The conflation of what is viewed as objective and white cultural bias has become a liability that has limited the scope of our media and stunted our capacity as Americans to see each other clearly enough to tell complete, nuanced and true stories. But no matter how much "mainstream media" has attempted to erase those of us who have been historically marginalized or those whose identities don't fit neatly into check boxes, *we're still here*. Our stories are no less valid, vibrant, real or necessary. Our stories deserve to be told with care and witnessed with the intention to understand.

The first iteration of this book was a collaboration with the brilliant Michael Maine as the inaugural publication of Menrva Labs Publishing. We took a chance on each other based on mutual values. I love what we created and remain grateful for that collaboration and the opportunity to put my work forward. A steep learning curve paired with a global pandemic meant we didn't quite launch the way either of us had hoped, but also what always happens when I finish a book is that I realize it's not finished. This one might not be either, but I'll try to turn it loose, this time with 8 additional essays and articles. I'm choosing to publish with Hinton for mostly the same reasons I went with Menrva, because my community is where I was first given a platform and it's only fitting that I relaunch this work with the creators of the *South Seattle Emerald* and Vertvolta Press respectively.

The unexpected journalist

It started in 2013 with brunch. Media justice activist Sabrina Roach invited me to her house for French toast. It was a cozy lively gathering where everyone did the two things you should do at brunch, ate heartily and laughed with one another. Sabrina introduced me to the co-founders of the *Seattle Globalist*, Sarah Stuteville, Jessica Partnow, and Alex Stonehill, with a few connective words; writing and study abroad.

The three of them were journalists who had traveled the world writing and recording audio stories. They had co-created a documentary filmed partly in Seattle and partly in Iraq called Barzan and now they were teaching journalism at the University of Washington. In 2006 they found some funding to put together the Common Language Project which evolved into the *Globalist*. The intention was to tell stories that transcended borders.

After teaching English in Japan and Chile respectively for two and a half years, I had returned to the States to get my master's degree in international education. My intention was to lead a study abroad programs for youth of color, but I had found it difficult to get a foothold in my profession. At the time I was in recovery from my dream job of taking youth to Guatemala. I loved the youth and thrived in the work itself but felt constrained by a combination of toxic masculinity and toxic white saviorism that eventually became too difficult to navigate. We had a lot to talk about.

I fell into a rant about the ways in which people of color are excluded from study abroad programs and how the white solution is to mistake color for economic status and throw money at the problem. Yes, money is sometimes one obstacle that people of color face in making the decision to study abroad, but we are always making a way out of no way, finding scholarships, hosting spaghetti dinners or circulating GoFundMe pages. The challenges that go unmentioned are the fact that many of these programs were not designed with us in mind. And part of this is due to who gets funded to design these types of programs.

I told the story of the black girl who went to South Africa on a study abroad program only to arrive at a white homestay with a family that had a dog that was trained to bite black people. There is a global misconception often perpetuated by white media that the US is a white country. Still, what kind of negligence exists that a university would send a student to such an unsafe environment? What if that student had been white? Would it have been acceptable for them to stay in a home with people who harbored such hatred? What would they have learned about South Africa? I shared my own experience of being black in Spain on a predominantly white program and the microaggressions I experienced both in the group of my peers and in the host country itself.

Alex turned to me and said: "That sounds interesting. You should write about it." (I later realized this was his tagline.) I had unwittingly pitched my first story. I went home, wrote a couple pages and emailed it to him. To my surprise he published it with minimal edits and sent me a check.

I had a blog and a degree in creative writing, so me writing something was not much of a stretch. I'd even taken a journalism class in high school and been published in the *Madison Times* and the *Capitol Times* respectively, but the idea of being a real journalist was foreign and not especially appealing.

Despite my ambivalence, money was money, and writing for money was an exciting proposition. After my first article, I followed up with another. Within a few months Alex offered me a column mostly so he could put me on the editorial calendar and gain some input into what I was going to write about. I didn't pitch ideas the way you're supposed to, I just wrote whole unsolicited articles and submitted them. It was several months before I learned that's not typically how it works. I did a lot of things out of sequence and created a steep learning curve for myself and my colleagues, but I was good at the work and I never missed a deadline so there was a lot of grace for me.

When the invitation to have my own column arrived, I told my dad that I was going to be a reporter. The first thing he said was don't be that asshole who sticks the microphone in the face of the person who just lost their kid. What a gut check. His words challenged me to think critically about the role of journalists. We tell the facts, we report what happened, but so much of what has been written about my community has been narrated by people from outside of it with no context to understand the facts enough to articulate the full truth. I wanted to tell stories from my community, but never at their expense.

In the early 1900s W.E.B Du Bois wrote about the theory of double consciousness in his book *The Souls of Black Folk*. His work explored the idea that to be Black and American is to know the world through dual understandings, that of the white mainstream lens and that of our own cultural perspective. It is this double consciousness coupled with a Black feminist upbringing that made me skeptical and critical of journalism for the ways it has been used as a tool of systemic oppression to vilify and misrepresent people of color, but it is also what positioned me well to become a counter narrative and tell more complete stories than what had become the norm.

Through years of conditioning by white media, we have been taught that journalism is sensational, concise and didactic, and should be narrated without emotion or bias. That is not who I wanted to be or how I wanted to write. I needed to create a new paradigm of ethics. I wanted to tell more complete stories, to create a space for nuance, balance, authenticity, and perspective. Could I do this? Could I be the journalist that didn't lose myself or my voice? There was no guarantee that this was possible. I had no road map, but the Globalist was new too, just barely six months off the ground and I loved what we were trying to build. The *PI* had closed its doors and the *Seattle Times* seemed to be in a decline. The *Stranger* had gone from indy to establishment. Journalism as we knew it was dying. Standing at the funeral suddenly there was an opportunity to right some wrongs, to stop begging for representation and trying to get a foothold into the mainstream.

I took a chance that together we could do something I hadn't seen done. I had never worked with an editor before, and I was hesitant to invite anyone to critique or censor my writing. One of perks of invisibility is that you don't have to follow rules. No one was listening to me anyway; I could say or write whatever I wanted. But here was this invitation, this opportunity to be heard.

Alex was a patient editor. Sometimes I would pitch an idea and he couldn't see the story, but he was open to letting me try. He asked smart questions that helped me to reframe and clarify my words and sometimes poked holes in my arguments so that I could see where I needed to shore up my research. Working with him made me a stronger writer. Despite my misconceptions about journalism being a dry concise form of writing stripped of all personality, I found myself with an editor who was interested in my voice and my perspective. The Seattle Globalist showed me who I could be as a journalist and what I could contribute to a field poised to acknowledge its own failure to represent communities of color in an equitable and accurate way and ripe for a reinvention. It opened a door for me, a pathway to a platform where not only did I get to say what I wanted to say, but where there were people who wanted to hear it.

In 2014, my column took second place at the Society of Professional Journalist Excellence in Journalism Competition and the Washington Press Association awarded me first place in the editorial category of their Communication Contest for *Black History Month: The Same Old Song and Dance?*, a piece I wrote about a minstrel performance at Spectrum Dance.

It felt like an inside joke to update my bio with the title of award-winning journalist when I still didn't really think of myself that way. This was all an experiment. I had imposter syndrome because I didn't see any models for the way I wanted to engage, but I didn't let that derail me from the work of writing.

Also in 2014, I wrote my first viral article. I was on deadline for a story about a Somali woman. She had been kidnapped by her family who then tried to force her into a marriage when they found out she was gay. We spent hours together. Her story was the stuff of movies, but in the end for fear of retribution from the family she had so narrowly escaped, she begged me not to publish it. This was that moment where if I were Lois Lane I would have had a huge headline. I sat there staring at my phone knowing it contained hours of our interview. At this point I didn't legally need her consent to write the piece, but I decided to respect her request. Pissed and disappointed, and still on deadline for my column, I drafted up a quick piece I had been kicking around about my neighborhood.

Who's Afraid of Rainier Beach? was a game changer. I went to bed and woke up the next morning to see 30 comments in the comment section with more posting every few minutes. And long comments too. Someone had shared it on the Rainier Beach Facebook Page and the thread there was heated and expansive. What struck me most was not the contention, but that people were actually engaging with what I wrote and with one another. They were sharing their Rainier Beach stories.

Our editorial meeting that week was abuzz. Until that point our tagline *Where Seattle meets the World* had been a guiding post around content. We mostly talked about international issues, and though the 98118 is lauded as being one of the most diverse zip codes in the country, the piece did not have a strong link to anything global. And yet our readers were saying that this was important and that this was something they wanted to hear about. Writing this piece expanded the scope of our coverage. I knew tons of people in my community through my work as a community organizer, but this was the piece that introduced me to them as a journalist. I started fielding pitches. People came to me with events they wanted me to attend, books they wanted me to read and stories they wanted to share.

Sarah Stuteville connected me with Marcus Harrison Green. He came to me for writing lessons and we became friends. He started the South Seattle Emerald, which seemed like an answer to the outpouring of energy that showed up in response to my Rainier Beach article. People in the Southend were sick of being misrepresented in mainstream media. I started writing for both publications. From time to time Marcus would invite me to edit articles. I discovered I really liked being on the other side of that process.

I had done some freelance writing coaching but now I started putting together one-off classes. When the *South Seattle Emerald* started an internship program, I worked with the first cohort on the basics of writing. Through the *Globalist* I was invited to teach a *writing with voice* workshop as a part of a series of pop-up workshops to train folks throughout the city on the basics of journalism and to cultivate new contributors. I loved and still love working with new writers. It felt powerful to open the door for them in the way Alex opened the door for me.

I didn't limit my teaching to one genre. In 2015 I woke up from a dream of my grandmother with half of the curriculum for a class that evolved into my signature course, the Mixtape Memoir. After retiring from teaching middle school English my grandmother took a memoir class for senior citizens through the University of Iowa. They produced a slim anthology called *Harvesters—The Stories of Our Lives*. She gave each member of her family a copy for Christmas. I think I read it at the time, but I hadn't looked at it in over a decade.

When I awoke I went to my bookshelves and dug around until I found it, then flipped to the section labeled Barbara James. There was a grainy black and white wallet sized portrait of her next to a bio followed by three short piece *Choice, An Unexpected Call,* and *One Monkey Don't Stop the Show*. I sank down on the carpet, still feeling the intensity of the dream and reread her words, amazed how in 5 pages she explained so much about herself and our family.

I had never written a memoir. I hadn't even read that many of them, preferring fiction and poetry. I felt intimidated to put myself out there like I was some kind of expert, but my grandmother had spoken and I knew I had to teach this class. I taught the first version at the Amor Spiritual Center, and it called in an eclectic collection of writers ages 25-75 from a range of different backgrounds. The work they produced was resonant and heartfelt. They reminded me of how impactful it can be to provide a space for people to share their stories.

I began with music because I'm the kind of person who can hear a song on the radio and get completely transported into a moment in my past. What I used to love about making a good mixtape was the way you could choose songs to tell a story and they didn't have to be similar to be on the same tape. You could use music to tell a story but it didn't have to be linear. I loved supporting others to write the soundtrack of their lives.

As a columnist and a freelancer for both platforms respectively, I was building my own prolific mixtape. I didn't have a specific beat. Instead, I was given freedom to cover whatever caught my interest from city council meetings and political topics to art events, profiles, and movie reviews. I continued to write about study abroad programs, specifically my own. After taking over 200 youth abroad to Guatemala and Japan respectively, I took what I learned and piloted Many Voices, One Tribe, a study abroad for young writers of color.

My article *Why I Started a Study Abroad Program for People of Color* was the first of a series chronicling our adventure to Mexico. Before we left, Sarah and Jessica met with my youth cohort for a Journalism 101 workshop that helped them to frame the writing we would do abroad. It was an incredible experience, in many ways one of the most fulfilling journeys of my life, but it depleted me emotionally and financially and schooled me on why so few BIPOC people start study abroad programs. It's the chicken and egg of needing money to get legitimacy and needing legitimacy and a proven track record to get money. People were fine to trust me to lead youth under the guidance of a narcissistic white man, but despite my degrees and my experience folks we reluctant to trust that I was competent to do it on my own. It was heartbreaking and I was exhausted. I needed a job.

I had recently completed a second stint as a community organizer for the United Food and Commercial Workers and had a temporary contract with

Powerful Voices, supporting 13 teenage girls to prepare workshops for Girlvolution, an annual youth led social justice conference. I applied for a diversity fellowship with *Yes!* Magazine. It was the first and only time I applied for a full-time job in journalism. I was afraid that turning my passion into my day job would kill the joy, but again- I needed a job—and I figured a year fellowship would give me a chance to see if this was where I wanted to go career wise. I had reservations about the way that the position was structured. Many news outlets when faced with criticism over their overwhelmingly white demographics decided to solve this through creating token positions and that's what this felt like, but I liked the magazine itself and the opportunity was undeniable.

Life had other plans for me. Though I was a finalist, the fellowship went to Marcus. I ended up accepting a position as the Program Manager for Young Women Empowered (Y-WE). I continued writing and through Y-WE I designed and facilitated a summer camp for young writers called Y-WE Write. I also led a school year track in our Y-WE Lead program called Y-WE Represent which was all about connecting youth to different forms of media to give them the skills to represent themselves.

Through Represent I was able to create a pathway into journalism, not just for the youth in our program, but for the mentors as well. Mahroo Keshavarez, Esmy Jimenez, Aisha Al Amin, Samantha Pak, Vivian Brannock and Namaka Auwaee-Dekker became contributors to the *Seattle Globalist* and the *South Seattle Emerald* respectively. Esmy became a *Globalist* Apprentice then served on the board and went on to become an immigration reporter with KUOW. Mahroo won *Seattle Globalist* Community Journalist of the year in 2016.

As a fellowship finalist I was invited to pitch to *Yes!* Magazine. I wrote a story about an innovative center for domestic violence survivors that was using the science developed in the NFL around traumatic brain injuries to treat women and children who had been abused. They paid me more for that article than I had received for any article I'd ever written, but after submitting my first draft I didn't hear from them for months. Having primarily worked with the *Globalist* and the *Emerald*, I was used to the quick turnaround and personal interaction that smaller organizations accomplish with ease. To have worked my ass off to craft a compelling piece and then to have it disappear into a void felt disrespectful. After six months and several emails my editor resurfaced. She had some clarifying questions. I returned to my sources, feeling super unprofessional to not be able to tell them when the piece would post. I completed my edits and the piece was published, but it left a bad taste in my mouth.

If this is what journalism is like in other organizations, maybe I didn't want to invest in organizations that didn't seem invested in me. People are always claiming that the reason newsrooms are so white is because there aren't qualified candidates of color, but to me it seemed that in the same way most study abroad programs were not created with people of color in mind, neither are most newsrooms and that makes a difference in terms of retention. I felt tokenized and devalued from the start. In the words of Lauryn Hill "Respect is just a minimum."

Around this time I started doing a lot more arts coverage. My favorite perk was getting to see any movie at the Seattle International Film Festival for free. I rearranged my work schedule to eat popcorn for breakfast. People sent me free tickets to plays, performances or art openings. My weekends and evenings were packed with events. Some were transformative and breathtakingly inspiring, some were mediocre or very strange, but I enjoyed the spectrum and people seemed to really resonate with my arts coverage because whether I liked it or not, I fully engaged in it.

I was introduced to the managing editor at Crosscut and invited to pitch some stories. I visited their newsroom in Pioneer Square and met some very friendly white people. They invited me to apply for a fellowship to cover arts and it was tempting since I was mostly doing it anyway, but after my experience with *Yes!* Magazine I wondered if I had been too willing to be tokenized. I was having the existential conflict of wanting to write and take advantage of open doors, but not trusting white institutions to navigate professional relationships equitably. Since this wariness was more about me and where I was at than anything that happened with Crosscut, I compromised. I didn't apply for the fellowship, but I did pitch a few articles. I worked well with Greg Hanscomb and Joe Copeland and felt respected in our interactions and proud of the articles we published together. Still, I felt more comfortable working with publications that prioritized diverse contributors in their staffing model and not just in their fellowships.

In 2015 I was invited to go to Honduras with the Seattle Sounders to cover a community service project they were doing there. This blew my mind. The Seattle International Foundation flew me to Central America to write. I was an international correspondent! After a harrowing landing in Tegucigalpa on the world's shortest runway we were ushered to the American Embassy where they tried to scare us into never setting foot outside of the hotel. I ignored this completely and within the first couple of hours of my stay, I discovered a hunger strike, interviewed the strikers, and got a machine gun pointed in my face for taking pictures of the presidential palace.

I wrote three pieces, one about what it was like to attend the Sounders game, one about the Seattle International Foundation refurbishing soccer fields for kids to keep them engaged in community centers and not in gangs and one about the hunger strike and the egregious government corruption that had caused several deaths because the president stole $350 million dollars from the national health plan. This was one of the most outrageous news stories I have ever covered and yet no one seemed to care about it at all.

That same year I wrote an article that went viral about POC yoga. A white woman named Laura Humpf owned a yoga studio in Rainier Beach. Someone got ahold of an email she sent to her students announcing that her studio would be hosting a POC only class and gave it to local conservative shock jock Dori Monson, who turned it into a national story about white oppression.

I reached out to Laura for an interview, but at that time she was fielding death threats and too traumatized to speak with me though we did eventually talk off the record and became close friends. I was able to interview Teresa Wang the co-founder of POC yoga and wrote an article called the *Vitriol Against People of Color Yoga Shows Exactly Why It's Necessary* because while many other news outlets were covering the same topic they were doing so in a way that made white rage seem like a rational response to being asked not to participate in a healing ritual for people of color. At Teresa's request I am not including the article in this collection because the whole thing was so traumatizing for her that she would rather it be buried, but I'm bringing it up because this moment in our community is too important not to discuss, so I'll try to share the lesson though not the full story.

Why people cared so much more about white people being uninvited to one yoga class than the thousands of Hondurans who actually died because their corrupt politicians stole money from hospitals I still don't understand. Also why people felt compelled to normalize an intensely violent and anti Black response to BIPOC people attempting to heal felt incomprehensible too. I ended up going on Dori Monson's show which was like being trolled in real life, but it felt important for me to not be silent. I was sweaty palmed and angry after seeing the ways this news story traumatized Laura and Teresa. They weren't the only ones negatively impacted, but they were the face of the story. POC yoga never actually shut down, but it did go underground which meant that many of us who wanted to take it lost access.

One thing I love about writing is the luxury of second drafts. There are no second drafts on the radio. You only get one chance to say what you have to say and to say it correctly. I held my own for the first half of our conversation then I shut down, but I learned a lot from the experience. And I was proud of myself for working through my fear. It made it easier the next time I had to do it again in an even bigger and more public way.

The POC Yoga article was my first significant experience with being trolled. Yes, *Who's Afraid of Rainier Beach* had tons of comments, but most of them were people really trying to have a conversation. We shut down comments on the POC yoga article because too many of them involved racial slurs or violence. Alex was the first responder to these things, but sometimes I saw them before he could shield me and it was jarring. I live in a very liberal bubble and very naively assumed that everyone was taught basic respect for others. Trolls made me question my commitment to everyone having first amendment rights. And then there was the distinct before and after moment of the 2016 presidential election where trolls hijacked our political system and we all had to live with the repercussions of white privilege left unchecked. I digress.

The trolls taught me an important distinction around the ethics of storytelling. Now when anyone can record a video and post it online or write something and find a place where people will read it, what separates journalists from trolls? Some would say research, facts and legitimacy of the platform. I nerd out on research and facts, but they aren't immune to bias and neither are news outlets. I think the best journalism comes from a deep love and respect for all humanity, a commitment to bringing the truth to light and a curiosity about the story. We all want to assume we're right (I'm guilty of this too…I love being right), but true journalism is an interrogation that is less about right and wrong and more about finding out what is happening and all the whys behind it. It's in that space where we're willing to explore where all the magic is possible. There is nothing magical about trolls. They shit on all the magic and pretend it's a prelude to a conversation and nothing has been more damaging to journalism as we know it.

My writing was pushing me into more public forums. Almost a year after writing *Black History Month: The Same Old Song and Dance?* Donald Byrd, the director of Spectrum Dance, asked me to have a skype meeting with students at NYU to de-escalate a protest. Based on my review of his show, the Black Student Union had decided they wanted no part of it and were going to block it from being shown. The dialogue was fascinating to me, as was the idea that across the country someone was reading my words and using them to educate their own opinions.

Joe Copeland from Crosscut pitched a story idea to my new editor at the Globalist Venice Buhain. They were looking for a female reporter to do an experiential piece on burlesque. Venice declined, but passed it onto me and on a whim I said yes. Crosscut paid for me to take a six week Burlesuqe 101 class (which was super expensive). Of course, I didn't really know what I was getting into, but like most things, that didn't stop me. I had gone to the Burlesque Nutcracker and imagined it would be something like that, an ensemble routine in riske costumes. Instead it was a solo performance and I was totally out of my comfort zone. There is a vulnerability to writing that sometimes feels like you're stripping for an audience but this time literally stripping was involved. *The Making of a Burlesque Dancer* won me a first prize at the SPJs that year. That same year, 2016, I was awarded a Globie for being *Seattle Globalist*'s Journalist of the year.

Dressed in a fuchsia ball gown I gave my acceptance speech in front of 300 people including my mom. I finally felt like a journalist. It wasn't the award itself, but the body of work that earned me the distinction. I had written over 70 articles. I had given voice to so much that had previously gone unsaid and, in the process, told the stories of my community and created a new framework for how journalism can be.

Also, that year I got scooped for the first time. Rich Smith from the *Stranger* is credited with breaking what ended up being an internationally covered story about performance artist and social justice consultant Natasha Marin's Reparation Project. I wrote two pieces about Natasha Marin's Reparation project, *Reparations ReImagined: Can Online Giving Counter Systemic Racism* (which posted 20 minutes after Smith posted a placeholder article) and *Shrine of Asshats: Seattle Reparations Project Slays Trolls*. I subsequently wrote *Calling Out (And Calling In) White Media* and began to be more vocal about the hazards of what journalist Jose Vargas called #journalismsowhite. I was invited to share my views at Seattle Town Hall and on KUOW, Seattle's NPR affiliate.

In 2017, I returned to speaking about my neighborhood. Now the question was no longer who feared Rainer Beach, but rather who would get to live there in light of an intense gentrification. *Brad and Becky are coming to Rainier Beach* (*Brad and Becky and coming for Rainier Beach*, had been the original title, but Marcus changed it at the last minute) struck a nerve. I don't think I said anything that people didn't already know, but I gave a voice to a conversation we were all politely avoiding.

In 2018 after my property taxes skyrocketed, I wrote another piece called *The Displacement Tax: An Update from Gentrification Ground Zero*. The peril of including myself and my story into my work means that then I'm out there to be judged. The comment section was visceral and included long diatribes from my new white neighbors who had been waiting for the opportunity to confront me for making them feel "unwelcome" with my lawn signs which told the story of gentrification and why my house is NOT for sale. There were also long rants from my new woke white neighbors who had read Ijeoma Oluo and Robin D'Angelo and wanted to affirm my experiences as a part of their allyship. In the end I think they started a book club.

I was invited back to On the Record with Bill Radke on KUOW, this time with my dad (who was great) who spoke about his challenges with finding housing in Seattle. I was invited to speak on a panel about gentrification at the Governing for Regional Equity and Inclusion Conference. This felt awkward because the other people on the panel worked for government agencies that provide low-income housing. They were there to present all the ways they were addressing the challenges of the Seattle Housing crises. I listened to the other panelists and agreed that the work they are doing is a great start. I was doing my best not to criticize, but finally one of the participants in the audience raised her hand and said "That's great, but none of what you are doing is going to help Reagan stay in her home."

Writing this article was expensive in ways that I anticipated, but still couldn't quite prepare for. When it posted on the Rainier Beach Facebook page, my neighbors googled my property and began to post my personal financial information online. Everyone wanted to talk to me, but I had said what I needed to say in the article. Anyone who had ever driven past my house and saw my signs knew where I lived. I began to feel unsafe in my own home. I already had a security system, but I bought and installed cameras and took down all of the lawn signs except one so it would be less identifiable from the street. I don't regret what I wrote. I stand by it, but the experience forced me to really think about whether journalism was still bringing me joy.

I did the thing I set out to do. I used my writing to amplify the stories in my community. In much of my writing I found myself simply stating the obvious. But given the response, the way that people began to seek me out to share their stories or to invite me to cover their events reminded me that my feeling of invisibility is one shared by many in my community. They needed to be witnessed as much as I did. But how long will we still need to be the counter narrative? It is a heavy weight to bear, always having to explain myself and my perspective, which is not as unique to me as people seem to think. I long for when Black, Indigenous, people of color can shift from the margins to the center, to help journalism have a much needed conversation with itself around the whitewashing of what it means to be objective and what media must do to wield it's power responsibly and provide balanced and representational coverage.

The changing of the guard had begun. Sarah, Jessica, and Alex decided it was time to leave the *Globalist* for their next adventures. They asked if I would consider taking over as Editor in Chief or Executive Director, but I had fallen in love with Y-WE. Also I saw the toll it had taken on them. I didn't feel prepared to take on that level of responsibility, though ironically now I am the Co-Executive Director of Y-WE. It is no small feat creating a sustainable organization, managing personalities, and endlessly gathering resources, but that's the non-profit life. I wish I could say I outgrew my hesitancy, but I don't think that's true. It's just that my love of the Y-WE community and knowing I needed to step up in order for us to thrive became more important than my fears.

Marcus left the *Emerald* to take a position with the *Seattle Times* and I declined that role for the same reasons. I felt well received and welcomed by the new leadership who made sure to let me know there was a place for me.

In September of 2020, The *Seattle Globalist* took its last breath. I felt blindsided. It was devastating to lose the incubator for my (and so many others) start as a journalist. I was so angry and felt so guilty to have not been able to support with an intervention. It deserved more of a fight than it got, but in 2020 many of us were fighting for our lives and our health and the *Globalist* was one of many organizations and businesses that didn't survive. Fortunately the *South Seattle Emerald* has grown and continued to thrive, absorbing many of the *Globalist* contributors. It is a platform that truly serves and supports our community. I am proud to have contributed to both orgs.

Though it felt like I would lose momentum, I decided to take a break from journalism to focus on youth work and my other writing. Since I was never conventional in my approach it seemed silly to cling to the idea that if I didn't publish regularly people would forget about me and I'd never get a chance to do it again.

In 2020 I only published one article: *The Tea on Our Juneteenth Blackout And the Necessity of Black Healing Spaces.* This was the backstory of how and why Mary Hall Williams and I (with three days' notice) raised $25,000 and took over the Capitol Hill Occupied Protest for a 12 hour Blackout to recenter Black grief and Black joy at what was supposed to be a space where Black lives mattered.

I hadn't planned to write about it, but the experience was so big that we created a national news story and the way it was being covered by mainstream media was so reductive, I felt compelled to come off my break to get it right. Fox news stuck a camera in my face and when I looked down the street there were armed proud boys headed our way. The proud boys never made it to the field. CHOP security took care of that, but there was so much that happened in the span of 12 hours that I had to write about it just to get it out. Someone from Antifa posted a video and it was retweeted with a snarky comment by the 45th president of the United States.

Getting trolled by Trump was something many journalists experienced to varying degrees of trauma. Some wore it like a badge of honor, others felt terrorized, but the president didn't troll me as a journalist...he did it to me and Mary as activists, as Black women who dared to hold space for Black grief in public. In a time of viral Black death it was ubiquitous to see pictures of Black folks holding picket signs, screaming into face of police dressed in riot gear or waving off tear gas, but rare to see actual mourning. Mary and I wanted to create space for a fuller spectrum of Black humanity. We dressed our city in flower crowns, fed folks and gave them a space to do art and yoga and to bring our grief to an in-person ritual where we could set aside our rage and defensiveness long enough to feel our sorrow.

My work had often blurred the lines of subjectivity, but I had never been the story in quite this way and it was deeply unsettling. We stepped onto Cal Anderson field with no illusion of safety knowing that white supremacists knew where we would be and what time. This wasn't some stupid radio show. Shit got very real and I'm still processing, but I'm proud we had the courage to see it through. Our flower crowns and thought leadership rippled out across the city. Black folks all over Seattle started popping up with grief and joy work, creating more spaces of healing and it was beautiful.

My life is very different now. I never stopped writing, but now I only publish when the story really calls me. I don't go looking. I just live my life until I stumble upon an article that feels like its writing itself. In 2021 when a homeless man wandered onto my property, I wrote Who Can We Call to ground the defund the police movement into the real live context of trying to navigate around the systems we've created. In 2022 I published one more piece about Rainier Beach, my most expensive and vulnerable piece of writing yet, about someone shooting two bullets through my front window.

It's been almost 10 years since I wrote my first article. I still haven't run out of things to cover. There are an endless wealth of stories and fascinating people, but I was never only a journalist. I'm a poet, a children's book author, a novelist, now a song writer, an educator and the steward of an incredible organization that is far more than a full-time job, but a calling. I'm also the producer and cohost of a podcast called The Deep End Friends. After years of interviewing incredible people for profiles, I realized I didn't want to edit what they said down into sound bites and even just leaving our conversations in written Q&A format didn't seem to capture the nuance. I wanted people to be able to listen in. In 2021 I was invited to be a distinguished visiting writer for Seattle University where I taught another round of Mixtape Memoir. I don't know when I'll teach it again, but I'm sure my grandma will let me know when the time is right.

2023 finds me looking back on where I've been and how far I've come. I am so grateful for all the support, encouragement, feedback, and opportunities I've been given that have made this possible. I'm grateful to still be here: writing, learning, and evolving.

~Reagan E. J. Jackson

The
Hood

Who's Afraid of Rainier Beach?

When I tell people I live in Rainier Beach I get a variety of reactions. Sometimes people politely nod as if to indicate that they might know where that is. Sometimes they live there too and we try to figure out if we're neighbors. But too often I get that incredulous "WHY?!" reaction.

I actually had one person say "And you bought a house there?" while shaking his head. This guy used to go to school in Rainier Beach at a time when crime was much higher. He visited my house once and spent half his time peeking out the window to see if his car was being stolen. His paranoia made me wonder what I was missing.

Should I be afraid? Of whom?

Growing up in Madison, Wisconsin in a predominantly white west side neighborhood by a lakeside park, the closest I came to the ghetto was watching Boyz in the Hood on cable.

Like anyone who has ever had any exposure to U.S. media, I learned that the "hood" was nowhere I wanted to be. It was dangerous and in order to live there you had to be dangerous too—or very poor with nowhere better to go. And of course that's where black people lived.

To this day when people ask me where I'm from, they side eye me when I say Madison. One of my roommates in college upon meeting me for the first time blurted out "but you're black," as though I couldn't possibly be black and a Wisconsinite. And now here in Seattle my neighborhood precedes me, giving me some unexpected street cred.

When I first moved to Seattle I lived in the North End in the U- district then later in Wallingford, Greenwood, and Greenlake. During those years I was often the only black person on my block, something that was familiar, but not ideal.

I wanted to live where other people of color lived, but was often discouraged from considering the South End. That was described to me as Seattle's hood, a place synonymous with drugs and crime.

In 2011 I moved to Beacon Hill. I was still one of the few black people on my block, but rather than being surrounded by white people my neighbors were mostly Asian and Mexican. I loved hearing Spanish spoken on a regular basis. Beacon Hill felt like a community to me in the way Wallingford—with its neighborhood watch groups and email list serves—never had. I began to question what I had heard.

Yes, there was crime. Someone broke into my neighbor's car once, but the same thing had happened in Wallingford. In fact when I lived in Wallingford there were a rash of home invasions, car thefts and vandalism, yet no one had ever described Wallingford to me as a scary place to live.

So what makes a place "the hood?"

Most people think of it as the poorest part of any city, the place people of color live because they have no other choice (as though anyone who did have a choice would want to live in a white neighborhood).

That is not how I would describe Rainier Beach.

There is no crack house on my street. I don't know all of my neighbors, but the ones I've met haven't struck me as gang banging thugs or prostitutes. They wave and say hi if I'm out in my yard or if they pass me on the street. Mostly they are a mix of first generation immigrants from Mexico, Cambodia, Vietnam, and East Africa and U.S. born people of color, mostly African American. My neighbors are people with kids, people who get up and go to work every day, who walk their little ones to the school bus and work out at the corner gym. One neighbor is a landscaper, one is a cab driver, one is a retired guy with a fondness for tinkering with old cars. I've never seen him in anything but a very comfortable looking blue bathrobe that he wears on his short walks with his dog.

The people who live on the corner are by far the loudest. They like to play Al Green on Saturday afternoons while breaking out the BBQ. Mostly it's laughter and loud talking—annoying at times like the perpetual siren songstress of the ice cream truck circling the block— but not exactly something to be afraid of.

Yes, the property values on my side of Seward Park Ave are much lower. Yes, people of color live here, but many of us live here not because we have to, but because we want to live around other people of color.

So the question becomes is it still the hood when the people who live there do so by choice?

Recently I've begun to attend meetings of Rainier Beach Moving Forward, a coalition of my neighbors who have gotten together to be strategic about making Rainier Beach a safe and beautiful community for its residents. They have partnered with Puget Sound Sage and local business owners to host a community art walk, a Back to School Bash for Rainer Beach International High School and to plan a community farm.

What's unique about Rainier Beach is that unlike the Central District and Columbia City, the gentrification hasn't come yet. Most of my neighbors bought their houses in the '90s and have no intention of getting pushed anywhere. Organizations like Puget Sound Sage and South CORE continue to do their part to empower people to stay in their homes.

So I am living in one of the last predominantly mixed communities in Seattle—and while I'm not saying it's all rainbows and unicorns, it's home. It's a place I feel comfortable and a place I feel invested in.

If it's the hood, then I guess that's where I belong.

Seattle Freeze Thawing in Rainier Beach

Thursday morning. 11AM. Bob Marley is blasting, the air is warm and wet with chlorine. I'm looking fly in my new black and white swim dress about to get my cardio on with 50 strangers. It's time for deep water aerobics at the recently remodeled Rainier Beach Community Center (RBCC).

I live in the 98118 and what they say is true, we really are an eclectic microcosm of the world. The last time I went to a water aerobics class was in Arizona. My mom and I were the only black people in the pool and I wondered if we were going have to have to flash our passports to keep from being deported. Thankfully, my experience at RBCC was the complete opposite. Waving their arm floaties beside me were men and women of various ages, ethnicities, nationalities, and body shapes. Diversity personified.

That got me thinking about Seattle and how segregated it can sometimes feel. While we coexist near one another, we don't often mix. This made me wonder what Rainier Beach Community Center is doing right. Not only were we in these classes sweating next to each other, the locker room afterwards was filled with strangers in various states of dress actually chatting with one another as though somehow we had found a magical antidote to the Seattle Freeze.

"I see a lot of interactions with diversity. And of course having a brand new center it is beautiful to be there," says Nelson Lopez, a community health advocate with Neighborcare for the last eight years. "I think it helps not just minorities, but people of any ages from toddlers to teens to retired or older adults. There is always something at the center for everybody."

Located just a few blocks away, Neighborcare is one of many organizations affiliated with the community center. Neighborcare has created a program to subsidize the pool for patients in need of more physical activity.

"I think the success comes from providing ample programs that reflect the needs of the community," adds Tiffany Bigham of Rec Tech. Rec Tech provides a free computer lab housed at the community center where anyone can use the computer with no restricted sites, no time limits, and free print-ing. "Basically it's free and benefiting the needs of what the community said they would like to see," explains Bigham. In addition to access to the com-puter lab, Rec Tech provides daily tutoring for kids between 4-5pm and con-tinuing education courses for adults

The Center also hosts a variety of activities: drop-in basketball, water classes for all ages and abilities, tots' classes, Officer Cookie's chess club, marching band, Zumba, African dance, the S.E. Youth Orchestra, a Youth Speaks weekly writing circle and more.

"It started out as a race and social justice issue, about delivering services out of a facility to a community that really needs services," recounts Chris-topher Williams, Acting Director of Seattle Parks and Recreation. "We've been working on a new community center since at least 2004, 2005 when we knew the school district was going to demolish the old school and build a new school next door."

In 2008, during the recession, Williams approached then-mayor Michael McGinn with the idea of debt financing the development of the new Community Center. Now the 20 million dollar facility is being paid for partially through revenue generated from the pool.

"This is just a kid-rich neighborhood. There is a lot of need for and a lot of demand for youth programming here. In consciousness we just didn't feel like we could continue to meet that demand in a 50-year- old building that was hardly adequate to serve the most diverse neighborhood in the city, " explains Williams.

The activists of Got Green also viewed the community center as a social justice issue. "There was this missed opportunity during the time when it was being reconstructed about how the city spending in construction could have created jobs," says Michael Woo, Founder of Got Green. Woo described the two main issues as being who would build the center and who would run it.

The City approached the YMCA about taking over day-to-day oper-ations.

While community activists were ultimately unable to influence the con-struction process, their voices were heard when it came to the YMCA. "Not only did the Y not have a good presence, but people were worried about the fee structure for the use of the facility," says Woo. "It didn't happen because the community spoke up." Part of the concern was for the displacement of city employees who had previously worked at the community center. Resi-dents wanted to make sure they got their jobs back.

According to Martha Winther, Recreation Center Coordinator, from before and after the remodel, at least 30% of the staff live in Rainier Beach and even more in nearby sound end communities. The staff demographics, like the population making use of the center, reflect the diversity of the neighborhood.

"Of course we want to be welcoming to everybody," says Winther, explaining the fee structures and scholarships available to reach out to the economically disadvantaged in the community. "Some of the things we've done intentionally are that we have our women's only swim on Sundays and that's not only for the Muslim population but for the Orthodox Jews." The reoccurring theme for what is working and why so many people are loving this community center is that despite the issues with the construction process, the Center itself is giving the community what it wants. What we want is a place to hang out and enjoy all kinds of activities with our neighbors.

Brad and Becky Are Coming to Rainier Beach

Six years ago I bought a house in Rainier Beach.

As a single person living on a non-profit salary, homeownership in Seattle seemed an impossible dream. With rents steadily rising, I went through the motions of finding a realtor and getting prequalified for a home loan anyway, just in case I got lucky and could lock in a place to live at a fixed rate.

What followed was a six-month tour of the South End's scruffiest houses. There was the house that had gutters on the inside (a DIY addition gone wrong) and the place with the hideous Pepto-Bismol carpet that smelled like a herd of llamas had died in the walls.

One house we saw was totally haunted (I mean if you don't believe in the paranormal, I dare you to spend the night there). I was there for ten minutes six years ago and remembering the feeling there still makes the hair on the back of my neck stand up. It was discouraging to think this is what homes in my price range were like, neglected, run down, and in some cases toxic.

When we arrived at what would become my home it felt like a miracle. It wasn't on our listing, but after seeing so much crap, I begged my realtor to show it to me.

"It's probably out of your price range," she warned.

I didn't care. I just wanted to see something beautiful to remember what it felt like. I mean once upon a time weren't houses affordable? If you had a decent job, even if you weren't a Microsoft millionaire, but perhaps a teacher, a mechanic, a bus driver, was there ever a time you could just save up and buy a house without having to mortgage your soul? Is this what they mean when they talk about the dying middle class? You're either rich or in my case, you're not The house was empty and move-in ready. The fireplace, the big kitchen, and back porch, even the roses that blessed the front yard were nothing short of what I'd placed on my vision board the year before. It was everything I'd been looking for. I put in an offer the next day.

Fast forward a couple of years. My property value had already increased by $80,000 and was steadily rising. I don't remember exactly when the solicitation letters started. It didn't seem like a big deal at the time. I'm sure I just mistook it for junk mail and recycled it. But like the first ant at a picnic, there wasn't just one. It was a harbinger of a coming onslaught. Now I get at least a couple letters a month.

They always begin with *Dear Homeowner... Mostly they come from predatory realtors and developers who claim to just want to chat with me to make sure I understand the value of my property. Oh, and that they are willing to pay cash.*

Occasionally I get handwritten notes like the one from a couple in Bellevue who "just happened to be driving around my neighborhood" and fell in love with my house.

After that one, I went outside and looked around my yard to see if someone had accidentally put a for- sale sign up. Nope. That letter bothered me the most. Rainier Beach isn't exactly on the way to anywhere. If you're in the neighborhood, it's on purpose. Just like that emotionally manipulative, "We're just a nice couple" routine also felt very intentional. It pissed me off.

It's not like I'm unfamiliar with gentrification. I've got a lot of friends who used to live in the Central District and some who once lived on Capitol Hill. I've spent a lot of time thinking about what it must feel like to be pushed out, but I hadn't really thought about what it would be like to be the one left behind in a neighborhood that has completely changed.

About a year and a half ago my neighbors across the street disappeared and a pile of mattresses bloomed on the corner. The house lay vacant for quite some time. I noticed a white woman trying to get in and I approached her. She informed me that she was a realtor and that the house had been foreclosed on. While we weren't super close, I had shared a couple of meals and even celebrated a birthday with those neighbors. We always spoke when we saw each other. Still, there were no goodbyes.

I watched as the house that had been painted yellow and orange with turquoise trim was gutted and repainted gray with black and white accents. The East African family on the corner disappeared too. I don't know if they got foreclosed on or not. They were replaced by a Mexican family who lasted less than six months. Now a white family lives there. A white family bought the house across the street too. I'm sure they are lovely people. They put a Black Lives Matter sign in their yard. We wave to each other if our paths cross in the morning, but I can't bring myself to welcome them properly.

Every time I see that sign I think if my life really mattered you would understand that in this white ass city, living in a POC neighborhood has been one small refuge.

When I started my house search, I drew a map from Beacon Hill south through Mount Baker, Columbia City, Hillman City, Brighton Beach and Rainier Beach. I chose to move south after living in the North End for years because I wanted to put down roots in a community of color. I moved to a street predominantly inhabited by immigrants. My neighbors were Mexican, Filipino, Cambodian, Vietnamese, East African, and African American. My neighbors are landscapers, cab drivers, grocery store clerks, and teachers. Some worked at Boeing for years and are retired now.

On the rare weekends when I'm not working I like to curl up in a blanket with a cup of tea and peer out the window. In the summer especially it seems like there is always a birthday party filled with children or a barbecue bumping '80s music. This is the community I chose to invest in.

According to the *Seattle Times*, housing prices have doubled over the last five years. My salary certainly hasn't. And if I were to be on the housing market again, I'd be competing with Brad and Becky who work for Amazon. I find myself facing the same questions many of us face. If I have to move where will I go when I could barely afford this place? Skyway? Renton? Burien?

Now as I walk through my neighborhood I see a lot of for-sale signs. I watch for the telltale mattresses in bloom on street corners and wonder how long before that nice couple from Bellevue moves in next door. Then I check my mail and wonder how long before someone makes me an offer I can't afford to refuse.

The Displacement Tax: An Update from Gentrification Ground Zero

Rainier Beach is the new gentrification ground zero. I have a front row seat. Next month I will celebrate my seventh anniversary of being a homeowner. I have watched my neighbors get foreclosed on and pushed out. I have watched the house flipping teams come through and trim up the yards, slap up new fences, and paint over bright colors with the neutral blues and grays white people seem to prefer. When I walk through my neighborhood now, it's a lot less like the vibrant diverse place I chose to live in and a lot more like Pleasantville.

My house doesn't stand out much, but my lawn signs are like a loud middle finger. When I first put them up I noticed people slowing down their cars to read them. One lady rolled down her car window to explain herself. It seemed like she was hoping to engage in a longer conversation, but I let the signs speak for themselves. Now I think I'm ready to say what's on my mind.

Everyday I pass white people walking their dogs down the street to the bakery. I pass their newly fenced yards, see the beginnings of mother in law cottages getting built and feel envious of what two income families, tech industry money, and generational wealth can afford.

My home has doubled in value, which would be good if I wanted to sell it, but since my plan was always to live in it, the increase in value is a problem. During the first 5 years I lived here my property taxes varied, but only enough to cause a $20-40 difference in my monthly payments. In the last two years my monthly payments have gone up by $284.

My new neighbors aren't bad people. They are that specific brand of Seattle liberal. If you could sum them up in a lawn sign it would be the one that says: In this house, We believe Health Care is a Human Right Black Lives Matter Women's Rights Are Human Rights No Human Is Illegal Science is Real Love is Love.

Their beliefs aren't driving my property taxes up, but their presence is.

So much about money and land is a mystery to me. My parents owned a home when I was born, but they sold it when they divorced, something my dad still laments. So I grew up living in apartments.

Neither parent was able to buy another house until I was 17 and by that time I was getting ready to leave Wisconsin for college and my new life in Seattle, so I wasn't really involved.

Buying my house was terrifying. I had a great realtor, a white woman who knew bankers and attorneys, and leveraged her connections to make my dream a reality. She sat patiently with me explaining how the process worked. Still, the day before I signed the papers I sat on the floor in the empty house in the room that would become my bedroom and had a panic attack. I sobbed on the phone with my mom.

What if I can't do it?

I'd never missed or even been late with rent before, yet somehow a mortgage, even a fixed rate mortgage felt different. What if something major went wrong? How would I afford to fix it? This was more debt that I could wrap my mind around.

My parents for the first time actually weren't that comforting. Either you can afford this on your own or you can't, they told me independently of one another. There was no safety net. I had saved up for my down payment and based on my salary I knew I could make the payments. It was everything I didn't know that scared me the most. I didn't ask them to co-sign the loan and they didn't offer. This was me adulting.

Fast forward to two years ago. I was invited to facilitate a conversation on the film, Race the Power of Illusion for the Delridge Neighborhood and Development Association. I met up with my co- facilitators to pre-screen the film. Since gentrification was very much on my mind, I agreed to lead the portion about structural racism and the Federal Housing Administration.

The film was illuminating. Like 13th , *Healing Justice*, and other films that talk about the impacts of racial oppression, it isn't new information, but there is something jarring and powerful about seeing it all together. I understood how red lining worked, how banks refused to loan money to people of color for the purpose of buying houses in certain neighborhoods.

But what I didn't know was about equity. There is a clip in the movie where they talk about how white families have been leveraging the equity in their homes to make repairs, pay off student loans and create generational wealth. The next morning I called my bank. Do I have equity?

Yes, they said.

For an institution that is committed to sending me junk mail, here was a key piece of information no one had ever mentioned to me. Though why would they? My financial dependence is much more lucrative than my financial freedom and with an institution that has historically gone out of its way to prevent people of color from creating generational wealth, what should I expect?

I went online to try to understand what this invisible resource was and what I could do with it. Then I called my bank back and it was like talking to a genie I didn't know existed. Within the next couple months I refinanced my house, knocking five years off my mortgage and paying off my student loans.

I guess I could have dreamed bigger, maybe remodeled my bathroom or painted my house turquoise like I've been wanting to, but my biggest dream has always been not to owe anyone anything. I have come to accept that, barring divine intervention or winning the Powerball, I will be paying off this house for the next couple decades, but if I could zero out all my other debt that would be miracle enough.

I look around my home and I love it. I replaced the beige paint with bright colors, furnished the rooms with comfortable places to sit and read, fun lamps, and shelves to hold my ever expanding book collection. From the outside my house is plain. I try to keep my yard under control. This summer, a financial gift from my dad allowed me to dig out all the invasive black berry bushes that were threatening to devour my back yard. But other than some interior paint, basic maintenance and the occasional repair my house has not changed in seven years. I haven't added a room or built a fence or gotten new plumbing or a new roof. So how is my home suddenly so much more valuable?

You know the answer.

The "real" difference between my house now and my house seven years ago is that now I have white neighbors.

So yes, I threw a temper tantrum -with lawn signs. I got out my art kit and repurposed my Nikkita Oliver sign to read "Gentrification Ground 0", because that is where I live. One sign didn't seem sufficient. So I made another, then another, culminating in a sequence that ends with "This House is Not for Sale." I knew these signs wouldn't change anything, in the same way that having a Black Lives Matter sign doesn't change the fact that we are still being shot in the streets. But in the way that art has always grounded me, it made me feel better to express out loud the silent conversation I'd been having with my neighborhood.

An older black gentleman who lives a block away walked over with his dog to tell me how much he loves my signs. He lived in the Central District for years because it was the only place blacks could own property. He owned two houses there, but ended up getting pushed south.

"Many African Americans who had paid off or paid down their mortgages after twenty or thirty years in their homes saw spectacular increases in the value of their properties particularly in the 1990s and the first years of the 21st Century ," writes Henry McGee in an article outlining the impact of gentrification on the central district. "One three bedroom, one bath, 1,200 square foot Central District home assessed by King County as valued at $1,280 in 1938 was worth $5,000 in 1960, $190,000 in 2001, and $355,000 in 2005."

And here we are, living history as it repeats itself in the Rainier Valley. The city of Seattle was clearly complicit in allowing property taxes to become a tool of racial oppression. So now what?

When we talk about the affordable housing crisis, of course those living below the poverty line, those suffering homelessness or housing insecurity, should be prioritized. But what steps Mayor Durkan is taking to address the issue of gentrification? This is an opportunity to reevaluate how "fair" market prices are assessed. With the help of my realtor, I am appealing my taxes (also something I didn't know you could do). But whether or not the appeal is successful, the problem remains. If the fair market value of my house is still contingent upon a homeowner's perceived access to generational wealth and, by default, the color of my skin, there is no winning.

The husband of the white couple who moved in across the street made a point to introduce himself to me. "I want you to know that I agree with you people," he told me and pointed at my lawn. I felt myself bristle at being called "you people," but I could see his hands shaking and I realized that this was an act of bravery for him. My signs had made him nervous to talk to me. I think my white neighbors think I hate them or that I am some militant angry black woman. I don't hate them, but I am angry.

I hate injustice. I hate that it's 2018 and we seem to be moving backwards, that everything the civil rights movement set out to accomplish seems to be getting reversed. I hate that I don't know if I will be able to absorb the next round of taxes and that I might have to sell my home. I hate not knowing where I will be able to afford to live. My neighbors are not some super villains ruining my life. They are just ordinary people who like me wanted to buy a house and live in it.

I don't hold my neighbors responsible for the structures in place to marginalize me. But if they truly believe everything their lawn sign says I need their help to hold our city accountable for creating a more equitable process.

If you are looking for something to do with your unearned privilege, call Jenny Durkan. Call the King County Assessor's office and ask them to make a dispensation for people who have been disadvantaged by structural racism in the same way they make dispensations for senior citizens. Tell every elected official that will listen (and even the ones who don't want to) that this is a problem. Take your beliefs and your caring hearts to the voting booth, but don't stop there. Take action. It's not enough to only care about people of color when we are living in desperate conditions. If my life matters to you, help me deconstruct these systems that keep me, and many others, living with the fear that in the next few years we will lose our homes, our legacies, and the tiny bit of wealth we've worked so hard for.

What's Not to Like About Uncle Ike's

"We was red lined in but now we black balled out so they can sell green… Ike is no uncle to me. How many brothers went to jail on this corner from moving dime bags. In a week he doing, what, a couple of hundred grand?"

Local rapper Draze's mournful track "Irony on 23rd" has become an anthem for people in the Central District who view Uncle Ike's, one of the city's most popular legal pot shops, as a slap in the face.

Since it opened in late 2014 the store has been a source of controversy for the reasons Draze outlines so eloquently in the song—from community members feeling voiceless in the process of land development, to the unfairness of a wealthy white business owner profiting from doing the exact same thing that many poor people of color are still in jail for.

So today, on 4/20, the pot smoker's holiday, community members plan to take their next stand against Uncle Ike's Pot Shop.

Protestors will convene at 3pm at Garfield High School before making their way to Uncle Ike's.

"Unity On Union" is the call to action. Organizers include Draze himself, the NAACP, Africatown, Mount Calvary Christian Center, The Black Book Club, Seaspot Media group and Third Level Events.

Ian Eisenberg, the owner of Uncle Ike's, didn't respond to my interview requests. During past protests Eisenberg has been mostly dismissive.

"I feel like I'm in a Spike Lee movie," he told the *Seattle Times* earlier this year when hundreds of protestors broke off of the yearly MLK Day March and forcibly shut down the store for a few hours. But a lot of other people did want to talk about Uncle Ike's—how it's become a symbol for uneven development in the CD and the displacement of a historically black community—and the specific legal and ethical issue of the store's proximity to its neighbor, Mount Calvary Christian Center, and the Joshua Generation Teen Center across the street.

Section 18A of Initiative 502 originally stated that marijuana could not be sold, "within one thousand feet of the perimeter of a school grounds, playground, recreation center or facility, child care center, public park, or library, or any game arcade admission to which is not restricted to persons aged twenty-one years or older."

But it has since been amended at the discretion of the city to only require retail businesses selling marijuana to have a 500 feet buffer when it comes to child care centers, game arcades, libraries, public parks, public transit centers, and recreational centers or facilities, or 250 feet in the case of property zoned downtown mixed commercial and residential.

Unless the city is now classifying the Central District as downtown, Uncle Ike's does not appear to meet the required buffer. But rather than put the burden of proof on the business owner, it has been up to the Mount Calvary to prove that the Joshua Generation Teen Center falls under one of the protected categories.

"So the law does not specifically say teen centers or it doesn't say churches or it doesn't say mosques," says Draze. "But I think the spirit of the law when they created it was trying to make sure we had discretion in protecting the youth."

Mount Calvary tried to argue this point in court for the purpose of getting an injunction to keep Uncle Ike's from opening in the first place, but lost on the grounds that the Teen Center was not open enough days to meet the criteria.

This didn't sit well with Reggie Witherspoon, who has been the Pastor at Mount Calvary for 28 years.

"To discredit my teen center and to disrespect my youth and to say it's not a legitimate teen center is asinine and very offensive," he said.

For him, the proximity of the weed store to his church is more than just a technicality.

"It's against everything," says Witherspoon. "It's the opposite of what we teach our young people relative to taking care of themselves, the impact of drugs, etc. So for them to have to see it every week is just not a good look."

He says he met with Mayor Ed Murray soon after he learned what Eisenberg was planning to do with the property, which had previously hosted a Mediterranean restaurant that closed after an arson in 2013.

"And I told the Mayor that if this were Magnolia and you were 250 feet away from those white kids in Magnolia, I don't believe you'd allow the store to open up," he says. In the end, he concludes, the city prioritized tax revenue over the well-being of the children.

But it's not just about weed. It's really about respect for the community.

"This is not an attack on anybody who smokes marijuana or who doesn't smoke or anyone who has a pot shop, that's not our issue," says Draze. "There is one pot shop in the state of Washington that is within the legal of 500 feet from where youth assemble. And it just happens to be in what is known as a traditionally black neighborhood in Seattle. I just don't think that's a coincidence."

Neither does lawyer Sheley Secrest, the Vice President and Chair of Economic Development for the Seattle King County chapter of the NAACP.

"These types of stores, weed stores, that doesn't happen in white neighborhoods. Mothers, parents, everyone would be outraged at the idea of a store selling these types of drugs within a 500 foot you know radius of where children hang out," she says.

Over the past few years, Secrest has spent a lot of time contemplating how development can be approached from the standpoint of community benefits.

"We want to be able to be a part of the development," says Secrest. "We want it to reflect our needs and our wants. We wanted to be able to see the beauty of our culture in our neighborhood so that's what this action on 4/20 is about. It's developing yes, but with a community benefits approach."

That might seem like an abstraction, but Jaebadiah Gardner of OnPoint Real Estate sees real ways to make that happen.

"In particular to our neighborhood, it really boils down to not being able to have the wealth and resources to acquire the things that we need to maintain our foothold," says Gardner, who recently won a Business Human Rights Leader award from the City Office of Civil Rights.

To him, lack of employment opportunities have also systematically prevented the community from being able to keep pace with the housing market. Gardner calls out the big employers like Amazon and Boeing and asks why they insist on hiring transplants when there are perfectly good local candidates who could fill those positions.

"It's not just about white people coming in and pushing us out. It's more about what job employment are we not getting, A, and B, how do we come together as a community to acquire real estate in the Central District in a productive way?" asks Gardner.

Gardner views protests as a Band-aid, and hopes this incident with Uncle Ike's will be a catalyst for the community to come together to take preventative measures.

"I'm going to host a pretty informal community meeting to literally just lay out the lay of the land in the Central District, to just inform everybody where development projects are going on. Because its also a foresight thing," says Gardner. "I don't expect a single mom or the grandparents who take care of their kid's kids to be on top of this, so I feel like my duty is to make sure that my company informs the community and hope the community uses the information to its best advantage."

"The eyes of the country are looking at Seattle to see how we handle this."

Draze is looking forward as well—though his gaze is turned towards how an informed community can make pragmatic decisions about its elected officials.

"Uncle Ike's is not our focus," he explains. "It might seem that way. But let's just say that our focus is our elected officials, our state liquor board etc, they're the focus. Ian [Eisenberg] doesn't have the power to change this beyond moving, and he's already proven that he doesn't have a heart, not for us, not for these issues."

If you're looking for more irony, consider the parallels between the city's handling of Uncle Ike's and the push to shut down hookah lounges last summer. Both are cases of businesses operating on the blurry edges of the law. But while the Mayor threatened to shut down the mostly Somali-owned hookah lounges, driven by the perception of them hosting a criminal element, he seems to be going out of his way to protect Uncle Ike's.

"That right there is a shining example of institutionalized racism. If you have the resources and you're white and you're able to do things that you know black people couldn't do," says Gardner. "We've been selling weed for hella long and we've been getting in trouble for it, and now it's okay? For real? Now it's okay? Because you've got a license? Because you can afford to get a license?"

"They need to know it's wrong, that they blew it," says Draze in reference to the Mayor and the State Liquor and Cannabis Board. "The community knows it's wrong and wants them to do something about it, and if they don't, jobs will be on the line down the road. It's not a compromise."

But the stakes are even higher than what happens with Uncle Ike's and Mount Calvary. Draze views Seattle as the guinea pig for what is likely going to happen across the country.

"The eyes of the country are looking at Seattle to see how we handle this, how we do this, so let's make sure we do it and do it right," he implores.

"I just want to invite people to come out, sign the petition, and let their voice be heard."

Rainier Beach — A Beautiful, Safe Place to Live?

This fall marked my 10th anniversary of owning a house in Rainier Beach, making this the longest I've ever lived anywhere. This year, instead of hosting a celebratory gathering or painting another wall, I stood sobbing in my living room, trapped in a nightmare while my neighbor boarded up my window and hung a sheet of canvas to keep the glass from further falling into the house.

When I arrived home on the evening of Oct. 26, 2021, I knew something was wrong.

I noticed there was a hole in my new sheer curtains. The carpet, which I recently replaced, was crunchy with tiny shards of glass and the fine, white dust of fibers.

What Makes a Hole in a Curtain?

I called a friend, the way I have learned to do when there is something scary I have to deal with alone — like a spider I have to trap and remove or squash if it gets too jumpy. I didn't hear anything. There wasn't a burglar. For the most part, things seemed as I'd left them, but there was a circular chunk missing from the marigold-yellow wall of my dining room. It should have been obvious, but my first thought was "What makes a hole that size in a curtain? An animal? A giant moth? Something with teeth?" It wasn't until I pulled back the curtain and saw the window that I understood. There was no animal. This was a bullet hole. Two bullet holes.

Two bullets had come through my window, sliced through my curtains, and sailed over my couch and coffee table. One came in high, ricocheted off the ceiling leaving a scorch mark, and lodged inside the white molding of my living room wall. One came in at head level, piercing the walls I'd just had painted berry fizz. The bullet hit so hard it knocked a chunk of plaster from the wall behind it, blowing white dust across the room.

"I have to hang up," I told my friend. "My house has been shot." And then, "Oh, God, I'm going to have to call the police."

I don't know which felt worse. My sanctuary had been violated, and in order to be made whole by insurance, I would need to invite the further violation of the police. It wasn't until I was on the phone with the dispatcher explaining what had happened — for what would be the first of so many times — that it really hit me. I started to cry. "Was anyone injured?" the dispatcher asked me. "No," I said, though it wasn't true. This hurt me in ways I still can't articulate.

An officer arrived promptly. He was polite, but he didn't take off his shoes. There was glass and it was safer that way, but it still bothered me. The process was compassionately brief. We both took pictures to document the damage. He asked for duct tape and taped two silver crosses over the bullet holes like Band-Aids to keep the heat in. From the outside, they looked like small grave markers.

He gave me a card with his name and phone number and an incident report number. Another house down the street was hit too, but no one was injured. No one died. It could have been so much worse.

When things are shitty, that's what people tell you. "It could have been worse," as if somehow that makes it better. The officer seemed very interested in the trajectory of the bullets and where the person would have been standing. Were they on foot, were they in a car? Did I see anything? Did I have any reason to suspect I was targeted? He asked if I wanted him to try to dig the bullets out. I asked if it would help him find who did it, and he said no and that he'd have to break open the wall even further, so I declined. My house took those bullets for me, and they remain in its bones.

I called my parents. It was too late to call my insurance company, but I composed an email with pictures and the incident number, and then I got out the vacuum and cleaned the carpets and the couch. I wiped down the coffee table and the windowsill and vacuumed again, thinking that in all the endless hours of Law & Order or whatever casually violent movies or TV shows I've watched, you never see anyone vacuuming.

The Part They Don't Show on TV

Calling insurance, explaining what happened. Calling contractors and glass companies, explaining what happened. Getting referred to an insurance adjuster. Explaining what happened. Realizing three days later your bookshelf is still covered in dust. Bursting into tears. Wiping everything down. Compulsively vacuuming again. Watching a spider crack develop between the two bullet holes as the rainstorms beat against the house. Wondering if the window will break. Scheduling an emergency therapy appointment, explaining what happened. Crying until you puke. Going to work like nothing happened, because you don't want to have to explain what happened. Taking a day off of work, because each time you have to make a call, you have to factor in time to have an emotional breakdown. Calling more window companies, because COVID-19 has ruined our supply chain and most of the companies the insurance agent recommended have shut down or are scheduled out and can't fit in your repair until March 2022. Realizing your urgency is no one else's urgency. Staring every day at the holes in your beautifully curated walls and the crack growing larger in your window. Talking to your insurance agent and adjuster and backup adjuster again. You know them all by name and recognize their voices. Buying replacement curtains. Asking neighbors to come help hang replacement curtains, because you are too emotionally exhausted to do this alone. Explaining what happened.

Declining multiple invitations to stay at your friends' houses because you want to sleep in your own bed and have done the strange mental calculus of assessing safety as the number of walls between you and the front window. Asking a friend to go through the multiple phone calls and convoluted bureaucracy it takes to get a copy of the police report, which tells you only three useful things: the name and address of your neighbor who is at his house doing the same thing, the time of the shooting, and that no one was reported dead or injured. They don't know who did it. They don't know why. The term "ongoing investigation" seems nebulous. Call your friend who knows people who know people involved in gangs, start your own ongoing investigation. Receive no answers.

Expect no accountability. Experience bouts of paralyzing rage. Thank God and whatever angels helped you to miss the shooting by 12 minutes. Wonder how much bulletproof glass costs. Get the wall patched. Watch it dry like a splat of oatmeal. Get everything repainted. Contemplate the duct tape crosses on your window and painting a mural around the bullet holes. Realize the crack has grown larger.

Come home one day to find the window is all the way broken; a huge piece of glass has sliced through the curtains you just replaced, and it's raining onto the new carpet you're so precious about. Cry some more as a neighbor boards it up to keep the rain out. Realize your neighbor, who you initially thought of as a gentrifier, is now a friend. You can't sleep in a house with no front window, with wind and rain playing the plywood like a drum. Find a place to stay. Wait for the repairs, which continue to be delayed. Wonder about actual justice, and know there is no point in holding your breath. What's done is done.

When the window finally gets replaced, I rearrange all the furniture so the couch is against the wall. I have to practice sitting in my own living room again five minutes at a time, like exposure therapy.

The Things We Say and the Things We Don't

Even after explaining what happened over and over, I don't know how to talk about this with my friends. Some conversations have been nourishing and grounding; others have made me feel judged and victimized.

I feel sad, angry, exhausted, frustrated, and violated. There is a deep well of grief inside my heart at the loss of sanctuary. Unexpectedly, there is also shame. I didn't do anything wrong, but when people ask me if I plan to move or want me to come stay with them, it makes me feel like I should be ashamed and afraid of this place where I chose to live. Anyone who knows me, and any stranger who has read my work over the years, knows I rep Rainier Beach hard. Something about this happening feels like a betrayal of that. Like I vouched for this community, and it didn't live up to my ideals. I know this isn't fair. Whoever was out shooting was not doing so on behalf of the community and probably wasn't even in their right mind to be considering the collateral damage. It's not logical, but it's how I feel.

I find myself wondering if friends will now be afraid to come over for dinner. Should I be afraid to host them? Will they be safe? Will I? When will I feel at home in my home again? A few days after the shooting in Rainier Beach, there was a shooting in Northgate, and a man died. I wonder if anyone has decided that Northgate is a dangerous and bad place to live. I also wonder about the impact of the pandemic on people's economic and mental stability and how that will color our access to safe neighborhoods. I don't want this to be the thing that makes me give up on Rainier Beach. Does this one experience define my relationship to my neighborhood?

A Story of Home

This home has been my sanctuary. When days are hard, I come home and rest. I can cry or scream or be mad, and no one bothers me or tells me I am bothering them. I paint murals on the walls and cut roses from my yard for my table and take long baths in my beautiful deep tub. When days are good or there is something to celebrate, I light up the grill and host back porch lounge sessions. These walls hold so many memories: birthdays and slumber parties, podcast recording sessions, so much laughter, so much peace.

Last year, I had wheelchair ramps built so my dad could come live with me. He stayed for several months, and I was so grateful to be able to share my home in this way. Thankfully, he moved to Portland a few months ago, because if he were still living with me, he would have been at home. I try not to think of what might have happened if he had been home during the shooting. There are some things insurance could never cover. Windows and walls can be fixed. But the reparation for a sanctuary, returning to a sense of normalcy after this kind of violation, is another process entirely.

On Fear and the Fallacy of Safety

I didn't choose this neighborhood for its reputation of safety. I wanted to live around other BIPOC-identified folks, and, depending on who is telling the story, that can be seen as a dangerous proposition.

When you come home to a house that's been shot, it's hard not to feel like safety is performative — a nice idea, but hard to execute with so many uncontrollable variables. Even before this, the concept of safety for me existed in a form of suspended disbelief. There are times when I might feel safe, but I rarely confuse that with actually being safe. How could I, when it's common knowledge that bad things happen to people like me regardless of what neighborhood I'm in?

Black women in America live some of the most toxic superlatives. We are most likely to experience rape, assault, violent crime, generational poverty, intimate partner violence, structural and systemic violence, and bias that leads to us being paid less on the dollar than everyone else and having inequitable access to housing, jobs, and basic social services. We are most likely to be under-medicated and disbelieved in medical situations (ask Serena Williams about that), to die in childbirth, to be disproportionately punished in school settings, to be routed into the school-to-prison pipeline, to have Adverse Childhood Experiences that result in negative health outcomes through the rest of our lives.

The list is long. And it is worth acknowledging that there are many folks, such as trans and Indigenous people, experience parallel oppressions. I'm not here to play the oppression Olympics. No one wants to medal in that. I simply want to bring some awareness to the fact that often, conversations around "safety" seem tone-deaf and impossibly ridiculous in the face of my lived experience.

I am making a choice not to fill this paragraph with numbers or statistics, though these things are all easily Google-able, along with the very public deaths of Sandra Bland, Breonna Taylor, Charleena Lyles, and ... you know the names, you know the stories. The numbers are not how I know I am vulnerable. I know I am vulnerable because I have the lived experience of harm. I exist in a community that holds a generational memory of lived experiences of a broad spectrum of ongoing, daily harm and trauma.

The closest approximation I have to safety is an optimism that, though I will 100% experience harm, I might live beyond it to have other experiences too. And that I also have a generational legacy of resilience and of cultivating an unbothered stance. Black women make it look easy, but spoiler alert, it's not. It's expensive. Living in this country takes literal years off our lives and puts us in impossible situations regularly. There are some days where I will Michelle Obama and take the high road. There are some days where I will get knocked down and have to just lie there wallowing in rage and grief while I catch my breath. And there are some days where I've got my sword in one hand and my sage in the other — ready to do battle.

When my friends ask if I feel safe at home after this, I have to ask myself, "Did I ever?" I think a better question is, "Am I afraid?" And the answer is, "Sometimes," but I face it and work through it, because that's not how I want to live my life.

Unpopular Opinion: Guns Create Gun Violence

Though I know how to clean, load, and shoot a gun, they don't make me feel safer. I never want to be in a position to end up shooting and possibly killing someone. I don't think I could survive the weight of that, even if it was in self-defense. People with guns are more likely to kill people. This is true with or without intention. NPR just put out a story about the rise in accidental shootings during the pandemic, while kids are quarantined at home with their gun-owning parents. Not everyone is equipped to handle the responsibility of gun ownership. We get it wrong when we focus more on maintaining our right to do something rather than focus on what we're actually doing.

The National Rifle Association has been having a juvenile, well-funded temper tantrum about this for years. Their game is to convince us that not having access to guns infringes on our rights, rather than admitting that such unrestricted access endangers our lives. As usual, death is more profitable than investing in new ways of living that might be beneficial to us all. But that doesn't make it right. I would rather build a world where people would feel safe enough to go unarmed than to continue arming people who compromise everyone's safety. Whoever shot my house had no right to put me in danger or damage my home, but they were given access because America cares more about money than it does about safety.

When I first moved to Rainier Beach, I attended several meetings of the Rainier Beach Action Coalition. The group was just in the beginning stages of drafting up a community vision for making Rainier Beach a beautiful and safe place for all. I loved this mission. I loved that there was a group of neighbors coming together to host the Back 2 School Bash, to distribute backpacks full of school supplies, to feed the community, and to actively disrupt danger by providing corner greeters. This was exactly the kind of community I wanted to participate in.

My house getting shot has surfaced for me the ways in which I have normalized the inaccessibility of safety. That is something I am carrying with me everywhere I go. And it's not healthy or fair or okay, and I don't want to. I want to have a lived experience of safety in my body, in my home, in Rainier Beach, in Seattle, in this country. I have been in survival mode for so long that I've stopped dreaming into this possibility.

It's time to dream again. The window has been replaced, the walls patched and painted, but a deeper repair must also take place. It's not enough to be unafraid. It's time to stop normalizing and accepting the unacceptable. We can do better, for ourselves and our families, for Rainier Beach, for Seattle and beyond. If the pandemic has taught me anything, it's that it's entirely possible for the whole world to change in the blink of an eye. When it's important, we can move mountains. And this is vital. It is time to reimagine safety in a way that is radically inclusive. We've started the conversation about defunding the police, but what about defunding gun lobbies? What about teaching meditation in schools and shifting punitive practices to restorative ones? What can we be doing to cultivate a culture of connection and accountability that can lead to safety? We owe it to ourselves and to the next generation to create a framework where all communities can truly be called beautiful and safe.

Who Can We Call?

It was a rare sunny day in January and the curtains in my dining room were drawn open to let the light in. I sat fidgeting with my sewing while on a Zoom meeting for work. Out of the corner of my eye, I saw a man come into my yard.

He had a lean build and was of medium height, in his late 20s to early 30s, possibly mixed-race Black and Asian, dressed in dark loose clothing. My house sits on a hill, back from the street, with no fence bordering the front, but a chain-link fence neatly marking the division between my lot and my neighbor's. In the summer teenagers from a house across the street had taken to sitting at the bottom of the hill by the sidewalk. I startled them mid-hang out when I went to water my plants, but we introduced ourselves to each other and established that as long as they didn't leave garbage behind I didn't mind them sitting on the edge of my property. It didn't feel invasive since they were mostly on the sidewalk. If anything, during this time of social isolation, it was comforting to hear them laughing and giving each other shit. For a moment you could almost forget that it wasn't a normal summer.

But this man wasn't in public space. He had climbed the hill and entered my side yard and seemed to be heading towards the back, which dead-ends in another fence. Since March 2020, I've worked remotely from home and been occasionally surprised by people in my yard. It mostly turns out to be meter readers or my neighbor collecting his wayward chickens, but this was not that. I excused myself from the meeting, threw on some shoes, and walked out to the yard.

The man didn't seem as jarred by my presence as I was by his. In fact, he glanced up at me, but didn't say anything, but crouched down to examine my grass. I cataloged the layers of vulnerability to the situation. Here was this stranger, a man, possibly homeless, who seemed mentally unstable (because who just rolls up into someone's yard like that?) and then me, a woman, home alone and unarmed in slip-on clogs, which are not the best shoes for a fight.

"Can I help you?" I asked.

"Oh I'm just feeding the birds," he mumbled in a soft voice, not making eye contact. His movements were slow and stilted and I didn't sense hostility, but I wondered if that would change when I set a boundary.

"I need you to leave," I said.

He stood and looked up then, but not at me. I tracked his gaze to the bare-branched tree behind me that still held a few apples most of which, given the season, were rotting.

"Is it the apples? Is that what you want?" I asked. "I mean why would you come back here?"

"Actually I was just looking at this tree," he said pointing to the pine in my front yard. But then he was looking at the apples again.

"You can have some if they're any good, but then you've got to leave. You can't be back here," I reiterated.

So he walked to the tree and reached up to assess the apples and determined they weren't fit to eat. I went into the house and got two apples from my fridge. He pulled a gray scarf over his mouth and nose when he reached for the fruit, which is when I realized I had forgotten to put on a mask. It was a strange moment to realize that this person who just made me feel so vulnerable was himself vulnerable and not just from COVID-19. I wondered what had happened in his life for him to end up wandering aimlessly into strangers' yards in the middle of the day. Was he a sign of things to come? How many Washingtonians are a paycheck away from being in the same situation? But I also really wanted him to leave and he was not moving very quickly.

"You've got to leave," I told him again and that seemed to piss him off.

"Oh I can't be here?" he said aggressively. "Fine," he added, and as I watched him descend the hill to the sidewalk I wondered how many times he'd been told that. I went inside, locking the door behind me, and sat by the window watching to see if he would really leave or if things were going to escalate. He moved in front of my neighbor's house and reached down and threw something on the grass. It looked like a handful of dirt, but maybe it was seeds since he had mentioned feeding the birds.

I had my next meeting, but it was by phone so I sat distractedly trying to monitor the situation. I told my colleague what had just happened and that the man was still outside. I definitely didn't want to call the police, but I wondered who I could call.

My colleague's husband advised me to call 911 and coached me to ask for a mental health professional. He explained there was a program that got routed through 911 dispatch, but that I could request someone other than police. So I tried that, but the dispatch operator said that an officer would first have to come out to make an assessment before referring a social work intervention.

"I don't want to do that," I said. "Can't you just skip that part and call the mental health professional?"

The operator reiterated that it didn't work that way. Of course not, because the people who put this system in place obviously haven't been traumatized by the police.

Officer Friendly stopped being friendly to me when I was a teenager and a cop showed up at my door at 10 p.m. with questions about some graffiti. My friends and I had discovered the gymnastics gym by my house had drop-in sessions where we could play on the equipment and jump in the pool of foam blocks. When I asked the cops why they were questioning me they said it was because they were approaching anyone who went to the drop-in sessions and wasn't a regular ... read: wasn't a little white girl enrolled in their gymnastics sessions. They closed the gym to non-members after that and every time I walked past it I felt the weight of unwelcome, and the shame of being accused of a crime I did not commit.

Being accused of vandalism was actually one of my more positive encounters with the police. Mostly I do my best to avoid them, but almost every Black person I know (myself included) has had at least one awful experience personally or had a family member or close friend brutalized, criminalized, or worse. But if somehow you've been lucky enough to avoid the firsthand experience, Black Lives Matter has brought viral black death and the insidious state-sanctioned genocide to the forefront of our collective consciousness.

I refuse to watch the 8-minute and 46-second viral video of George Floyd being murdered by the police, but after Sandra Bland and Philando Castile, I can't see flashing lights in my rearview mirror without my heart rate speeding up knowing that all of the parts of who I am, an educator, a writer, a daughter, a voter, or even the fact that I haven't done anything wrong, could be rendered irrelevant by the assumptions made based on the color of my skin. That feeling: palms sweating, wondering if today is the day I become a hashtag and get posthumously tried in the court of public opinion for why I must have deserved it, is now just the everyday trauma of being _____ fill-in-the-blank with your marginalized identity of choice.

I experience this as a Black woman, but I don't think it is any less the experience of others who are visibly not white or don't fit the gender binary.

So why, when it is OBVIOUS that many of us have been traumatized by the police, are they the designated gatekeepers for mental health assessments? Why are the police who we turn to when their very presence and uniform might be enough to cause a mental health crisis? Who wants to play that kind of Russian Roulette? Would I be able to forgive myself if the police came and harmed that stranger? Or if he ended up criminalized over rotten apples? Or what if they got trigger happy and came for me? We all know what happened to Charleena Lyles.

Also killed in their homes: Atatiana Jefferson, Breonna Taylor, Aurora Rosser, Stephon Clark, Botham Jean, Michelle Cusseaux, Janisha Fonville, Akai Gurley, Tanisha Anderson … and so many more. How many more will be murdered?

What should we do when the very people who we are told to depend on to protect us have broken our trust and taught us to fear them more than any criminal?

I watched the man double back and walk past my house slowly. He stood in front and threw a handful of something on my lawn again—maybe it was seed because shortly after a flock of blackbirds descended on the grassy hill adding a Hitchcockian note to an already surreal situation. He crossed the street to do the same to my neighbors before disappearing down the block.

I was left with several questions. What happens if he comes back? What happens if someone else comes? What happens if they aren't just feeding the birds but trying to break in? And who can we call when shit happens?

I posed the question on the Rainier Beach Facebook page and sparked a wide-ranging discussion. My neighbors posted lists of resources, some more relevant than others, to deal with a broad variety of issues. Suggestions included the Crisis Connections 24-Hour Crisis Line, Union Gospel Mission, American Medical Response, the National Suicide Prevention hotline, 211, and more.

The moment had passed, but out of curiosity, I began to call down the list of numbers to see who was on the other end and what they could do for me. First I called the American Medical Response number (206-444-4444). It rang 8 times before someone picked up and when they did, they told me they could send an ambulance, but since there wasn't a medical emergency that wasn't what I needed. They told me I should call 911 to get an OSU officer (Operational Support Unit) … also not what I wanted or needed.

I called 211 and got a busy signal. I called again and got put on hold and their call back system never had anyone call me back, so I do not recommend this if you are having an issue that requires a timely response.

This also happened to me a couple of years ago when someone I knew was exiting a DV situation and needed to find a shelter. I called 211 to get referrals and spent 6 hours on the phone just to be told there wasn't a free bed from Shoreline to Tacoma. Many people have recommended this resource to me, but when I tried to use it, it did not work. Imagine being a person in imminent danger, having the courage to finally leave only to be confronted with closed doors. That person is safe and doing much better now, but only through their own scrappiness AND NOT BECAUSE THEY WERE ABLE TO ACCESS HELP THROUGH ANY OF THESE SYSTEMS.

Next, I called the 24-Hour Crisis Hotline (866-427-4747). Someone answered on the second ring, which felt reassuring. They asked for my name and zip code then we talked about the situation. Even though it had already been resolved, it felt good to talk it through. The operator suggested I connect with my neighbors to do some safety planning. But that is a complicated task, navigating our varying levels of comfort and cultural practices around conflict management not to mention the logistics of trying to get together during a pandemic in an area that is rapidly gentrifying. The Crisis Hotline echoed what everyone else had: that for removing someone from my property, police were my best and only resource.

So where do we go from here? We as a community have been vocal about defunding the SPD because, for many of us, it is a resource that has traumatized us. But what do we do in the meantime?

One thing I noticed during COVID-19 is the proliferation of mutual aid popping up across the city. Nowhere was it more visible than this summer during the Capitol Hill Occupied Protest. The CHOP was by no means a utopian experience. It was gritty and weird and complicated, but also incredible. Medics set up first aid tents and did triage for injured protestors. Restaurateurs donated food so that anyone from any walk of life could get something to eat. Social workers and therapists set up resource tents. There was even a security force that came to our assistance when we organized a Juneteenth Blackout and Proud Boys showed up. As needs arose, the community stepped in to meet them. Again, I am not trying to idealize CHOP, but that energy of people coming together to organize systems of support on all levels is what we need moving forward.

While the police may have cleared out the CHOP, displacing homeless people and scattering organizers, they can't erase the networks of people who answered the call of community and came together to build something different. Imagine a mutual aid of safety that is rooted in community care and restorative justice practices. What if instead of police being the ones to assess the situation, a team of crisis specialists was called instead? People trained to deal with mental and physical health situations with mediation and de-escalation tactics in addition to first responder training.

I want to live in a place where I can call a number and know there is someone on the other end who will actually help me. Don't we all deserve that level of safety? Isn't that an inalienable right? I want to be able to call someone if I feel unsafe without having to worry if making the call itself will put me at further risk. And I want people to stop pretending that all of us get that in the current iteration of the status quo.

The insurrection on January 6, 2021, did a lot to throw that into sharp relief. After our summer of tear gas-filled protests, simply to have this country and our police recognize the validity of Black lives and to advocate that justice be served to the murderers of George Floyd, Breonna Taylor, and Toni McDade, it was infuriating to see the gentle handling of white supremacist terrorists bearing confederate flags and nooses laying siege to our Capitol to steal the last remnants of our broken democracy. In the same way Dylan Roof got a trip to Burger King after slaughtering 9 church parishioners, we witnessed video footage of those Capitol Police opening the gates, just as we watched police show up in full riot gear for every Black Lives Matter protest. And noticeably absent was the footage of Capitol Police shooting Ashli Babbit. Ask yourself how many videos of Black death have you seen? I don't fault police or journalists for trying to have some sense of respect for human life, I just question the hypocrisy of when these standards are applied.

We know which side you're on. Your white sheets are showing. And this is part of the reason King County declared racism a public health crisis. I feel insane just having to write this article. I feel insane to think that I live every day without any expectation of ever being safe, not even in my home, and that is my normal. Fuck this shit.

Since March 2020, our whole lives have changed in ways we probably could have never imagined were possible. And now, even when life feels surreal, we have a unique opportunity to advocate for the society we want to live in. Though it can feel overwhelming, not knowing where to begin, I just can't help thinking that we deserve better. The rage, trauma, and grief we carry is too great a burden. It is time for us to create the systems we deserve.

The Struggle
#blacklivesmatter

Black History Month: The Same Old Song and Dance?

Bright red curtains part. A spotlight travels across an all-black stage. Everyone in skin tight black body suits with floppy afro wigs and black face. I mean black like shoe shine, like tar, like coal, black with chalk white rings around their eyes and smiling mouths.

I'd never seen a minstrel show. The closest was probably "White Christmas" with Bing Crosby, which was a bunch of white people singing, dancing and telling corny jokes. All very family time TV appropriate, (when that still meant something). It seemed so innocuous.

But "The Minstrel Show Revisited" performed by Spectrum Dance Theater was anything but.

I caught the second night of a three night run at the Cornish Playhouse at the Seattle Center. This performance, choreographed and directed by Donald Byrd, the Artistic Director of Spectrum Dance Theater, was an updated version of an original work Byrd presented in 1991.

Throughout the 19th century, minstrel shows were a uniquely American, extremely popular form of entertainment where white people put on black face and pretended to be black—and later black people put on black face pretending to be white people pretending to be black people. These shows included singing, dancing, and jokes that perpetuated and amplified, some might say solidified, the majority of the stereotypes about black people still prevalent today.

What better time than Black History Month to revisit our racist past and pay homage to our racist present.

I want to say I knew what I was getting into. I understood the premise of using minstrelsy as a tool to expose stereotypes and conduct an experiential form of social commentary.

"You can't erase a conscious moment," Byrd explained during the post-show discussion.

He expressed his hope that the minstrel show would be a wakeup call to make the audience really acknowledge the ways in which we are complicit in the systems of oppression and hierarchy. He wanted to create this specific show as a call to action, a hard ask in our passive-aggressive, politically correct city.

When the first performer appeared on stage in a black and white suit best described as cartoonish, and his lips parted in a garish grin, I felt my stomach turn.

I sat in the smoky darkness beside the friend who invited me. This was a show where a black woman and a white woman could sit side by side and have a completely different experience.

There is something so private about the all too public, everyday humiliations of racism. The white clerk following me around the mall, the white hand of a stranger on the bus reaching out to pet my hair, the note of surprise and the "you speak so well" as though I couldn't, shouldn't possibly be so very educated.

These are the discussions I avoid having with my white friends, partly because I am sick of rehashing the same issues and partly because I am exhausted from being used as a tool for someone else's education.

There was something equally intimate about this performance and the way the mask of blackness grinned at me, mirroring back every biting image of who white America perceives me to be. The dancers leapt and spun and tapped and swayed their way across the stage, every movement exaggerated, every expression so vivid. Coonery personified.

I sat there thinking of my own mask, of all the things I don't say, the unexpressed rage dwelling quietly within me. bell hooks calls it a killing rage. Lorraine Hansberry compared it to a raisin in the sun, but so few of us have the luxury to burst, to rot, to fester openly. I like my life outside of jail, and not bursting, not punching someone in the face when they so cavalierly dehumanize me makes that possible. Honesty can be dangerous. Though perhaps not as dangerous as before. I'm not at home arming my ADT because I think the Klan is going to lynch me (but then again I don't live in Florida).

I was triggered and stuck in the front row, my mind pin-wheeling with thoughts and feelings as more and more black faces appeared, dancing to rag time piano music.

Then suddenly the house lights came up and Donald Byrd himself stepped spritely onto the stage, not in black face (although he did appear later in the show in full regalia), just as himself. He informed us that we had reached the audience participation portion of the evening.

Chagrinned, I dropped a whispered F bomb because simply witnessing this performance was already becoming a lot to ask.

Six people did volunteer, and were prompted to tell whatever offensive jokes sprung first to their mind. People love to say the thing that is forbidden and here was the chance to speak aloud the derogatory humor graffitied on our collective subconscious. There were jokes about gender, race, nationalities, sexualities, even blondes. Jokes I never heard.

More than the jokes, the laughter jarred me. Who was laughing and why?

Down went the lights and out came that face again. That haunting face, that nightmare clown made even more frightening by its relevance to today. The music was old, the shuck and jive, a familiar dance, too familiar, generations out of date and yet I felt like this so called "re-visit" was just an unveiling of a reoccurring illness with which we are still so very afflicted.

The show continued with the cartoon suited dandy giving a monologue list of every derogatory term you can possibly think of and some you might not have even heard of. The list was robustly inclusive. But as the show progressed the focus narrowed back to the ever present dichotomy of black and white.

After the intermission, a new character was introduced, a white woman. She was the first person beside Byrd to appear onstage bare faced and I was a bit startled that she was white. The black face and costumes had given such anonymity to the dancers that I had assumed they were all black beneath the paint. Assuming anything in the context of this show is a mistake. It is so nuanced and deep on so many levels that I could probably spend months wondering what really happened.

The white woman wore a wig of blond ringlets and pranced around clad in a black bustier with knee high fish nets and heels. She held two tambourines—and believe me, no tambourines have ever been quite so menacing. She danced the dance of the predatory white woman, a dance I'd seen up close just a few nights ago at the bar. But this version ended with a black man in a noose (whereas the bar version ended up with a black man following her into a bathroom).

From there the show revisited several other familiar stories of Mammy and Scarlett O'Hara and the good old South, culminating in a chilling staged reading of the actual transcripts from the 911 call made by George Zimmerman.

The performance begged the question: What does it mean to be black in America now? What is the difference between black history and black present?

After two and half hours of sitting in the dark, made darker by my own thoughts and feelings, I had no idea how to process the performance. I find it difficult to even frame the show as a revisiting, when the issues it addressed are so ever present in my daily reality.

For me the questions remain:

What are our next steps? How do we co-exist in a way that is less damaging? What action should I take to be part of the solution?

And how do we transition from black history to black future? From stereotypes and caricatures to real people having real conversations and seeing one another for who we really are?

Do Black Lives Matter in Seattle As Much As Tacos Do?

"Whose lives matter?"

"Black lives matter!" echoed out across Rainier Avenue South last Saturday as protesters from two rallies—one beginning at 23rd and Union and one beginning at the Rainier Beach Community Center—converged just south of the Interstate 90 corridor. The group marched back to Rainier and MLK to block off the entire intersection.

The protest, which lasted more than four hours, was one of many held across the country as a part of a national day of action in solidarity with Baltimore after the murder of Freddie Gray.

Gray, whose spinal cord was severed while in police custody, is the most recent in a long list of black people slain by the police. Some were killed for petty crimes, some killed for no reason beyond the fact that armed police officers felt "afraid."

For black people, causing fear has become a crime worthy of a death sentence. After the acquittal of George Zimmerman in Florida in the death of Trayvon Martin and the decision in New York not to indict New York police officer Daniel Pantaleo, who choked Eric Garner to death, we've learned that not only do our lives not matter, but that we cannot reasonably expect those responsible for those deaths to be held accountable because their fear is more important than our right to exist. This injustice isn't new. Eric Garner, Walter Scott, Tamir Rice, Michael Brown, Trayvon Martin, and Amadou Diallo are names permanently etched into our collective psyche. But the list is so much longer, spanning not years or decades, but across centuries of systemic brutality.

And there are so many names we will never know, those disappeared, kidnapped, tortured, murdered and left to pollute rivers or decompose in unmarked graves. In 1964 as "Freedom Summer" began, the search for missing civil rights workers James Chaney, Andrew Goodman, and Michael Schwerner uncovered the corpses of black college students, Henry Hezekiah Dee and Charles Eddy Moore. They had gone missing that spring. Also found was the body of 14-year-old Herbert Orsby and five other unidentified Mississippi black folks whose names were never known.

Even in death they were not equal. No one searched for these men except for their families and local communities. However, the FBI and other agencies led a search for Goodman and Schwerner, two white northerners who got too close to the truth of the black experience. The bodies of Goodman and Schwerner were found shot once each through the heart, but Chaney, the black civil rights worker who was with them, had been beaten and then shot multiple times.

This genocide is not endemic to the south or to white police or even to a particular time in U.S. history. It's simply made more visible recently by people catching these crimes on video and sharing them with the world. But even when the truth is evident, there is still no justice. In a recent Saturday Night Live sketch, comedian Michael Che commented on the fact that six officers had been charged with the murder of Freddie Gray.

"It's a vital and first step on the path to those officers being acquitted," he pronounced to the titter of audience laughter. But really it's a little too true to be funny.

A few days before the rally, I attended a workshop on creative activism. During the workshop, facilitator Cambrie Nelson posed the question: What is activism? Was it marching in the street? Was it getting people to take the stairs instead of using the escalator? Was it throwing lit flares at the police? And was the purpose to effect change and if so how could change be quantified?

At the workshop, I realized the root of my depression was the feeling that nothing will ever change. Every February, we drag out footage of MLK talking about his dream and then we have self-congratulatory lattes in our Obama mugs because, gee, haven't we come so far since then? Yes and no. We aren't where we were. But where we are is a country that is OK with the fact that people who look like me are four times more likely to be killed. Houston (and Seattle, and the USA), we still have a problem.

I joined the Seattle BLM march near Orcas Street to fully immerse myself in it. Since the dismissal of the case against Eric Garner's murderer, I have been too angry to allow myself to feel. Who wants to feel when reality is so overwhelming? When the names of the black people murdered every 28 hours start appearing on your Facebook feed daily, it's hard not to drown in hopelessness.

"Black lives matter!" we shouted in unison, quoting the now ubiquitous Twitter hashtag. As we walked with one another, yelling, chanting and singing, with the police surrounding us every step of the way, we were met with a variety of responses. People stared.

Some took out their phones and filmed us, some drove by and honked their solidarity, a few raised up black power fists, but few actually took a moment out of their own lives to walk with us.

At the end of the march, people spoke not only about the murders, but a wide spectrum of issues facing black people. Topics included police brutality, gentrification, racism in the school system or the criminal justice system. 10 year-old Eridon Stewart demanded an end to these killings. She pointed at her own brown skin and affirmed its beauty. At such a young age, despite living in this racist patriarchal society she learned to embody what the rest of us struggled to chant—that her life matters.

That moment cut through my anger, my weariness, not just from the hours of walking, but from the years of ceaseless attacks on my people. Her speech shifted something in me and restored a sliver of hope. If this young woman could somehow remain intact, then it might be worth it to keep marching, to keep shouting, to keep affirming the truth of this movement. Our lives matter.

Now its time for Seattle to affirm the same. In this liberal bubble where pets are treated like people and everyone must recycle and compost, in a city with the nation's highest minimum wage, where we regularly tout our progressive values, I felt a disconnect. In the middle of the street on a gorgeous sunny Saturday I looked around at the 200 others in attendance and wondered, where is everyone else? Why aren't there thousands here standing with us?

Shortly after the march, I caught the light rail to the International District for the Taco Truck Showdown and had my question answered. Half of Seattle was shoved into the two-block corridor lined on either side with food carts peddling tacos from every ethnic background. There were pho tacos, duck tacos, Hawaiian tacos, curried goat tacos, chicken tikka tacos and so much more. And people were lined up for hours to stuff their faces.

In the face of such dedication—just getting a taco was a 45 minute commitment—I wondered what it would be like if black lives were as important as carne asada. A girl can dream.

#blacklivesmatter At a Crossroads

After the grand jury acquitted Darren Wilson for murdering Michael Brown, I wanted to punch someone in the face.

I've been pissed off since Trayvon Martin, no, since Amadou Diallo. No wait, I've been mad since Rodney King. I don't know when grief and rage became a normal part of my experience of what it means to be black in the U.S. It's just something I live with.

But since the verdict, I've found myself at the bottom of a deep and silent depression.

It's not like this is the first time or the second or the hundredth time that someone with my skin color has been denied justice while their murderer walks away at least half a million dollars richer.

That verdict and many of the subsequent racist commentaries in the media confirmed for me something I already knew: I am not safe.

Despite being theoretically protected by the constitution and by our laws, if I were shot today by the very people we are supposed to entrust to uphold justice, it is likely that my death would be meaningless, just something that happened that no one would have to take accountability for.

This is our America. This is what our collective consciousness has created and allowed to persist.

I love protest rallies. As a community organizer, I was the go-to yeller, the one with a bullhorn in hand. Yet lately, it's been really difficult to even want to be near people, especially white people— even those who are allies.

Dear white people: I don't want to talk about your feelings or hear your condolences. I certainly don't want to stand next to you at a protest and listen to you say, "Hands up, don't shoot." No one is shooting at you. These are the words I haven't said. This is what lies within my silence.

I have withdrawn from friends and deliberately avoided having this conversation because I really do know in my heart of hearts that the white people in my life are doing the best they can. I also know it's not good enough. I know that whatever activism I have done up until this point has also failed. Collectively these travesties of justice state clearly that whatever we've been doing is not working. It's almost 2015 and we are still not free, not equal, not protected under the constitution. We are still three-fifths human.

One of the few things I've taken solace in have been the Facebook reports of protests overseas, people in Madrid and Tokyo standing in solidarity with the people of Ferguson. Those pictures have meant more to me than I can fully articulate.

The protests here have left me sad and feeling isolated, yet somehow knowing someone an ocean away is moved to stand up for my human rights gives me hope.

I was 16 the first time I went abroad. I traveled to Senegal with my mother and, though we were only gone a month, being in a black country after growing up in Madison, Wisconsin was like taking a deep breath after being underwater. I didn't know it could be like that: that I could be anonymous, look around and see only black people in every direction.

It gave me an inkling of what it must be like to be white, to be the norm: to know that when someone follows you around in a store, it's probably to help you or if they do think you are stealing, it's more about ageism or classism.

When I'm in the States, my color is the first thing everyone sees. Depending on where I travel, color is still an issue. But there is no racism quite like the racism I experience here at home—perhaps because it is my home.

So the question is still where do we go from here? I can't pick a new country out of a hat to start a new life in, nor should I have to.

Moreover, who is to say I would fare any better anywhere else? What I have come to realize is that these verdicts not only compromised the civil rights of black Americans, but have also put the U.S. in violation of the United Nations Declaration of Human Rights.

By my count, we are failing in Article 3: "Everyone has the right to life, liberty and security of person"; Article 6: "Everyone has the right to recognition everywhere as a person before the law"; and Article 7: "All are equal before the law and are entitled without any discrimination to equal protection of the law. All are entitled to equal protection against any discrimination in violation of this Declaration and against any incitement to such discrimination."

While protest pictures are nice, my request is that the international community step in to support us to do what we seem to not be able to do for ourselves. We are at a crossroads. Help us to create a climate of human dignity and accountability.

During a conversation with a friend, I was reminded of how all of humanity has benefited from the existence of black Americans, that even through our most dire trials, through the Civil Rights Movement, abolition and fighting to end to slavery, who we are and our struggle for liberation and equality has elevated not only our own consciousness, but the consciousness of our nation and in fact, the consciousness of our world. He reminded me that these very injustices occurring today might be the catalyst for our evolution as Americans.

As I meditated upon his thoughts. What occurred to me is that if all of humanity is going to benefit from our suffering, then all of humanity is also responsible for helping ensure that this never happens again.

Never again. That's what we said about the Holocaust, that is what we said about Hiroshima and Nagasaki.

In order for those words to apply now, it is not enough for us to act as U.S. citizens, in this age of globalization we must act collectively as human beings, as global citizens to change the course of our future so that our great grandchildren aren't still dealing with this bullshit.

The Necessity of Black Joy

The second annual "Where Does Black Joy Live? A Day of Dance and Celebration" was held last Sunday afternoon at Othello Park. Drawn by the beat, a gorgeous sunny day, and the promise of community, I found my way to a small concrete stage at the center of the grass. There Dani Tirrell, the creator of the event, and his friend Alexander Jackson greeted me with smiles and hugs.

"I don't do titles," said Tirrell. "I'm trying to take myself out of titling myself as a dancer. I'm a creator and I think we all are and we put labels on what it is we create which means we are stuck in this box so I'm trying to get out of my own box and say I just create stuff, and its all movement based, but I just create stuff."

Tirrell's latest creation has been a series of house music pop up dance workshops. "I grew up with house music. In Detroit being queer and black and going to the clubs it was all house music," explained Tirrell. "And it was, it's just a style of music that speaks to something deeper inside of myself. It's really where I find my spiritual place."

For this gathering, Tirrell took his love of house and love for black community and used it to curate a space for black joy. The Facebook invitation framed the event beautifully, acknowledging the challenges we've all experienced and posing a vital question. "Yes there is pain, anger, fear and hurt. Yes people from the African Diaspora are still getting killed. Trans Black Women, Womyn and Womxn and still getting killed. But can we find a moment of Black joy?"

The first gathering took place last summer. About 30 people attended. For Tirrell it was part birthday party and part love offering for community activists. "Black people are tired," he said. "We're exhausted and it was really last year the height of just protests and people talking about black bodies being killed and I was just like I need some joy." This year's celebration coincided with the memorial of the dance legend Kabby Mitchell III, who was the first black dancer at the Pacific Northwest Ballet. Mitchell passed away in May at the age of 60 due to coronary artery disease. Both Tirrell and

Jackson danced at his memorial earlier in the day before arriving at the park to continue the celebration.

"The party is still going and will be still going because you can't celebrate his life in a day because he has done so much for this city and this universe," said Jackson who is an instructor with the Northwest Tap Connection and was also mentored by Mitchell. "We can't just celebrate him in a day."

Jackson didn't attend the event last year, but was happy to dance this year. "Baby to be honest I think we're a lot more comfortable in our blackness this year," said Jackson. "It took Trump being president, well first it took Barack Obama being president to give us the confidence that we knew we already always had to know at the end of the day honey we are beautiful and we can do anything we put our minds to and so look at us, we are here honey and there is something so beautiful about that."

As the sun sunk lower in the sky, more people arrived, some bearing chips and even a couple of pizzas to share.

"Ya'll need to introduce yourselves to one another," Tirrell intoned frequently. "This is not going to be a thing where people come and nobody speaks."

An hour into the event, the first white person arrived. I wasn't surprised. I've lived in Seattle long enough to expect that sort of entitlement, but I did find myself feeling annoyed. Tirrell greeted her with the same warmth that he greeted everyone else. "If white people want to come they need to bring a black friend or something to offer," said Tirrell. "But I'm not going to tell them no."

Kate Benak, did not bring a black friend, but she did bring a massage table. "I'm a healthcare worker. I'm a licensed reflexologist. I'm on the board of Washington Reflexology Association," said Benak.

In the wake of the Black Lives Matter Movement Benak has found herself drawn to black communities. In a recent conversation with two black women, Benak had a personal revelation. "They said health care for black women is the worst of any demographic. Through Planned Parenthood they were telling me the statistics and all that and I thought I'm in healthcare and I can do something about that," she said. "That's why I'm here."

Though her intentions were admirable and I wanted to support her burgeoning allyship, I couldn't help but feel robbed. Suddenly this pop up dance party was no longer about my joy, but about her education.

Over the years, my life has been inundated with well meaning white people who have asked me to share my experiences about what it is like to be black. Well meaning is generous, if I were to be honest: they are white people with privileged curiosity, seeking to have a deeper understanding of race without wanting to admit complicity with systems of oppression or acknowledging the depth of trauma they ask me to re-live in order to educate them. They prioritize their own education over my well-being without a second thought. This has been a recurring phenomenon throughout my life and I am exhausted.

Living in this toxic environment where even social media feels like a landmine of exploding trauma from the latest police shootings and hashtags to the unexpected craziness of former childhood friends turned racist assholes in post-Trump AmeriKKKa. I would say I have PTSD, but that denotes that the trauma has ended when truly our struggles are unending.

So the idea of taking a few hours to gather together with other black people, not to discuss race, not to bitch about white people, but to simply disengage and dance and laugh and remember our own humanity is truly powerful. The very best way white people can show their allyship is by not interrupting that time, by not centering their needs to feel included or their desires to "help." There will be time for us to come together as a human collective, to educate one another, to argue, to navigate healing and justice, and to do the difficult work of fixing what is broken between us. But there must also be time for black people to come together in the privacy of our own communities to laugh and cry, to dance and love, and enjoy one another.

"We're not worrying about whose looking, we're not worrying about whose judging, we're just like baby this is us and we're going to do and be ourselves and just let us be us, for us, by us," said Jackson. "We are going to live in our black boy, black girl joy honey and love it and just embrace it."

Accomplices vs. Allies

Living in the self congratulatory liberal bubble of Seattle I find myself surrounded by white allies. Allyship here is a common concept that I used to believe meant being willing to acknowledge and stand up for someone else's humanity.

Recently I came across a blog post by Indigenous Action Media that challenged my thinking and introduced me to a concept that I am intimately acquainted with yet didn't have a name for, the Allyship Industrial Complex.

This term describes the lucrative industry of social justice self help that has arisen from the mix of well-intentioned people wanting to do better with our capitalist culture.

Starting in high school and through my graduate program I took several courses on social justice and have since participated in workshops either as mandated for professional development or as a facilitator. Mostly we have the same conversation. Power and privilege exist. Tears ensue, sometimes there are heated arguments, sometimes there is heated silence, sometimes we all tip toe around the minefields and pretend we are more evolved than we actually are. This was interesting when I was 16 and having that moment of discovery that white people legitimately didn't believe that racism still happened or that systemic oppression was actually at thing. At 36 it's old and I am constantly left to wonder…okay now what?

I am surrounded by allies and yet the systems of oppression remain unchanged. It's nice that white people want to talk about race and make their kids watch Eyes on the Prize. I greatly prefer this to cross burnings, lynchings and slavery. Despite the daily evidence to the contrary something in me thinks that we have the capacity to do better. Last week Town Hall hosted a conversation between Mychal Denzel Smith, author of *Invisible Man, Got the Whole World Watching* and Marcus Harrison Green, *YES!* Magazine Reporting Fellow and founder of the South Seattle Emerald. Smith's book is an exploration of black masculinity, but also of intersectional oppression and the myriad of contradictory roles we play in one another's lives. During the discussion Smith spoke candidly about the ways in which patriarchy has weakened the struggle for black liberation by black men, sometimes intentionally, sometimes inadvertently, perpetuating supremacist culture against black women.

Smith encouraged us all to examine our beliefs and our behaviors and to be honest about the ways in which we are all complicit in the systems we claim to abhor.

"Because you should look back on your own behavior and you should be appalled," he said outing his own shortcomings. "The next thing you do is say how do I get better? And it's a learning process continually and an unlearning process because so much is indoctrinated in you as a means of replicating these systems."

Often we resonate the most with a specific part of our identity, but we are all intersectional beings that experience an ever evolving level of power, privilege, or oppression depending on circumstance. When I think about allyship my first instinct is to examine it through the lens of race. But truthfully while I may experience oppression as a black woman, there are other ways in which I hold privilege for example by being born in the U.S. to a middle class family. As someone cis-gendered I have had the privilege to choose whether or not to acknowledge or learn about what it means to identify as non- binary or transgender.

Simply taking the time to be self aware and willing to see the sometimes unflattering truths about the beliefs we hold in our hearts and minds has been and will probably always be a part of "the work" we must do to evolve in our humanity. But that is just the beginning. "So once you've gotten uncomfortable, and someone has unseated you from the comfort of privilege, what are you willing to do to change that, what are you willing to let go of, what are you willing to lose?" asked Smith.

In trying to answer that question for myself I first had to delve deeper into the idea Smith posed as Accompliceship, transforming an ally into the ride or die getaway driver in the heist we planned together.

The indigenous action media writes: "The risks of an ally who provides support or solidarity (usually on a temporary basis) in a fight are much different than that of an accomplice. When we fight back or forward, together, becoming complicit in a struggle towards liberation, we are accomplices."

Their thesis is a great deal more radical than what Smith had to say in that it involves a decolonization and repatriation of native lands that would leave the majority of us homeless. However they both align on a simple truth that something has to give.

"And that's part of the problem is that so many of us are not willing to lose anything, and we're not willing to stand up and we're not willing to tell that truth in the difficult situation and we have to recognize that's where change happens."

Many of us have given something to be considered an ally, whether it is suffering through arguments with family and friends or sacrificing some modicum of privilege to align yourself with the struggle. Now the collection basket is coming around a second time. What will it take to move forward from here? What are we willing to give?

During a recent sermon about commitment, my friend Reverend Allen Mosely shared some southern wisdom in the form of this analogy. When you make eggs and ham, the chicken is involved, but the pig is committed. Similarly I think the greatest distinction between allyship and being an accomplice is in the amount of skin in the game.

There may be some effort involved, even perhaps some discomfort, but in general the chicken gets to go on about its business whereas the pig is forever and irrevocable changed by it's commitment. Given the toxic political climate and the blatant disregard for black lives, queer lives, women's bodies and so much more, it's time for allyship to be recognized not as the end goal, but as a step in a process leading towards something deeper. But what's next and how do we get there?

As I began to grapple with these questions I was given an unexpected gift from a young woman I met recently. She is an alumni of Young Women Empowered and someone also seeking to transition her allyship into something more tangible. She began with her family and has been doing what she can to get them to acknowledge their privilege. It was through our processing conversations that she reminded me of how much she has gained from deepening her understanding of power and privilege, how she has formed bonds and turned acquaintances into family by being willing to see them and meet them where they are.

It can be scary to face the loss of privilege, to risk jeopardizing your primary relationships and support systems to stand in solidarity with people you may or may not have anything in common with. But rather than clinging to what we must sacrifice, we must remember that ultimately we are regaining our humanity. We are regaining our sanity, that our liberation is intrinsically intertwined with that of every other person on the planet. If one of us isn't free, none of us truly can be.

"Our role is producing sanity," explained Smith. What that sanity looks like remains to be determined, but is something we must co-create with one another. Like it or not we are already accomplices, the question becomes to what end. Are we partners in the crime of continuing to perpetuate the systems that dehumanize and oppress us or are we partners in co-creating something new?

Reparations Reimagined: Can Online Giving Counter Systemic Racism

At first I thought it was a joke, or some really radical performance art. Artist, activist, and "tired black woman" Natasha Marin invited me to participate in her Facebook event called Reparations to be held Dec 17-31. The cover photo showed a white guy holding an armful of kittens like a creepy, wiggly bouquet.

"I invite People of Color to ask for what we need to feel better, be happier, be more productive by posting in this space. These may be both material and immaterial requests," the page read. "I invite people who identify as white to offer services or contributions to People of Color in need of time, energy, substantive care, and support."

Below this were a list of sample scenarios on what this might look like: people of color in need of simple things like a warm meal or a massage, to the more complex like the need to vent at white people.

But scrolling down the posts on the page, the theoretical asks and offers had turned real.

By the time I saw it there was already a long thread of participants: white people offering to clean and organize your house, take care of your kids, pay for your trip to the spa, buy you groceries and read your resume, people of color asking for sculpting lessons, paid vacations, jobs, and rides. And I thought, for real? This is actually happening.

40 Acres and a mule

When I think about reparations my mind instantly turns to 40 acres and a mule, which allegedly was supposed to be given to black folks after the civil war. Unsurprisingly the same government responsible for slavery, the genocide of Native Americans, the internment of Japanese people, and a lot of inhumane institutional policies and practices against all non-white people never got around to distributing that wealth.

This is a bit of a sore point, particularly when what's left of Native American survivors received sovereign land and casinos and Japanese descendants of the internment received an apology for how they were treated and their cash settlement.

Over the years, several Republican politicians have asserted that black people don't need reparations because all slave owners are dead and racism ended when Barack Obama was elected. This country doesn't really owe us anything—not an apology, an acknowledgement of wrong doing and certainly not land and animals. Oh, and we "get" welfare.

But then, having grown up in a non-agrarian community, I have no idea how much land an acre actually is. And what would I do with a mule? Ride it down I-405 on my commute to Kirkland? I don't spend much time thinking about reparations because I'm pretty sure I have a higher chance of winning the lottery.

But this concept is not reparations for slavery. "I think there's no way you can make up for slavery," said Marin over brunch. "But we can comfort each other right now in the present. There are people who I feel like need comfort and support and care. Material goods. And there are tons, tons of white people who are well meaning and want to do something to help and rather than stay in these isolated worlds, why not make a space where people can connect?"

Though created by a black woman, it's not even specifically targeted to black people, but to all people of color in an acknowledgement of the shared history of systemic oppression. Rather than putting the onus on systems and government to fix the imbalance of power and privilege, what Marin has done is to allow white people to acknowledge the ways in which they have been privileged and to take that privilege and redistribute it in a very personal way.

"Lend your car to somebody. Write somebody a reference…be a job reference for somebody. Take your whiteness and like vouch for somebody on a rental application. How much does that cost you?" Marin asked and answered. "Nothing, but time and these are actual measurable ways that white people can help people of color. It's also about recognizing in these acts where your privilege lies. The effect I think has been people actually getting to know each other right now."

After the back to back murders of Alton Sterling and Philando Castille, Marin says her Facebook page was filled with angry and grieving people.

"So I thought let me throw up a Reparations page that just allows people to offer what they can as a way of assuaging their guilt or I don't know, making it feel like they are actually doing something as opposed to just watching police brutality videos and feeling like crap."

The event posted last Friday and already there are hundreds of offers and requests on the page, most of them centered around Seattle, but also Baltimore, Miami, even as far away as Chile. One woman wrote to Marin suggesting she create a website. Another volunteered to help. So over the weekend a new platform was created.

The response hasn't all been positive. Marin has been inundated with trolls calling her the N word and a racist. However, local benefactors have volunteered to donate $1 for every racist email or post she has to deal with. Is this charity?

"I don't think of this as charity, I think of it as good people, regardless of what color they are, get a good feeling from being able to help somebody," said Marin. "Your network can help you find that person that can help you. And this is basically a bunch of people of all different colors taking advantage of the fact that we have these networks that connect us."

While fascinated by the concept, I also felt a deep discomfort with the idea of asking white strangers for help. My first instinct was that I don't actually need help. I have a job that pays the bills. I own my own home. Yes I am still impacted daily by systemic oppression, but I am better off than a lot of people.

While the southern side of my family struggled with poverty, the northern side managed to eke out some generational wealth due to my great grandmother's line of haircare products and the fact that she founded the first black beauty school in Des Moines, Iowa. This afforded my grandmother and subsequently my mother the opportunity to pursue higher education, which ensured that I grew up in a stable middle class environment.

That being said, I spent the majority of last week sobbing in strange places, ducking into bathroom stalls, crying in my car and on the disgusting yoga mat at my gym, then trying to pull it together enough to make it through my work day. I've been pretending at normal for so long that I have created a new normal where I can function surprisingly well and contain my internal turmoil to 10 minute intervals of depression before washing my face and moving on.

I know I must sound crazy, but let me just state this fact. I live in a country where it is not a crime to kill me. I live in a country where I am casually dehumanized on a regular basis and told to get the fuck over it.

I don't just live here, I was born and raised here. Generationally there are no records of any of my relatives living or dead that aren't from here.

America is in my blood and it is toxic. So in reading Marin's invitation to ask for what I need and to open myself up for the purpose of restoring my faith in humanity, my first instinct was "no thank you."

Let me explain: In asking me to receive, I would also have to give, I would have to trust that this interaction wouldn't put me into contact with people who would further damage me. We talk all the time about white fragility, but damn it as a black American woman I am hella fragile right now and while I really could use a hug, a massage and $100 million, I barely trust white people not to shoot me in the street. I am also used to being the person who gives, not the one who receives.

What can we really ask for?

In processing my own relationship to the page, I reached out to others to hear their perspectives.

"I would not participate in reparations the way others might," said writer Anastacia Reneé Tolbert, a black woman with her own concerns about vulnerability. "but I am a staunch supporter of reparations and I feel like we all want things. Some of them are not quantified by materialism. I would like a million apologies. And if a white person could type I'm sorry, I'm sorry, I'm sorry and send it to me, I would be happy with that."

Bettina Judd, professor of gender and women studies, also a black woman, said she plans on participating in the experiment.

"I think it's a brilliant way to put reparations back on the table as a real thing and to see how the micro-aggressions that we experience, the everyday experiences of racism, the seemingly benign experiences of racism, can be at least mitigated by some benign acts of kindness that would otherwise not befall black folks and other folks of color."

Judd hasn't decided what to ask for yet. "I'm with Anastacia in that there is not enough to give, so it'll be…no matter how many things one might ask for it won't be enough, but that's just going to be the condition of our healing until we're healed."

While reparations is a concept based on repair coming from the outside in, I've always thought my healing was my own responsibility and something I would just have to spiritually bootstrap without any hope of apology or systemic acknowledgement.

But reading through the posts forced me to consider what I might need in a real way, but also what I would be willing to accept. I found that there was a difference between the two, that there were things I couldn't bring myself to ask for regardless of whether I felt I wanted, needed or deserved them.

It made me wonder what's really at stake in this personal act of giving and receiving? What scared me most about the idea of asking for what I need is first having to admit that I have needs and then second the idea of admitting that to a white stranger and asking them to help fill the need.

But then I began to think about the love and support I've received over the last two weeks. Without me ever asking, friends of all colors have called me to check in, brought me food, and cried with me when I could bring myself to cry in front of them. And I have felt closer to them because of it.

Maybe strangers need to feel closer to one another, maybe we need to connect in order to begin repairing the incomprehensible state of inhumanity our country is in. Maybe white people need to know that I am hurt and have needs. Maybe people of color need to know that there are white people out there who feel as devastated as we do and who want to be good human beings.

With this in mind I made an ask. Art has always helped me through hard times, so I asked for a gift card to my favorite art store to replenish my paint and glitter supply. Within an hour a woman responded, not with money, but with a care package of actual paint and glitter. Through our brief exchange I felt a glimmer of that hope that Marin is trying to create, that there is some possible remedy to all this hurt and separation, but I also still acutely felt the risk of trying.

White people get on board

I was curious to hear from people who were making offers what made them take the risk. Dan Joslin, a white man from Tacoma posted an offer that included: small tree pruning, hauling, groceries, poetry, and art supplies. No one has taken him up on it just yet:

"If someone doesn't want to be involved or they just want to take me up on it that's fine," said Joslin when I contacted him. "But if there's an opportunity to work for somebody for the day or help somebody who needs it, I'd love to be able to meet with them and share a smile and a laugh and I would love for folks to take me up on it."

As I watched the newsfeed over the weekend, I saw a reoccurring theme. Regardless of what the asks and offers were, the magic of the page lay in the connection.

"For me I think it can only be good. It's gonna be something that I feel passionate about and hopefully the people that are on the other end of this that I'm meeting and engaging with...that I'm able to bring something to their lives that they wouldn't otherwise be able to have," said Joslin. " I'm not looking so much for me, I'm looking for the outreach and the way to communicate in multiple different ways with people that I might not have otherwise met."

Jane Hinton a white woman from Seattle found herself similarly fascinated by the page.

Hinton responded to a request from a woman of color who was transitioning into a new job. After years of working in the non-profit sector, she offered resume editing as a form of support.

While she believes the approach is innovative and powerful, Hinton worries that there will be white people who use it as a vehicle to assuage guilt committing to broader change.

"The part ... that makes me nervous is that it's on an individual level and you can't just do the individual work, you have to also do systems changing work," she said.

"No matter how much work you do politically or how many times 1 have conversations about race with my white relative, no matter how many times I vote or sign a petition, or I march or whatever the different political actions are, there is this desire also to make impact individually," she went on. "That's the beauty of the experiment. It allows me to say oh I have this skill or gift because of my privileged position and I can share it." Where do other POC fit in?

As I scrolled down the feed, one woman identified herself as mixed race, Filipino and white. In her post chose to both ask and offer.

Esmy Jimenez, who identifies as Mestiza is an undocumented immigrant from Mexico and felt unclear on how to approach her involvement. "I absolutely think this is a fascinating event and I really like how people are stepping up and saying okay this is how I can contribute. But there wasn't really guidelines for everybody else who wasn't white or wasn't black. That made me a little nervous frankly."

Marin wants to make it clear that everyone is invited to participate. "Its absolutely broader than black and white. People of color are welcome to choose how they identify and whether they want to participate in offering or asking."

For now Jimenez has been content to watch and wait, as she discerns what is hers to give or receive. Despite her nervousness, Jimenez says she will participate in the page. "This whole like being nervous and not acting is not helping. That's the opposite of progress. So you better go do it and learn from the mistake rather than not doing that all."

Through this project, Marin is encouraging people to connect with one another to assess and quantify their own privilege in relation to their intersectional identities, for the purpose of improving the everyday lives of people in our community. "But what I don't want is for white people to do any asking," Marin said. She wants to be clear that the appropriate way for white people to participate is solely through giving.

"Maybe you can't stop racism in the United States, but if you can help a single black mom have a 90 minute massage you've actually done something substantive to help somebody," said Marin.

The purpose of the project is not absolution. "It's not like a pardon from racism… you still have to check yourself and make sure you're living in a way that matches your beliefs," Marin said, "but it's a place to start."

A care package of art supplies no matter how lovingly given could never equal the weight of what I've endured in my 36 years of living life as a black woman in America, but the gift isn't just the material item, but that through the giving and receiving a humanizing connection is made between strangers.

There is a difference between allyship and being an accomplice. Marin has taken this concept and put it into action. What are you willing to give? What are you willing to receive? What can we as a community do to redistribute the balance of power and privilege?

The Scariest Thing About *Get Out*
is Black Trauma

I hate horror movies. They linger. Long after the screen goes black, I am reliving every cringe-worthy moment. So when I saw the preview for *Get Out*, I was like wait: Is this a horror movie or is this racism? Is this a horror movie about racism?

Oh hell no. I definitely don't want to see that.

Eventually, I succumbed to curiosity and peer pressure. True to the genre, *Get Out* is a movie that lingers, but in a very different way than most. It's the subtle violence that gets under your skin. Writer and director Jordan Peele does a masterful job of creating scene after scene filled with micro-aggressions, white privilege run amok and downright awkward racist interactions.

The movie begins with Rose (Allison Williams) and Chris (Daniel Kaluuya) making googly eyes at one another, establishing themselves as a couple in love. All the black women sitting in my row (myself included) gave a collective eye roll.

Becky meets a Brother. Okay. That's only the plot of like 900 other movies (#savethelastdance #guesswhosecomingtodinner #Othello). And Rose is the quintessential Becky, perky and progressive, the daughter of parents who would have "voted for Obama a third time" if they could.

They discuss their plans for Chris to meet Rose's family. Chris asks if they know he's black. Rose says no, because she is entirely too post- racial to have really noticed that he is black, let alone mentioned that to her equally post-racial family. She also lets it slip that he is the first black man she's ever dated (yeah right) which so perfectly frames the paradox of white people wanting to be both color blind and congratulated on their sophisticated race relations at the same time. Chris calls his friend Rod (played by comedian Lil Rel Howry) who tells him pretty much everything everyone in the audience is thinking. *Don't go. This is a bad idea. Something isn't right!*

But of course, Chris goes anyway, because white people inviting you to white spaces with other white people that may or may not be cool is actually an everyday kind of thing. What follows is a montage of the way too true shit that happens when you are black in white spaces, beginning with a slightly new twist on an old classic, the D.W.B. (Driving While Black).

While on the way to the countryside, they hit a deer. It's jarring. They are both stunned. When the police officer arrives, though Rose was the one actually driving, he asks to see Chris' driver's license. One of them is stunned by this. One of them is not. You can guess who.

So Rose pulls out her white feminist crusader cape. After a short and snarky assertion of her white privilege, they are back in the car and on their way. Here you see that first crack in the lovey dovey "we are a couple" façade. It's that moment where two people realize they were raised differently and have completely different understandings of what just happened and why.

Read: that moment when Chris remembers that Rose's whiteness can be dangerous (#EmmitTill) and Rose realizes for .5 seconds that the post-racial bubble she likes to live in might not have room enough for two.

Throughout the movie we watch Chris rationalize his relationship, again and again, bestowing unsolicited silent forgiveness for all this bullshit simply being with Rose requires of him, and all the lies and mental gymnastics it takes to keep believing "it's not that bad."

Except it is that bad.

When they get to the house, Chris can't wait to call Rod. This is a thing. When that crazy and or crazy making racist thing happens, no matter how cool your white friend, colleague or partner is, you have to call your black friends or family members to debrief because they actually understand how you feel and can make you laugh about it. Unsurprisingly, the humor in this movie is a big part of what makes it work. It's what kept me watching as the storyline drew us into worst case scenario after worst case scenario.

I promise not to drop any more spoilers. Everything you previously read takes place in the first 15 minutes of the movie. And, come on, it's a horror movie, so you kind of know what's coming, twists and turns, bloodshed, and general scariness. But I will say this, it was funny, it was scary, it was honest, and now I can't stop thinking about it.

As I left the theater I was inundated with memories of my first boyfriend, a white boy from Two Rivers, Wisconsin that I met at church camp. He came to Madison to take me to my homecoming dance, so when he invited me to be his date to his school formal, I begged my parents to let me go.

Lengthy conversations ensued. You want to go where? With who? Stay where? Really? My parents were very hesitant to let me go and told me flat out that they didn't think I would have a good experience, but true to their parenting style they decided that they would let me make my own mistake, but not without support. My dad drove me to Two Rivers. He met the boy and his parents (gave the boy the stare down that black fathers are famous for) and then left me there to endure one of the most awkward and humiliating experiences I have ever had.

There were times during the movie where I wondered if Jordan Peele had secretly followed me around Two Rivers to write down the things white kids and their parents said to me. Then I realized, no, this is actually a universal black American experience, but one that for the most part goes unsaid.

We watch documentaries about slavery or the civil rights movement. Racism is depicted as fire hoses and dogs, confederate flags and white sheets, all open and obvious. It's rare to watch a movie that openly addresses the intimate injustices, the small ways in which your white friends fail you, not by saying the fucked up thing themselves, but by putting you in a situation where that trauma can and does occur.

Sometimes it happens so quickly or it's so subtle that they don't even notice. You go home feeling terrible and needing to process and for them it's like it never even happened. This movie lives at the intersection of this disconnect. It takes a long festering wound and picks at the scab until you're left bleeding and raw.

Get Out puts white people on blast in an intense and at times entertaining way, but it also spills the tea on black folks. We have been enduring racial trauma for so long that we have normalized it to a certain extent, learned to laugh about it, learned to side eye, suck it up and drink about it. It's a survival tactic. But what happens when you just can't anymore? What happens when your worst fears are realized and there is no turning back? When you can't keep pretending over and over again that whiteness isn't a psychopathic disease systematically trying to silence, dominate, infect, subdue, and kill you?

Chris shows so much compassion. You can tell he really wants to make it work. He wants to believe that his girlfriend is genuinely a good person. He wants to believe that he just has to endure the unpleasantness and that this will just be a fucked up story to laugh about at the bar. But whiteness is coming for him and the choice is clear: stay and submit, or stand up and get out.

On Fear and Anger and Fighting Back

Jab, jab, straight. V dip, hook punch. I keep my feet moving and my guard up, in sync with my partner. It's the 11th session of a 14-week boxing class called We Fight Back and we are finally sparring. My shirt is soaked through with sweat and my muscles are screaming, but I am grinning through my mouth guard. I've needed this.

It's been 16 years since the last time I wore a pair of boxing gloves. I was lighter then, in the best shape of my life. I am a different fighter now, more grounded and strategic. Even with less stamina, my punches knock my partner back a few steps and land with a satisfying thud.

I love sparring. The adrenaline, the sweat, the way power feels in my body. When I am fighting it's one of the few times I feel like all of me is in alignment. My mind is never clearer. But my love of fighting has always been complicated by my relationship to violence.

Throughout childhood, my dad tried to get me involved in martial arts, but I considered myself a pacifist until middle school when bullying reached a fevered pitch. Though I never started a fight, almost daily the fight found me. I stopped worrying about hurting people and started worrying about getting hurt. A boy in my class hit me with a brass edge folder slicing a gash just a quarter of an inch beneath my eye. Any higher and I would have been permanently blind. As it was, I had to get stitches. I was humiliated, but worse I was angry.

This was no casual emotion. It was a raw primal Incredible Hulk anger, what bell hooks would call a killing rage. Every time I saw that kid I wanted to smash his face in. I began to have violent fantasies, each more warped than the next. My rage became a source of shame and fear, confirmation that I was truly a terrible person. My parents were concerned. My dad kept pushing me to take karate, but I steadfastly refused because I didn't trust myself. I thought if someone taught me how to really fight I might actually kill someone.

I didn't start boxing until my senior year of college. My junior year was simultaneously the best and worst year of my life. I moved to Spain to study Spanish and fell in love with cream sherry, flamenco music and beach lounging. I also lost my best friend in a car crash and I was roofied.

I don't know what drug it was, but I still remember every moment. A stranger bought me a drink. I was perpetually at a party those days, so it was a pretty common occurrence. But almost as soon as I drank it I knew something was wrong. I tried to convince my friends to take me home. They didn't want to leave the bar, so they put me in a cab.

By the time I got to my apartment building the drug had taken hold and I was completely immobilized. The cab driver had to carry me out of the car. He took me to the entrance of my apartment building and laid me across the marble steps. First, he paid himself by taking all the money from my pocket, then he reached inside my shirt. My whole body was frozen, but I was lucid. I couldn't move, but I could scream and did. This was sufficient to scare him away, but then I lay there alone in the middle of the night on the streets of a foreign country feeling terrified and praying no one else would find me. I don't know how long it took before the drug wore off and I was able to feel my arms and legs again, but it felt like hours. I know I am lucky and that it could have been so much worse. Still, I had never felt so powerless in my life.

The rage I had been so careful to suppress rose up in me larger than ever and it would not go away. I was mad at my friends for abandoning me the one time I needed them. I was mad at myself for being reckless, mad at God for taking my best friend, and mad at every person, place or situation that had ever made me feel powerless. It was the kind of fury that burns you from the inside out like acid. I had to find somewhere to put it. So I started boxing.

After a year of boxing, I got the opportunity to move to Japan. I traded fighting for meditating. I didn't fight again for several years when I took up taekwondo. I received my black belt in 2010 shortly before another travel opportunity took me away from my training. Getting my black belt was what cured me of fearing my own power. With skill came discipline and being in control of my own body gave me the peace I had been searching for.

I have endured an entire lifetime of people fucking with me. Even now I feel like I am constantly fighting to assert my humanity, to be allowed to live in this world. I think that's why boxing feels so satisfying because for one hour a week when I feel the world pummeling me I can finally punch back. I can take all the rage and sadness and righteous indignation, shove it into my fists and punch until my arms are sore and I can't breathe.

Now trapped in the waking nightmare of having a president-elect endorsed by the KKK, the fight has only begun. We have elected a bully who has effectively normalized openly racist, Islamaphobic, and misogynist behavior. Hate crimes are already on the rise and it's no surprise when I turn on the news and our nation's "leader" is up on rape charges and caught on video unapologetically laughing about how he assaults women.

"So much of my life work has been around stopping male violence against women and challenging gender-based violence that I'm just so sick of women being raped and murdered and brutalized and beaten," confessed Ane Mathieson when asked what inspired the creation of We Fight Back. Mathieson and Megan Murphy, both social workers, teamed up about two and half years ago to pilot the first class. "I wanted to create an opportunity for women to fight and defend themselves from violence, but I wanted them to be able to do that for free," said Mathieson. "So I reached out to a friend of mine who is an MMA instructor."

MMA stands for Mixed Martial Arts. The first project involved eight women including Murphy and Mathieson. In addition to learning physical skills for self-defense, they hosted concurrent conversations about gender-based violence. "So that's been a big challenge," said Mathieson. "Creating a space where women can feel comfortable to start really talking about this stuff authentically but then not feeling like that means that can't have relationships with men or that it means that they have to hate every man."

After the first program, Murphy and Mathieson took stock of what went well and what needed to change. "The first cohort we had was all white women and we all knew that this was not okay," said Mathieson. While the program is open to all women, Murphy and Mathieson wanted to make sure it addressed the fact that women of color and queer identified women are disproportionately impacted by violence.

Another challenge was having a male identified instructor. This was a trigger for participants who had been assaulted by men, but neither Murphy nor Mathieson had previous experience with fighting. They decided to bring Genevieve Corrin as a third partner because of her experience with boxing and this paved the way for a new partnership with Cappy's Gym. Located in the Central District, Cappy's has been making boxing accessible for everyone since 1999.

The women in my cohort are a diverse mix of 20 and 30 somethings, some first-time fighters and some, like me, returning after a long break. There is a camaraderie that has grown between us over the past months. All of us have our own personal relationship to violence and fighting, some with more trauma than others, but despite the different motivations our goal is the same, to prepare ourselves for the inevitability of a fight.

For 20-year-old Azeb Tuji, We Fight Back was just something that sounded cool. "It just sounded so out of my comfort zone and something that I wouldn't be able to do and something like so kick ass that I was like yeah I need to do something like that for myself."

Tuji, a first-time fighter, recounts that the only physical fights she's been in have been with her brothers when she was a kid, but she is not new to confrontation. "I think the last couple of weeks I've been getting harassed and people are trying to talk to me more," said Tuji. "But instead of kind of lowering my voice or something or being like 'ok' I've been getting super angry and my fist are clenched and I'm just ready to go."

After an hour of physical training there is a short break, then boxers trade gloves for pens and notepads and reconvene for an hour of curriculum facilitated by Murphy and Mathieson. Often we begin with a meditation or a centering, a reminder that we are more than just bodies fighting, that we are minds, hearts and spirits too.

Sometimes there are experiential activities that get us on our feet and in our voices. And always there are robust conversations.

"I'm the person that comes up with the drills and the focus and themes behind each class every week," says boxing coach Olivia Mendez. "Prior to the start of any of the classes, we all sat and thought about the components. Number 1 who are we working with and what do they want to know?" Mendez began boxing 15 years ago after a bad breakup left her searching for an outlet for pent up emotions. "I think one of the canons that We Fight Back speaks to is that myself as a woman growing up when and where I did, I didn't have a lot of opportunities to experience my emotions," says Mendez. "I really struggled with how to cope with that confrontation."

This seems to be a common refrain. What do you do when conflict occurs? In our last class, Mendez described the three most common gut reactions: fight, flight or freeze.

We separated into three groups based on our default reactions then we boxed a round operating from that paradigm. After years of running away from my anger and trying to avoid conflict, I've finally succumbed to my base reflex, to fight. The first round I gave no quarter. I used my size to force my partner to back up, but then the next round Coach Mendez asked us to practice using a different response.

For three minutes I had to freeze instead of punching. It's one thing to take a punch and then return fire and a totally different feeling to just stand there. Though running away isn't my default either, when I practiced boxing on the defensive it at least gave me a sense that I was doing something, blocking and ducking, but just standing there frozen I felt like a victim.

For Tuji, We Fight Back has given her the confidence to unfreeze. When she's confronted with microaggressions from her coworkers, she has begun to speak up. "Even though it's like hardly saying it, I'm learning how to stand up for myself," she says.

For some like Mathieson, whose default is to attack, there is a realization that being reactionary is still no guarantee of safety. "I'm really mouthy and when men harass me on the streets I have a whole slew of tactics that I have to respond to them and I sometimes am really aggressive," she said. "There have been so many times where I'm like 'I am going to get my face bashed in'. One of these days one of these men is going to bash my face in and I really want to know how to defend myself in case that happens."

While it's been good to get back into my body, to engage with an incredible community of women and to experience the release that fighting provides, participating in We Fight Back has also brought to the surface a deep-seated grief. I'm tired of always having to fight back, of being told not to walk at night, or being made to feel as though my basic human rights are privileges.

This war I'm fighting in is not against men or white people, but against the white supremacist, heteronormative patriarchy which has done everything in its power to create, sustain and normalize bullying and rape culture. We live in an environment where we learn early on that our bodies are not our own, that we should expect to be judged by how we choose to dress or how willing we are to be complicit in our own victimization. It's exhausting and it's not just happening here, it's happening all over the world.

But so is the resistance.

More than a class, a community or even free boxing lessons, We Fight Back is a declaration that women are ready to stand in their power.

That's what keeps me coming back week after week, knowing that I am not only contributing to my own strength and self-empowerment but that I am part of a broader movement demanding justice in my community.

Calling Out (and Calling In) White Media

The first and only article I ever published in my high school paper was an assignment for journalism class.

It was about an event launching the newest *Norton Anthology of African American Literature,* edited by my shero Dr. Nellie Y. McKay and Henry Louis Gates Jr.

Despite the momentous occasion that people from around the country had gathered to honor, my little dinky high school paper was one of the few to cover it.

Why? Because that is how systemic oppression functions. What people of color think about, feel, do and achieve is often marginalized or not considered "newsworthy." This is nothing new.

My entire body of work is predicated on these truths: what I have to say is important, my life matters, and the lives of people of color matter. Our experiences deserve to be centered, validated, and shared.

To that end the articles I write are often stories that don't get told in mainstream white publications. And when I do write about "mainstream issues" (read: shit that white people care about), I write from a perspective and in a voice that is not often heard.

From time to time I've made a point to provide counter narratives when #journalismsowhite gets it wrong again. But for the most part I am less interested in being reactive and more interested in proactively promoting the incredible work that is taking place in my community whether it's art, activism, or just a great Southend brunch.

In the three years I've been a columnist for *The Seattle Globalist,* publishing articles with the Black Girl Nerds Blog, the *South Seattle Emerald, Crosscut,* and *Yes!* Magazine, I have never been "scooped" before. You would think I would have experienced this journalism rite of passage, but I have a pretty good guess as to why:

White media doesn't care about/wants to ignore/erase the things I write about.

So I was surprised and surprisingly pissed off when, literally 30 minutes before I finished writing what I still consider to be the most comprehensive piece on Natasha Marin's Reparations project, *The Stranger* popped up with a 5 paragraph nothing article "breaking" the story. The piece was a place holder, the entire purpose of which was to say hey this black lady used the word reparations and is asking for shit, who knows what's going to happen next.

After derailing my schedule to conduct interviews, spending hours transcribing and putting together a piece that actually delved into the nuance of the project and the historical context behind it I wanted to punch Rich Smith in the face. I called my editor to help me breathe through my rage. He was mad too, but he assured me my piece was better and that in the scheme of things that was more important than it coming out first.

Before long, Reparations.me went viral and I watched the story get picked up first by all the other local mainstream media, then by the *Washington Post* and even the *BBC*.

I was excited that Marin's project had become so well publicized. She is a fellow black woman artist (and a friend) who has been creating fascinating work for years with little to no fanfare. In fact the article I wrote about The Red Lineage she created just a few months back (you know before white media "discovered" her) was some of the first media attention she garnered, despite showing her art internationally.

But part of me felt furious to read the way white media took this really interesting project and smushed it into racialized clickbait. It's like journalists read the word reparations then didn't bother to read the rest of the project description. They took a project that centralized the needs of people of color and doing the work to create a bridge through this collective racial trauma towards some sort of healing and spun it into a story about black people begging for charity.

Not only did I feel marginalized as a journalist, as my story got shunted aside in favor of the inaccurate, mediocre whitewashed retelling, but then I got to watch white media marginalize black art and a black artist ... again. What is the point of "mainstream media" providing coverage of non-white issues if they aren't going to take the time to get it right?!

I decided to give voice to my frustration. First I posted the link to my article on all of my social media and asked my friends to read it and share it. Anytime anyone posted an article on the subject that missed the mark, I put the link to my piece in the comments to supplement the anemic narrative. Then I took it a step further. I went through every article written by a Seattle news outlet and began to send the writers my unsolicited critiques via the comments section of their articles (in addition to posting the link to my piece there too).

Yes. This was my version of a temper tantrum, me screaming at the top of my lungs that I had a voice that deserved to be heard. Strangely, writing critiques was the thing that pulled me out of my anger and returned me to myself. For the past several years I have felt a strong calling to teach writing. It began with a dream about my grandmother from which I awoke with the curriculum plan for a memoir writing class. Teaching that class has been such a gift to me. In empowering others to tell their stories and to use their voices, I found myself connecting on a deep level with my students and their lives.

Moreover, I found a universal truth: the common thread of their humanity woven through their stories. It didn't matter if I was reading about a young Korean woman's tales of religion and sexuality or an elderly white man's stories about coming of age in a small town. No matter how radically different their lives were from my own, there was something they said or felt that resonated with me.

As I began to critique the articles, those writers became human to me again and not simply agents of the faceless white supremacist patriarchy that is systematically working to silence me at all times.

They became my students. And if you have ever taken a class with me, you know that I am exacting. I demand a lot from you, but I do so with compassion because I understand what one must sacrifice to be worthy of the gifts writing has to offer.

So Dear White Media, here is the gift I want to give you. This simple truth will make you a better writer, a better person, and will prevent me from having to call you out on your lazy, tone deaf, apathetic attempt to include people of color in your journalism: If I can remember that you are a human being, then you can remember that all those people who may or may not look like you, dress like you, eat the same food, have the same color skin, or speak the same language are all human beings too. You may look at me and see my differences, but don't stop there. See all of me. Develop what columnist Sarah Stuteville calls a staring problem.

I am calling you in. I'm glad you want to join me in writing articles that move people of color's experiences from the margin to the center. It's about fucking time. And there is more than enough for all of us to write about.

But get it right.

Media is a mirror of our culture. This experience has highlighted for me the fact that the majority of journalism is not created with a respect for humanity. I don't know when or why, but this need to be detached and to appear objective has caused in erosion of our common sense.

What is needed now is for us all to become more connected. You can't report accurately about a community if you don't understand it and the best way to cultivate understanding is to engage and participate. You owe it to yourself. And yes, you owe it to the communities you've been charged with covering to be diligent, to ethical and to tell the truth. So please take this as an invitation to rejoin the human race. And do better.

The Tea on Our Juneteenth Black Out and the Necessity of Black Healing Spaces

Let me preface this with one important point of clarity: Mary and I don't owe anyone an explanation about what we chose to do. We are accountable solely to and for our community and to the call for Black healing to which we are responding. However, as a commitment to my greater calling as a healer, I have decided I will gift you with the additional emotional labor required to provide folks with more context. This is so people can educate themselves about the necessity of Black healing spaces and possibly expand their understanding of this work and our framing of it. You're welcome.

On Monday, June 15, 2020, Mary Williams posted an Open Letter to the Capitol Hill Occupied Protest (CHOP) on Facebook. In it she expressed her longing to take what started out as a powerful protest in services of defunding SPD and protecting Black lives — and has since devolved into a tent city encampment co-located with a quasi-political street fair — and make it a space of healing for Black folks.

She issued an invitation to co-create such a space in Celebration of Juneteenth and I said yes. In three days the two of us raised over $25,000 and made June 19, 2020, a day to center and prioritize Black healing at the CHOP.

Our event lasted for 12 hours. From 8 a.m. to 8 p.m. we held the central field at the CHOP as Black people came and went, made flower crowns, prayed for dead loved ones, wept, connected, laughed, lounged, painted, sang, danced, stretched, and released. The crowd ebbed and flowed as people left to attend marches and rallies and other various celebrations throughout the city. In the evening the field filled up as music began to play.

We enlisted the support of the entire community. We hired Mulu Abate to provide us with nourishing and delicious food as well as several Black facilitators and healers to share their expertise and healing modalities. Abiola Akanni led morning yoga. I curated two altars: one to honor and connect with our ancestors and one for forgiveness and to release our burdens. I also led a grief ritual.

Aramis Hamer curated an arts space and encouraged participants to make cards and write letters to their ancestors. Naa Akua led a sound healing meditation. Natasha Marin invited us to engage in Black imagination through conversations with strangers. The Black Femme Collective, which has been instrumental in organizing the CHOP, spoke about their work, and the day culminated in a dance party with DJ Dark_Wiley.

Myisa Graham set up a Storyorp style project and filmed Black people talking about their experiences of freedom and healing. Taylor Freeman was our logistical intern and Hunter Grier supported with sound and tech.

We also reached out to our non-Black allies for the support necessary to protect the space for our healing. Our allies of every ethnicity showed up beautifully in a variety of capacities. So many folks contributed to our gofundme page that we quickly exceeded our goal. Allies also showed up with an overwhelming wealth of donated supplies: snacks, cases of water, masks, hand sanitizer, homemade fans, musical instruments, sound equipment, sage, art supplies, and flowers. (Shout out to Alyssa for creating our flyers.) They also showed up with their bodies and formed a physical perimeter to deter non-Black folks from disrupting the space and to do the emotional labor of educating non-Black folks about the necessity of Black healing.

This was incredibly courageous and demanding work as individuals with white supremacist groups showed up — some of them armed. The majority of the people who showed to agitate were large white men, and the majority of the people who held the perimeter were women, so there were some very risky dynamics that presented themselves throughout the day.

When I spoke with my co-workers, the entire staff of Young Women Empowered unanimously agreed to support this event and provided a generous donation of staff time, money, and coordination. I can't express how much this loving display of solidarity and care has meant to me. Rose Waterstone, founder and Co-Executive Director of Y-WE, became the point person for coordinating allies and even hosted a Zoom call the night before where folks were trained in conflict de-escalation.

Why did we do this at the CHOP?

The CHOP itself has its origin story rooted in a protest against Black trauma and police brutality. In the first weeks of June, police used tear gas and rubber bullets at the intersections surrounding the CHOP in an attempt to silence crowds of enraged, outraged, and grieving people responding to the gruesome murder of George Floyd. On our minds and hearts also were Breonna Taylor, Ahmaud Abery, Tony McDade, Charleena Lyles, and the ongoing list of Black people who have been victims of the systemic genocide committed by the police—the very people we are told will protect and serve us.

Beyond the simple and agonizing grief of these tragedies, there is the deep and traumatizing fear of being next. Black people showed up to yoga at the CHOP on Friday in tennis shoes in case we had to run away from an attack. Re-read that sentence and let it soak in: the depth of our fear for our own safety even when doing very ordinary and everyday things. Feel that in your adrenal glands: the sweaty-palmed, heart racing panic attack of being vulnerable anywhere at any time simply because of the color of your skin.

Every Black person I know is soul tired and rubbed raw. I don't think this is a secret. I am stating an obvious thing. However, it is necessary to state the obvious because there seems to be a cognitive dissonance. Almost anyone I have encountered understands how hurt Black people have been in this country over the course of the last 400 years and in this year alone. Yet for some reason when two Black women decided to host a healing space for other tired, angry, traumatized, and grieving Black people in the epicenter of a space that was literally created in the name of centering Black lives, we were met with resistance, racial slurs, condescension, rage, indignation, questions, obstructions, and general fuckery.

Why? The answer is because the space we chose to curate did not center whiteness. I had a white man scream at me for being "a segregationist" which I find hilarious, offensive, and historically inaccurate to compare Black people conducting a grief ritual in the park to a whole-ass system that oppressed, marginalized, and harmed our people for decades. "We should all be together," I was told repeatedly. "What you are doing is wrong."

The Caucacity (this word is a contraction for white audacity) of white people thinking they have the right to dictate what my Black healing and grief should look like after a racially motivated murder is another side effect of the deeper mental illness of white supremacist conditioning. Imagine planning a funeral for your loved one and having someone crash it in order to center their needs because they didn't understand or approve of your customs. Imagine if someone came into your therapy session to scream at you that you had no right to heal and they were the only ones who could tell you what healing should look like.

Just stop. We didn't ask for your permission, your opinion, or your approval. In the same way that CHOP was taken, we used civil disobedience to take our healing to the CHOP. We responded to the needs of our community because that is who we are and what we do as Black women. It's what our mothers did and their mothers, and this is how we have survived. The difference is that this time, we chose to do publicly what we have been doing for generations in private as an act of freedom on Juneteenth, the very day we celebrate our freedom.

Why can't we all be together?

In this city especially, we are all together. All the time. We also have affinity groups that serve specific purposes. For example, I live in the South End in a community where there are many Orthodox Jews and East African folks. Due to their cultural norms, many women from both of these communities don't feel comfortable exercising in mixed company, so the gym and community center provide them with access to a female-only space in order to accommodate their safety and comfort. The gym and the community center are not segregated. They serve the entire community, and they are also responsive to specific needs that arise in the community, and no one is harmed through this process.

There are also groups like European Dissent. They are white people meeting to do the work of dismantling oppression and learning to become antiracist with other white people. The work that they do helps to create inclusivity because they unpack the things that make whiteness dangerous. And also, in doing so without requesting Black presence in the space, they are shielding us from doing the unnecessary emotional labor of retraumatizing ourselves for white education.

Even when we are "together," the experience I am having as a Black person in America is very distinct from the experiences other people are having. And my Black experience is different from that of other Black folks. We are not monolithic, but in this current political climate, in the wake of so much tragedy, many Black people are in pain. The specific Black experience I am having right now is trauma-filled and requires support, healing, attention, and space.

Here is another analogy. Would you ask a female-identified victim of rape by a man to process their assault in a therapy group with men? Probably not. Why? Because in that situation there is a high risk she would be uncomfortable and retraumatized. The fear and anxiety she would likely experience when surrounded by men would not be an indictment of the moral character of men generally, but a reflection of the trauma she experienced with a specific man. This does not mean that she will never engage with, love, or trust men again. It just means there is some repair work that needs to happen in order to create a space for her to be in community with men again. This is simple and intuitive.

But if Black people, who have just watched other Black people be murdered by white people, want to claim a healing space free of white people, it is seen as saying all white people are bad. That is ridiculous.

Dear white people

No one was even talking to or about you. The need to center whiteness is so relentless and habitual that when it doesn't happen, people lose their minds. We said Black people need a space to heal with Black people. Your inclusion or exclusion was never the point. However, we thought about it and decided there was a way that we could include you. We even gave you roles to play because we wanted to believe that the same community that has been screaming, "Black Lives Matter!" everyday, all day, for the last three weeks, might actually mean it. That you might support Black people not just in surviving but in thriving. We gave you the opportunity to make allyship a verb: to protect, defend, and support the full humanity of Black people.

Some of you showed up and did exactly that, and to you we are deeply grateful. Some of you really blew it. I'm talking about the white man who came into the space screaming the word "nigger" and had to be removed by no less than eight allies (thank you friends) and the Brown-skinned man who came up to me furious that Black people needed something he didn't understand or couldn't be included in. The "You Blew It" list is long. I was regularly challenged to account for my authority to name, claim, and organize my own healing. It is telling how reluctant people were to recognize, collaborate with, and/or yield to Black female leadership.

And then there was internalized oppression

Black people have been told for so long that we don't deserve to take up space that some people felt uncomfortable to enter a space that was designated as theirs. Some mixed-race Black-identified people expressed trepidation to enter the space for fear they wouldn't be considered "Black enough." Blood quantum is a colonizer mindset. If you identify as Black you are welcome. Black people come in every shade and we are here to heal together.

Some Black people chose to bring their white family members to Black sacred space. They chose not to acknowledge that, while that white person may be their safe person, their presence could make other Black people feel less safe. I met Black people who invalidated the safety concerns of other

Black people and centered the white fragility of their family members instead.

I also met one Black woman who showed up with a megaphone to announce a protest and framed her invitation as, "You can heal later, we need to go to this protest now." It felt shitty to have to pull her aside and inform her that, while she was welcome in the space both to announce the protest and be Black and heal, she was absolutely uninvited to decide for other Black people when and how it was appropriate for them to take space for their own healing.

I know some Black people are cringing reading these words, but I said what I said. And I said it in mixed company because we all need to start unpacking the ways in which the toxic culture of white supremacy is negatively impacting our lives. This is another conversation that usually centers whiteness, but the truth is none of us are immune, and oppression and discrimination are no less problematic when coming from other people of color. We all have a lot to learn. There is a huge amount of spiritual and cultural growth that must take place in order for us to even begin to have a new vision for a better society and it starts by telling the truth, calling out harm, making amends, and understanding one another.

For 12 hours straight, in addition to holding the spiritual and physical space, Mary and I coordinated facilitators and food, connected with media, answered questions, welcomed participants, and met as many needs and requests as we could. We did this while being disrespected, verbally attacked, threatened with physical violence, shamed, belittled, and dehumanized. And we will do it again if it means even one Black person is able to find a bit of healing, solace, and joy.

We did what we set out to do. I cannot count the number of Black people who thanked me with tears running down their faces for the moment of reprieve they were able to receive. "I can't breathe," is not just a protest slogan commemorating the dying words of Eric Garner and subsequently George Floyd, it is a whole-ass mood that aptly describes this experience of navigating the spiritual, physical, mental, emotional, and psychological terrorism currently suffocating Black bodies. But there we were. It was Juneteenth, our day of freedom, and despite every threat, we were breathing, loving, and living. And it was beautiful. Black people loving themselves. People of all colors showing up to support and affirm Black healing. This is what is needed NOW and always.

Additional FAQs:

Should we all be together mourning the deaths of Black people slain by the police and working every day to make sure not one more life is lost?

Yes.

Can we all be together and feel safe given what has happened?

No.

Do Black people need a space where they can process with other Black people about what surviving this genocide is like?

Yes.

Are we asking for permission?

Hell *no*.

Are we doing it again?

Yes. Next Friday and Saturday. Come through for another fire lineup. In honor of Pride weekend there will be a community ofrenda for trans and queer Black folk so that we can center our most marginalized. There will be a grief ritual, a writing workshop, art, delicious food prepared by Black chefs, flower crowns, music, dancing, and double dutch. We will be passing out safety kits created for Black trans femmes to protect themselves.

A Long-Awaited Cotillion

The running joke is that if I were gay, I would be married by now. Marriage and a child is something I have wanted for myself for a long time, but it has been difficult to find the right partnership. I used to wonder if it was because most men assume I'm gay, but I also think any man who would be a good fit for me would have to be comfortable in a queer world in the same way that he would have to be feminist and an anti-racist. So no, I haven't met this magical unicorn yet. I also think me being single is less about my perceived identity and more about who I am, a strong, smart, fat, fourth generation Black feminist with big opinions about everything.

It's national coming out day and my social media is full of my friends coming out for the first or the millionth time, sharing their identities as queer, non-binary, and trans. I also want to come out but hesitate because this day is not a day meant for me. I am coming out as straight. Though it's not a secret, there has been a conflation between my politics and my friend group and my assumed sexual identity.

When the privilege walk happens depending on how the question is worded I might step forward. If the question is do you identify as queer, gay, homosexual, trans or non-binary, I do not step forward. But if asked have you ever been discriminated against on the basis of your perceived sexual identity, I step forward. I have been called a dyke far more times than I have been called a nigger. It reminds me of an early Margaret Cho stand-up routine where she recounts the story of someone slurring her as a chink to which she yelled me back, "I'm a gook you fuck". It's equally awkward when I'm misidentified in polite ways, like the man who sent me an email inviting me to be a panelist to speak about my Black queer intersectional identity. It was a paid opportunity, and he was very complimentary towards the person he thought I was. I politely declined and directed him towards some actual queer people.

I used to attribute this misapprehension to a single closed door. During my freshman year in college, my roommate came out as a lesbian. I didn't know many other people, so we spent a lot of time together. After an isolating experience of high school in Madison, Wisconsin, I hoped to be more involved in Black community. My first step was to join the Black student union which was in the Husky Union Building, just one floor beneath the LGBTQ office. I went to the BSU office almost daily during my first month of school and at all times of the day, but never figured out when was the right time to go. The door was literally always closed and there was never anyone to ask. So sometimes I would go upstairs looking for my roommate. The LGBTQ office door was always open. Moreover, they had a comfy couch and free candy and condoms.

I outed myself as straight repeatedly, but this never diminished the welcome I experienced. One day Brad Benner, the president of the LGBTQ (this was before the other letters were added), arrived at the office for a meeting no one else seemed to know was happening. I offered to leave, but he said I should stay and then he asked us to go around the circle and suggest ideas for what we might do that year. I said a talent show would be cool and he said great, organize it. So, I did. It was a hit and has since become an annual tradition. When the student newspaper asked me if I was a part of the LGBTQ I didn't know what to say because I was and I wasn't. Somehow I had become their token straight girl. I can get along almost anywhere, but I'm not really someone that fits in most places, but in queer community we had that in common. I was welcomed and accepted and treated with respect.

When I sent my mom the article about the talent show, she asked me if I was a lesbian. I told her no and she expressed relief. This surprised me. I had never known her to harbor any negative feelings towards queer people in general or specifically the queer people in my family. When I pressed her, she just told me that my life would be hard enough without adding one more complexity to the ways the world might marginalize me. She talked to me about what it was like for her sister to come out, not just the first time to their parents, but all the subsequent times.

A family affair

Both my mom and my aunt attended Spelman College. They are 13 years apart in age, so mom went first and fell in love with Atlanta and the opportunity to be in Black spaces in a way that had not been afforded her during her upbringing in Des Moines, Iowa. In Iowa though my mom belonged to and participated in a beautiful Black community, she was often the only Black girl in her classes at school, an experience I lived during my formative years in Madison, Wisconsin. Having the opportunity to go to a HBCU, especially one located across the street from a male HBCU (Morehouse) was a dream come true.

My aunt Julie was initially excited to go to Spelman, but her experience was very different. There were three main factors, one was that she was in the honors program which meant she lived in the honors dorm which was separate from the rest of the student body in a way that did not position her well to make friends. It was also during the time of the Atlanta murders. People kept turning up dead, so there was a curfew and a heightened sense of danger that meant Spelman students were asked to be on a buddy system. The third challenge was that although Julie had been out to family, church, and friends in Iowa, being out as gay at an all Black, all female school in the south at that time didn't feel like an option. For my aunt safety was always a challenge. It didn't feel safe to be smart. It didn't feel safe to be Black. It didn't feel safe to be gay. She lasted a year before transferring to the University of Denver to finish her degree.

Much of my own relationship to my identity is tangled up in the ways my mom and my aunt move through the world. Julie is my aunt, but she is also my friend and a kindred spirit. She teases me about my terrible twos when she came to live with us in Colorado, how I would tell her I hated her. I grew out of this and came to really appreciate her as a person. Long after my mom and grandmother had gone to bed, we would spend holidays gathered at the kitchen table, just the two of us, laughing late into the night watching Jackie Brown on cable. Julie was the first person to ever name for me the unspoken tension around clothes.

On safety, intersectional identity and dressing the part

The James women like to dress. Julie too…although she is more of a nice slacks and polo shirt type of person, she also went through a vest and tie dapper stage. But my mom and my grandmother dressed like ladies and I was expected to as well. Now I do love dresses and feel as comfortable rocking a ballgown and a tiara as a vibrant African print jumpsuit or yoga pants and a hoodie. As I've grown more comfortable in my own skin my style has reflected that ease, but as a kid, much to my mother's chagrin, jeans and a hoodie were my armor. There was a safety in androgyny, both physical and emotional during middle school and high school and I was simply trying to survive.

It was clear I was going to be source of ridicule no matter what I wore, but my mom seemed determined to put me in clothing guaranteed to get my ass kicked. Her upbringing wasn't easy either. She was one of a handful of Black kids integrating a white school, but she was also a Riderette. She executed choreographed routines wearing fringed boots and a smart outfit. When I try to imagine myself as a teenager trying to be on trend in high femme attire and it's like a horror movie. This was something Julie and I had in common. It's not just that we dressed for comfort, it's that we dressed to be less visible. But to the boys at my school this was me "dressing gay". It's funny how just a short generation after mine boys can wear skirts and nail polish without people presuming their sexuality. But when I grew up binaries were enforced and homophobia and racism played a big part in how you were coded.

I was always "different", Black in white spaces or the wrong kind of Black in Black spaces. It was challenging to reconcile my experience of being Black with what I saw on TV or read in books. I didn't grow up in a neighborhood like Boyz in the Hood. I also didn't grow up on Martha's Vineyard with the talented tenth. I did briefly attend Jack n Jill, where a bunch of other middle class Black kids I didn't really know from various schools around Madison did their best to tolerate me while not really ever making me feel welcomed, understood or included. I was nerdy and sensitive and the only Black kid (not being raised by white parents) who chose to wear an afro in the 6th grade. Kids threw sunflower seeds at my head and called me a chia pet.

There seemed to be all these unspoken rules for everything from how I was supposed to talk, dress or walk, which sports Black kids played, what kind of grades we got in school or where we sat in the cafeteria. Black girls didn't do cheer they did drill team. They played basketball or volleyball and ran track, but never played soccer which was my sport of choice from ages 8-18. Three of my best friends (who were white) played soccer too and one by one as they stepped into adulthood came out as queer. They keep teasing me that it's never too late to switch teams.

I learned in middle school that I was bad at being Black, that most of my choices were the wrong choices and just being who I was from my vocabulary and diction to being chubby and having nappy hair were all wrong. The least I could do was dress plainly in ways that wouldn't get me mocked any further, though the way I dressed did get me called at best a tomboy and at worst a dyke. There was safety in masculinity. To dress more "feminine" might put me at risk of being sexualized. I wanted to avoid calling attention to my body at all costs for fear of dying of embarrassment.

And then there was the fighting. While you can fight in a skirt, I wouldn't recommend it and almost every day during the entire 7th grade I was in a fight. These skirmishes took place every recess and sometimes before or after school and were rarely, if ever, stopped by a teacher. I never started a fight, but my dad had taught me never to back down in the face of a bully. I started carry a lunch bag with a thermos that I could use as a weapon. What I lacked in speed and technique I made up for in rage and brutality.

I often wondered why I was such a weirdo. I watched as one of my best friends completely change her personas through clothing. One year she listened almost exclusively to Metallica and wore plaid shirts and black jeans, the next year she listened exclusively to rap and adopted a wardrobe of pristine white Filas paired with baggy jeans and a matching Fila gold chain. Though her style was always masculine, white girls didn't have to be feminine to still be seen as pretty. She also had far more Black friends than I did and seemed to move with effortless acceptance through community. I envied the way they treated her, the way she laughed at all the inside jokes. I always wanted to ask her how she did it, but one day we were hanging out and she turned to me and said something I never expected to hear. She told me she envied my authenticity and the way I never changed who I was to fit in. I would have though. If I knew how. If I thought I could pull it off. It felt ironic that the same adolescent insecurities would manifest in such different strategies.

The sole intervention came when I was 16 and my mom took me to Senegal. She was a professor of African American and Women's Studies and had the opportunity to do a faculty exchange at the University of Saint Louis. So we flew to Dakar then spent a month eating thieboudine, walking the sandy streets of Saint Louis, and immersing ourselves in the beautiful colors, sights, and people of Senegal. I watched the elegant women dressed in vibrant printed skirts and booboos made from stiff waxed fabric with waist beads subtly jangling together, their pace slow to keep from sweating in the relentless heat. I realized I liked pretty clothes and felt safe enough to explore expressions of femininity. I bought bangles and learned to tie wrap skirts. I even wore a little make up. Also having natural hair wasn't equated with masculinity or queerness in Africa.

Being in a country where everyone from the janitor to the president was Black completely liberated me from the narrow identity box I'd been put in. In Senegal it was an asset to be nerdy. After a week I had learned to count in French, greet people in Oulof and could haggle at the market. Being thick was desirable. I had to learn how to stop my American habit of looking people in the eye after my mom realized there was group of Mauritanian men at our hotel trying to figure out how to purchase our "services". Most women didn't look men directly in the eye unless it was an invitation. Though that felt a little scary, I mostly just enjoyed being seen as beautiful for the first time.

Being foreign in a foreign land allowed me the freedom to be myself because it removed me from the context that was forever misjudging me.

Fast forward to later in life, this trip is a big reason why I became so passionate about providing study abroad opportunities for youth of color. I wanted them to have access to the intervention I'd experienced because not only did it change my life, in some ways I think it saved my life. Just knowing that there was somewhere in the world, even if it was thousands of miles away, where I could be accepted as I was kept me hanging on long enough to get to college and from there life got better.

I spent my junior year abroad in Spain which is when and where I developed my fashion sense and met men who didn't assume I was queer and wanted to date me. Though I didn't ever join the BSU or pledge Delta Sigma Theta like all the women on my mom's side of the family, I did eventually find Black community, ironically in Japan where I taught for two years after college.

I have never felt more foreign in my life than when living in rural Japan. I literally had people stop me on the street because they had never seen a Black person before and wanted to take my picture or ask me questions. I was part of the Japan Exchange and Teaching Program which hosted 3-6,000 foreigners a year as Assistant Language Teachers. During our first conference in Tokyo I met 3 Black teachers, Candace, Donata, and Jerrold who became my family. For the next two years we met up frequently, traveling to each other's homes or going on trips together with an assortment of other teachers and friends we gathered along the way. It was the first time I ever felt like I belonged. And their acceptance of me gave me confidence, made me feel more comfortable in my own skin.

The F word

While it has taken me more time to embrace certain parts of my identity, being a feminist has always felt intuitive. When I was 9 years old my mom and her colleague Abena Busia published an anthology called Theorizing Black Feminisms: The Visionary Pragmatism of Black Women. More than a book, my mother's scholarship, her philosophy on other mothering and pragmatism was steeped into my upbringing from the conversations I had to media I consumed and the events I attended. I had a robust council of mentors including Dr. Nellie McKay who did more than explain feminism to me, they modeled it in their daily lives and careers.

I love Alice Walker and I respect many womanists, but I do not count myself among them any more than I identify with White feminists, so in that way I am on the margins of the margins because neither identity encompasses the liberation or accountability that is intrinsic to who I am and who I hope to be in the world. I can't be a feminist the white way, because their feminism does not challenge racism and is complicit with marginalizing those of us who have intersectional identities. I can't be a TERF because nothing truly radical would ever need to exclude trans people. I can't be a womanist, because their doctrine allows the toxic masculinity of Black men to go unchecked. I believe that every person has value. I believe that every person regardless of any of the ways they identify deserves respect, compassion, and equal consideration under the law...even people I don't like or respect or feel compassion towards. For me feminism isn't just a blanket statement that men and women are equal, it transcends binary thinking and is an action, a movement, a practice, not just a philosophical ideology.

Though there is an affinity or recognition I share with queer folks that is a solidarity forged from the pain of being oppressed based on identity, what binds me to queerness is not oppression, it's the positionality of my Black feminism, specifically this core belief around the innate value in every person irrespective of the ways they identify. There is a freedom in this ideology that speaks to queerness and provides space for the co-existence of a full spectrum of being that does not have to fit inside a box and can be as contradictory or as complementary as it wants to be.

Just because I don't identify as queer does not mean that I haven't learned anything from queerness. There is a great debt I owe to queer community who taught me the joy and necessity of chosen family, the importance of radical welcome and the bravery to live authentically in the fullness of who I am.

What the youth are teaching me:

When I returned to the States, I got my Masters in International Education with a focus on social justice. My intention was to design study abroad programs, which I did. To date I have taken over 250 youth abroad to Japan, Guatemala and Mexico respectively. But for the last 8 years I have been working at an organization called Young Women Empowered (Y-WE).

Y-WE is the program I wish I had as a youth. It's an intergenerational community of belonging that invites youth to come as they are and explore not just what they want to be, but who they want to be, in a space where they won't be judged for their answers. And just like the LGBTQ office held a door open for me all those years ago, we open our doors with a radical hospitality that encourages everyone to bring their whole self and be welcomed.

We center the needs of BIPOC youth ages 13-19 through a series of programs that cover a full spectrum of content from career readiness to environmental justice to creative writing, sewing, jewelry making, computer coding and more. Despite the name, we not only serve young women, but also adults, non-binary youth, trans youth and youth who don't yet know how they identify. The youth especially have been a source of unending education for me. Growing up in a place where everything was a binary...you were either Black or white, gay or straight, man or woman, these kids have introduced me to a whole world of grays.

Being queer or trans used to be a death sentence. In some places it still is. The Human Rights Commission and Black Lives Matter websites tell these stories of continued violence and death that queer and trans folks are facing. According to the Trevor Project more than 50% of trans and non-binary youth have considered suicide. And yet, the youth bring an unexpected playfulness to the ways they approach gender and attraction. There is a freedom to this fluidity and the ways in which I see them changing their pronouns or sometimes their names to most accurately reflect the person they are evolving into.

I wonder what it would be like to approach identity in a way that felt less limited by the societal expectations of who we are supposed to be and what those check boxes denote. I watch our youth accept and reject labels or customize them in ways I never imagined possible. What if we didn't have to exist in a binary or even on a spectrum, what if we could all fully inhabit our identities in a way that leaves room for growth and evolution, that doesn't guarantee the continuity that you will always be the same you, but allows for an endless cotillions where you celebrate the you that you are in that moment and the next and the next with equal acceptance.

The youth are out now in the bravest way, tenderly hopeful that they can wear their nuances in public and be well met. It's not to say that there is no fear, shame, complexity, or consequence inherent in these declarations, but that there is also at times a celebratory boldness. These youth belong to themselves. And their courage pushes me to imagine and work towards a world where we can live in a way where our authenticity is welcome and there is always enough space, compassion, and acceptance for all of us to belong. And that even I, a cis gendered, heterosexual, plus sized, fourth generation Black feminist can exist in the fullness of all my identities and be met with love.

The
World

Why I Started a Study Abroad Program
for People of Color

The two most influential forces in my life have been writing and travel. Growing up I always wanted to see the world (any place outside of Wisconsin would do). Just before I turned seventeen, my mother took me Senegal.

It's strange to think that one month could change my life, but it did. I fell in love with the food, the people, the baobab trees, and the sandy streets. While jarring to wake up to the unfamiliar cries of roosters intermixed with the Muslim call to prayer, I awoke each day feeling more alive and more myself than I ever had.

It's like simply being somewhere else gave me the freedom to reinvent myself, only I wasn't becoming someone else, I was becoming the me I really wanted to be. Through it all my journal was my constant companion. I wrote to document each miraculous day and in the writing began to sort through my feelings.

Being raised in a black feminist household made going to school a challenge. While academically I was well equipped to succeed, my values, my interests, my vocabulary, and my natural hair were all completely different from my peers and even my teachers. In middle school and high school being different is usually equated with being wrong.

For one month, though I was a foreigner, being different didn't feel so wrong; it was expected. There was a place for me, a place where people appreciated my accent and my command of the English language, my hair, my body size and shape, my sense of humor. It was a trip that affirmed me and also inspired in me a passion for travel that has yet to be sated.

I spent my junior year of college in Cadiz, Spain. When I went to meet the cohort I would be traveling with, it felt like I was pledging a white sorority. I went to Spain with 30 white women, 5 men, and 2 other women of color and it was an amazing experience, but one that was clearly not designed with me in mind.

The welcome packet we received included a list of local businesses, the post office, popular cafes, places to shop and places to get your hair cut. Of course there was no one in the small town of Cadiz who knew anything about black hair. I had to travel 8 hours to Madrid to get it braided in an African shop. It may seem like a small thing, but the small things began to add up, like going out with my friends from the cohort and being told I wasn't an American because I didn't look like the other girls.

After Spain came Japan. I was placed in one of the largest prefectures on Honshu with 200 other English teachers from around the world, yet I was the only black teacher. In fact, I was the only black teacher in the 13 years the town had been hosting the program. It was a shock for everyone involved when I stepped into the classroom for the first time and was greeted by students screaming and hitting each other in disbelief.

During the two years I taught in Japan, I was met with screams repeatedly. Many of them were excited as opposed to scared, but it took me a while to have enough understanding of Japanese to know the difference. I was also followed around in stores, bitten by an autistic child who thought my skin was made of chocolate, and asked by a woman whose eyes were filled with tears why my mother had left me out in the sun too long.

Through it all, at no point during my travels was there any authority figure or program director who had any interest or relevant experience to help me process why my journey was so very different from everyone else's. What would it have been like to have felt heard? What would it have been like to have had someone who could help me process the nuances of my experience? For as amazing as my travels have been, how much more enriching would they have been with someone who really got it? These were the questions that led me back to school.

In 2006, I completed my MA in International Education from the SIT Graduate Institute. Since then I have taken more than 200 young people abroad to Guatemala, Japan, and Mexico respectively and been a witness to everything from homesickness meltdowns to shy kids break dancing, the creation of a sport named sumo jousting and the epic battle of stomachs at the all you can eat cake buffet (Cake Tabehodai!).

I was with young people for their first plane rides, their first time seeing the ocean, and their first time communicating in a foreign language. We celebrated small victories like successfully ordering a meal at a restaurant and learning the steps to a traditional dance for a parade, and big victories like planting 500 trees and building a school.

Every day was an adventure, an opportunity to navigate a new culture and a foreign way of doing things. The connections those youth made with one another, with their homestay families and all the people they met along the way fundamentally shifted who they are.

These excursions changed me, too.

In 1932, Dr. Donald Watts founded the Experiment in International Living to create a space of cultural immersion for the purpose of fostering peace. For many young people of color, "cultural immersion"—stepping out of their comfort zones to interact with people from different walks of life —is just everyday life, especially for those of living in predominantly white communities. But youth of color also benefit from building community abroad. We are at a time when it is vital for those youth to have these incredible experiences of foreign cultures, and also to observe their own culture from a distance.

During my year on campus, the entire International Education Program took a field trip to Boston for the NAFSA conference. I stood in a balcony overlooking a ballroom that held literally thousands of study abroad program directors from around the world.

There I was in my snazzy suit with my resume neatly printed ready to network and find a practicum. As I scanned the room, it was like meeting the other people in the Cadiz program only on a much larger scale. Here again was this sorority of upper middle class do-gooder white women with Guatemalan purses, Kenyan earrings, and Chinese silk scarves accenting their business suits.

There were 7 black women in a room filled with thousands—I counted. Over the next few hours I made a point to meet each and every one of them. The majority of them worked for SEVIS, a branch of homeland security in charge of deporting foreign exchange students. One was an administrative assistant to a study abroad director. Not one of them was a study abroad program director. NOT ONE.

I left feeling disheartened. It's a feeling that stuck with me even though I found a practicum, completed my thesis, and achieved my objective of taking youth abroad.

Every job I have ever applied for—even positions in organizations designed to work with youth of color—has been headed by white people. Even if they hire staff entirely made up of people of color, they are the ones who have the final say over the curriculum. And while I don't wish to disparage the good work they are doing, sometimes who they are gets in the way of their goals.

While increasingly there are more opportunities to go abroad and more people investing financial resources in sending our youth of color abroad, there has not been an equal investment in providing them with experiences that are actually designed to accommodate the complexities of who they are in the world.

Many Voices One Tribe was the culmination my long held dream. It was a study abroad program for youth of color. Our mission was to empower young writers of color to see world, to know themselves, and to define their own futures. We were committed to dismantling oppression, telling our own stories, and creating global community using travel and writing are the catalyst to a deeper exploration of our identities and our place in the world.

I piloted the first and only trip in 2015. There were just five of us: Jordan Chaney, my adult co-facilitator, and three youth, Azeb, Eyerusalem, and Zion. Though everyone identified as black, the joke was that there were never three such diverse youth, a Muslim, a Christian, and a Buddist, with varying gender and sexual identities and countries and ethnicities of origin. Yet there were united in their desire share the experience and each worked for months to help pay for their trips.

Here is an excerpt from our trip blog:

> It's quiet today, no raucous laughter from the ongoing stream of jokes and shade throwing, nor Spanglish chatter with whomever might be downstairs. For the moment its just me alone in my white stucco room with its long green curtains, light streaming in through the opaque glass of the balcony door. After huffing my way through zumba by the waterfront with David and Gabriel, I dragged myself home through the dense salty air to find everyone else taking advantage of the morning off to sleep in.
>
> Today we will write. Having been here a full week, the youth have selected the focus of the articles they will be putting together and even conducted some preliminary interviews. Now they will craft pitches to be sent to their editor at the Seattle Globalist. Then we'll have lunch together. Paola, one of our instructors is making cheese empanadas. So far the best recipes I've gotten this trip have been from Angelica, another one of our instructors, who makes a black-berry pudding to die for.
>
> After lunch everyone will have language lessons in the afternoon during which time I hope to visit our new friend Karma. Karma, once a student at the language school, has returned to Veracruz to

live for the year while she is completing her dissertation through the University of Chicago. Her topic, Afro-Mexicans. She is a black woman from the States and in meeting her I saw the kids' eyes light up. This may be their first trip, but I can tell already that these three have a lot of world to see and meeting Karma seemed to make that idea more tangible to them.

After yesterday's arduous bus trip to Papantla to visit the pyramids of El Tajin we are all exhausted, but content. I am delighted for this brief respite of air conditioning and solitude and in general for the way this adventure is turning out so far. For those of you who know me or have been following my column in the Seattle Globalist, you know that this trip is years in the making. It's been my dream to create a study abroad program for young people of color and these young people have made the reality so much better than I had even imagined. In this short time, though it sounds cliche, we've become a family.

I wasn't sure what it would be like to bring a group of black folks to Veracruz, but its been fascinating. One of the things that sometimes irritates me about traveling while black is the picture taking. In Japan, this was especially an issue. Everyone everywhere always wanted to take my picture. I got my first glimpse of what it must be like to be chased by paparazzi. Here in Veracruz, I get the stares, we all do.

There are the old women who want to pat my cheek and tell me how much they like my black skin, the catcalls of "morena"or "negra", and yes the random people who want to take my picture, but Zion, the darkest and tallest of us all, is the one everyone wants to take picture of now. "I feel like a low key Kim Kardashian or something" he confessed yesterday after we were mobbed by an entire family of Mexican tourist who wanted to take pictures of all of us, but then individually with only Zion. Rather than getting irritated, he seemed to enjoy his little photo shoot, and the next and the next.

Eyerusalem has been working on an article about comparative standards of beauty. She's snapped photos of every billboard between the here and the Zocolo and decided she wanted to take pictures of girls and women to compare the ads to the real women of Veracruz. Tables turned. I took the group to the Zocolo for their first experience of danzon, an elegant traditional form of ballroo dancing that the older generation is trying to revive. After a few loops around the square, Eyerusalem took out her camera and began approaching people to take their pictures. There were a few odd looks of confusion, not unlike what I usually feel when asked the same, but most people complied and there were lovely conversations started because of it. And usually at the end, the subjects pulled out their own camera phones to take pictures with the group, but it didn't feel quite as objectifying because there was reciprocity and human connection.

Human connection. That's really the key to this whole experiment. When I think about what moments have been the most transformative in my abroad experiences, what triumphs have stayed with me and lingered with them, it's all about the times when we let our guard down and get to know another. There is something healing about our time together that I'm not yet able to articulate adequately, other than to say that I really needed this.

Last week was our week of excursions and frenetic activity. I walked everyone to the point of exhaustion, but it was worth it. In addition to language lessons, we visited the Veracruz Museum of the City, we traveled to the state capitol Xalapa and met with the Human Right's Commission. We visited the Museum of Anthropology, set on several acres of land and complete with indigenous plant life in addition to Olmec heads and an incredible replica of El Tajin. We visited the ruins of Quiahuitlzan and hiked down to the sparsely populated beach at Villa Rica before climbing up to the Quebraduras. We danced in the Zocolo, made friends with a street dancing clown, and made Jordan's wish come true by visiting the pyramids in Papantla.

This week our pace will be a little calmer. We will be spending a bit more time here in el Puerto. There will be beaches and museums, one last long bus ride to Yanga, but mostly it is a time for deepening in the writing and conducting interviews. It's time to explore the questions we have about this culture and to seek answers in the community.

Five years after the trip, I stand by the work we did together. All three youth graduated from high school. Eyerusalem, who was the oldest, will graduate from Spelman this May. After her Freshman year she returned to Seattle to intern with me at Y-WE for the summer.

Sophomore year she went to Ethiopia for the summer to lead youth groups for girls to talk about self care. She has plans to become an educator and start her own organization. Azeb went to community college and has been working on film making. Zion went to New York for school, but ran out of resources and came back to Seattle to start again. He started to work towards an education degree, but then realized his real dream is in storytelling. He is an accomplished photographer and works for the Rainier Beach Action Coalition.

It was my honor to be a part of their journey and I was grateful for the opportunity to run a program from start to finish the way I wanted it to be. I stand by curriculum and have witnessed the transformative power of that experience, but the two years I worked towards that dream took a toll on me personally and financially. This heart work is something that must be done in community, but I am content to have planted seeds for the pathway forward.

Soup or Salad: Afro American Cultural Erasure in the US and Mexico

No one ever just calls it "Yanga." The tagline "the first free town in the Americas" is as much a part of the identity of this place as the myth of the prince turned rebel slave whose name the town bears. From the moment you cross into town you will be reminded of its illustrious history as a haven for 400 black slaves who won their freedom in a battle against the Spanish in 1609.

The walls of the public buildings and even some cafes are lined with black art. Black rag dolls and quasi-African trinkets, masks and sculptures pack the shelves of corner stores and markets. The slave trade may be long over, but the commodification of black images is commonplace.

During my 16 day trip to Mexico, I visited Yanga twice: once to see the sights and the second time to attend the annual Carnaval Afro Mexicano. My goal was to explore Afro-Mexican identity, retracing the path of the black diaspora through the history of the state of Veracruz and searching for understanding of the present black culture.

You can taste the African heritage all around Veracruz, in the spicy regional cuisine. You can hear it in the lyrics and beat of the live music played and danced to each afternoon in the Zócalo—the main square of the historic district in Puerto de Veracruz. I didn't go a day without hearing songs about la negra, la morenita, the black woman, the little dark one.

And yet, everywhere I went, my presence was met with long inquisitive stares and followed up with questions about my origins. No one mistook me for Mexican... Cuban or Dominican perhaps, but not Veracruzana. And yet it was plain that the diaspora had marked this area. So what happened to all the black people? I held out hope for Yanga. All the Mexicans I met assured me that black people lived there. I arrived in town with no real plan. By accident I ended up in the mayor's office. Upon discovering I was a foreigner wanting to learn more about Yanga, Mayor Gerson Morales Villanos (who everyone refers to as "El Presidente") dispatched Lubin, one of his aides and Andrés, the town librarian to commandeer a municipal vehicle.

I was escorted to the three main tourist sights: the statue of "El Negro" set against a beautiful mural depicting the rebellion, the museum in Palmillas, and the ruins of the haciendas built during the height of the slave trade.

Since 1932—when the town formerly known as San Lorenzo de los Negritos was renamed in an attempt to solidify Yanga's place as a black Mexican folk icon—tourists from across the African diaspora have made the same pilgrimage. The librarian made a point to show me picture of a delegation of dignitaries who came all the way from Ghana.

But it was at the Palmillas Museum just outside of Yanga, in a fascinating one-on-one with the director, archeologist and researcher, Fernando Miranda Flores, that it was finally confirmed for me the thing no other Mexican seemed to want to say directly.

"The group here lost their culture. Some traditions remain in terms of certain dishes and wood working customs, but now there is little left."

I settled in to hear once more the legend behind the pithy tagline. While it was Francisco de la Matoza who allegedly led the armed rebellion (since Yanga would have been 55 at the time and too old to fight), Yanga (or possibly "N'Ganga") was said to be the man with the plan.

The history gets murky and is fraught with fascinating mysteries, but the indisputable result was that Yanga and the community of people he liberated from slavery caused so much disruption to the trade of slaves and sugar, that the Spanish government ultimately found it more profitable to grant them their freedom.

Freedom is a relative term. Citizens of the town that would later become Yanga could not have alcohol or weapons. They were also not allowed to have any interactions with the other black people who would arrive in Veracruz, because those people would come as slaves and freedom was (and is still) considered a highly contagious ideal. It was more like a reservation than a town.

With no access to new black people, the population of Yanga intermarried with the local indigenous people. Eventually the women of Yanga became disgruntled with the town and most left to live in the Port of Veracruz where they found employment, often as domestic help and sometimes as prostitutes.

Of course that was just the story of one group of people there were those who came as slaves and were not granted freedom and those who came much later during the building of the railroad. After finishing up at the museum, Lubin and Andres took me to Mataclara to meet Florentino Virgen Castro, a musician and the first self- identified Afro-Mexican that I had the privilege to meet.

Louis Armstrong played in the background as he received us into his living room, a sepia hued space with framed photos spilling family history across the walls. His grandfather was from Martinique and came in the group of railroad workers. Over the course of the afternoon we spoke of his life and his family, the Yoruba religious traditions they had managed to retain despite the Catholic imposition that is present even in the name he carries. Virgen Castro expressed pride in his identity as a black Mexican and pride in persevering despite discrimination.

He took us to meet his sister and aunt, two black women who wore their hair natural and made sarcastic comments about all the people who had come from other countries looking for Afro-Mexicans.

"Aqui estamos," We're here, they said casually, but in their words I recognized the underpinning act of revolution. Throughout my trip I felt as though we were chasing ghosts, as though Mexico itself had eaten what was black and left only music and stories. We're here, they told me, despite all odds, in the face of adversity, after all this time.

At night I returned to my hotel room and flipped on CNN. I found myself glued to the events unfolding in Ferguson, Missouri. Mike Brown. Trayvon Martin. Eric Garner. Amadou Diallo. I feel ashamed when I start to forget their names, but the list goes on and on. It is too much weight to carry, too much grief, too much rage condensing like an unending storm always brewing in our collective consciousness.

I want to remember their names and stories because I am afraid that if I don't they will disappear, but every memory of injustice, of how black lives have gone from being bought and sold to having little to no value at all, is another way of disappearing me.

How many times can we relive this same tragedy and not feel like a part of ourselves was killed as well? This is the unspoken war, no longer North vs. South, this is the war of the U.S. against black people. It's a silent genocide and there is no winning. In this so called "post-racial" American since Obama's second term began it seems like all the covert racists have come out of the closet. Every few minutes there is more news of white supremacist rallies or, more anecdotally, friends being called "nigger" or in general white people just losing their damn minds.

The fear is palpable. What else but fear can explain why a trained officer would need six bullets to subdue an unarmed teenager who had already surrendered?

I returned to Yanga wondering if this was how its former citizens had felt, hemmed in by Spanish law, not allowed any weapons except for a locked shed containing guns that could be used in case of pirates. Their very existence dictated by their former captors, a balancing act: Free, but only so free. Human, but only so human.

Ultimately, in preserving their freedom their descendants lost the very culture and heritage they fought to save.

After an hour and a half of Mexican folkloric dancing (which is pretty much like river dance with lacy costumes), I sat in my plastic chair, sipping a warm corona courtesy of the mayor's aide, and watched four white Mexicans be crowned queens of the Afro-Mexican Carnival while the Orizaba symphony butchered a tribute to the Beatles.

In the crowd of the hundreds of people who attended I was one of a handful of black faces. The only act of the evening that had anything to do with blackness was Santo Negro y Las Chicas de Angel, a west African drumming troupe who played and danced for about a half hour, with no explanation of which country they hailed from or what the significance of the music was.

On my cab ride back to my hotel in Cordoba I found myself contemplating cultural erasure. Identity is a complex nuanced creation built on family, how you are taught to see yourself, and how other see and respond to you.

While the myth of the U.S. is that we are all a part of a melting pot, I think the more apt metaphor is that of a salad bowl, collectively forming an American identity from very unique cultural components. What I found in Mexico was the true melting pot, a soup brewed from black, Spanish, and indigenous cultures, now seamlessly blended to create one overarching Mexican identity.

While on my trip I met a white couple from the U.S. who have lived in Mexico for ten years. The husband shared his observations about the cultural homogeneity. He was excited about it—as though this were the perfect solution to all of the racial issues in the U.S. As though all the mixing were voluntary and not a survival strategy on the part of black and indigenous people.

"People get along," he said, vastly oversimplifying the dynamics and ignoring all the sacrifices made in the creation of this so-called beautiful unity.

In the U.S. we have managed to maintain distinct cultural identities. But society's violent response to our identity as black people continuously puts us in danger.

So what's worse, to lose your life because you are seen as a threat, or to give up your identity to no longer be threatening?

Soccer Fields and Chainstores: Weighing U.S. Influence in Honduras

You might not have heard much news from Honduras recently. If you did, it was probably about the violent crime that has gripped this small Central American country in recent years, lending to its reputation as "the murder capital of the world."

So when I got a last-minute opportunity to join a Seattle delegation headed to Tegucigalpa, Honduras, last month, I wasn't sure what to expect.

The Centro de Alcance "Mi Barrio" is located in a neighborhood in the capital city ironically named Colonia de los Estados Unidos (Colony of the United States). Nestled on a hillside overlooking a residential area, the center provides programming and support for 300 local youth. It's one of 46 centers in Honduras co-created by the U.S. Agency for International Development (USAID) in partnership with local community organizations.

After crossing an unmarked boundary the driver rolled down the van's tinted windows so we could see and be seen by the residents. "It's a sign of respect," Mauricio Vivero, the CEO of the Seattle International Foundation tells me. "That way they know we aren't gang members."

There seemed to be little confusion about who we were—to the youth at the center we were the U.S. citizens responsible for refurbishing their soccer field.

"We do two things," explained Vivero about the role of the Seattle International Foundation and why they jumped at the chance to partner with the Seattle Sounders during the team's trip to Honduras. "We help Seattle people and Seattle institutions do good in the world and try to facilitate that. And then we also have our strategic focus on Central America and that is where we spend a lot of our intellectual energy and our resources," he said.

The small delegation of Seattleites including Vivero, former Sounders player Roger Levesque, Sounders photographer Dan Poss, and Melissa and Bruce Seiber, two Seattle Sounders fans who won a contest to attend the Sounders game in Honduras, received a warm welcome. Levesque drew smiles from the youth and struck up a pick- up game the moment he dropped a soccer ball on the field.

The day before the official ribbon cutting ceremony, the field didn't look like much, just a few rolls of green AstroTurf laid out over a concrete corner. The field markers hadn't yet been painted and the goal posts were still being welded together, but this was not a deterrent to youth delighting in have a new space to play.

The center itself was not fancy. It didn't seem large enough to accommodate those it serves, at least by U.S. standards. It began as a concrete patch surrounding an existing kindergarten and has expanded to include a small playground, a computer lab, bathrooms and two multi-purpose spaces. Center director Ulices Garcia led us around the corner to a narrow strip of concrete. "That's going to be a gym," he said.

With Vivero as a translator, Garcia introduced the staff, the majority of whom are volunteers from the neighborhood. Despite its size, the center offers a wide selection of programming including gym time for adults in the early morning and after work and classes for youth in dance, art, and computer. At one time they offered vocational courses for barbers and hair stylists, but they have since converted the space into a mediation room to encourage a different approach to conflict resolution. Several of the volunteers have received professional training to run this new initiative.

"Our hope is that our community be totally clean of all that is violent, domestic violence and child abuse and also narcotics because there are a lot and that's why we work with youth here, making sure there are other opportunities so that they can avoid falling into gangs," Garcia said. "That's what we hope, that our community can get out of this development."

For 18-year-old Jon Carlo Josua de Cuba, the two years he has been a part of the center have been transformative. "It's a place where young people can go to have fun and it has helped a lot. It's helped me in the area of computers and video games. It's a safe place where we go to have fun, but also to help out a little."

When I asked him the most important thing he's gained from the center, Josua de Cuba answered immediately: "Values, and to be someone in life, respect, love, and being nice with everyone." Josua de Cuba now volunteers regularly and expects that many other youth who come through the program will choose to do the same. When asked whether he was learning these values anywhere else in his life, he shook his head. "The truth is, no."

The morning after our initial visit to the center 50 youth met with Sounders' coaches Brian Schmetzer and Tom Dutra, Levesque, and 15 members of the team's official fan club, the Emerald City Supporters for a soccer clinic at the national stadium. In addition to getting to work on their skills, they received goalie gloves, jerseys and shirts courtesy of the Seattle International Foundation and the Emerald City Supporters. Later that afternoon, officials from USAID, World Vision, and various other organizations showed up at the Centro de Alcance to make speeches and break in the new soccer field.

Ted Glenn from USAID was present to speak about the overall strategy. "What we've done in the USAID is follow the examples of experts... in places like Los Angeles, Chicago, and New York working with the Department of Justice, that National Institutes of Health and the Centers for Disease Control who have a real expertise in violence prevention in the United states."

The objective is to adapt best practices of these models to fit the Honduran context.

Honduras is a country continuously struggling with crime and poverty, largely due to gang activity and the drug trade. Nearly two- thirds of the population live in extreme poverty. Contributing factors include Hurricane Mitch in 1998, which wiped out 70 percent of their crops, causing $3 billion in damages and killing 5,000.

Yet according the CIA factbook, Honduras' natural resources include: timber, gold, silver, copper, lead, zinc, iron ore, antimony, coal, fish, and hydropower. The question no one seems to be asking is how is it that Honduras is so poor and yet so rich in mineral resources and farm land?

I pondered this question throughout my brief visit. Every time I got into a van or cab to leave the hotel, I thought about the relationship between the United States and Honduras as I passed what seemed like one continuous symbol of modern day colonization. Dunkin' Donuts, Chili's, Baskin-Robbins, and McDonald's signs proliferated the skyline. This was Honduras, the second most dangerous country in Central America and home to Forever 21, Sears, Burger King, Subway, and even Cinnabon.

Meeting Ulices Garcia and the youth at the Centro de Alcance made me believe that the U.S. government and organizations like the Seattle International Foundation are doing some good work to support Honduran citizens in their struggle against poverty.

Still I was left wondering how much of these problems were we responsible for creating? I also wondered whether Hondurans determine what they need within their own communities or are the U.S. business ventures and philanthropic initiatives an international example of white privilege? Is it manifest destiny moving south instead of west?

Why Isn't The World Talking About The Scandal in Honduras?

Everyone in Honduras is talking about Guatemala. It's been two weeks since Otto Perez Molina resigned as Guatemalan president after a crackdown on corruption by the United Nations-backed International Commission against Impunity.

Just southeast of Guatemala, many citizens in neighboring Honduras are requesting that similar investigations take place in their country, after Honduras President Juan Orlando Hernandez admitted that his campaign ended up with money from the national health system, resulting in patients' deaths.

Hours after arriving in the Honduran capital of Tegucigalpa, I found myself in a plaza downtown. It was filled with people walking in all directions and several street preachers proselytizing from makeshift PA systems. Across the square from the Metropolitan Cathedral of Tegucigalpa was an encampment of tents roped off with a sign indicating that the residents were participating in a hunger strike.

Not only were there activists, five strikers and a political street artist, but supporters were guarding the camp and providing water to the strikers.

The activists said the supporters were needed to protect them from disruption from police.

"Last night they wanted to try it here. They were going to come here and fuck with us last night, people sent by Mr. President. He's been sending people here that attack us," said 54-year-old Oscar Maldonado, one of three men on his 14th day of the hunger strike. "But we realized what their plan was and we denounced them on Radio Globo and on other radio stations too."

Two of the five men had been on strike for 36 days only drinking water with a little honey and some juice to survive. They spent 28 days on the corner in front of the Presidential Palace before deciding to relocate to the more populated square.

"Well we're more or less healthy," said Hernan Ayala, 42. "It's logical that we're weak and tired, but our purpose is to pressure the government until they install the Commission here." They plan to stay there indefinitely.

"The last straw was our actual president who is governing our country," explained Marco Tulio Medense, 69, a member of a group he referred to as La Gente Indignado—the Indignant People. "Why? Because this man, when he began to govern this country, took money from the State Department and in the first place from the Social Security fund. He took money for his political campaign."

In a press conference at the end of May, President Juan Orlando Hernandez admitted that his campaign fund mysteriously ended up with about $3 million lempira (about $140,000 USD) from an account that funds the national health plan in Honduras. However, he argued that he didn't know about it and therefore should not be held accountable, according to international news network teleSUR.

The network reported that allegedly more than $350 million USD in total was embezzled by the managers of the Social Security Institute, some of which was funneled into the current president's campaign fund.

The result has been catastrophic, particularly to impoverished communities. Activists say that more than 3,000 people have died because the hospitals could not afford to stock medicine or in some cases substituted actual medicine for placebo pills made from flour or common diuretics. Thousands took to the streets carrying torches symbolic of shedding the light of truth on the dark corruption of the government.

Demonstrations were held simultaneously in Tegucigalpa, San Pedro Sula, Choluteca, and Comayagua. The protests were bipartisan. Even members of the president's own National Party joined in. Though the president committed to returning the misappropriated funds, the protests have continued every Friday.

"For that reason we are walking the streets indignant," Medense said. "Because he can return the money, but he can't bring back the dead. And we are demanding that he leave office, and that the Commission against Impunity come and not only investigate him, but also the gang of delinquents that are running this country."

Maldonado said Hernandez' presidency has been corrupt, with allegations of nepotism as well as embezzlement.

"They are thieves completely. That's what they are. They want to lie to the people. They don't want anyone to realize that they're stealing so they make these secret laws. Why? So that no one questions them. Because if you ask questions they kill you. They send you to be killed," Maldonado said.

While his words may seem dramatic, dissent appears to be dangerous in Honduras. Four students were found fatally shot after participating in protests of education cuts, according to the BBC. UNICEF has demanded an investigation into these murders.

Yet so far the cries of the Honduran people have gone unanswered. In the face of demands for international intervention, the President Hernandez formed his own commission on corruption called the "Sistema Integral Hondureño para combatir la impunidad"—the Integral System of Honduras to Combat Impunity with the goal of having open dialogue.

As the subject of investigation it might seem inappropriate for Hernandez to be leading the effort to expose corruption, but no one else has proposed a solution.

Moreover, solutions are not forthcoming from the countries that capitalize on Honduras' many natural resources—a point Medense made by wearing little more than a loin cloth, a wig and shackles chained to his wrists.

"The shackles represent our in independence that was born in 1821 when the Spanish left us in 1821," he said. "In 2015 we have 195 years of supposed independence, but the truth is that we have never been independent because in 1862 foreign mining companies began entered Honduras to exploit our minerals."

"We liberated ourselves from the Spanish to become occupied by the American and other countries' companies here," said Medense.

For example, after 1998's devastating Hurricane Mitch, the Honduran government lowered regulatory standards in the mining industry, and now Canadian companies control the majority of mining rights in Honduras.

While happy to participate in the development of Honduras and to reap the benefits of the various natural resources, the government of Canada has also been notably silent on the issue of corruption.

What about the U.S.? When I asked, U.S. Embassy officials in Honduras and D.C. wouldn't tell me what role the U.S. has in supporting Honduran citizens during this latest political clash. I was incredulous. So, money from the U.S. can build a soccer field or fund all the community centers we want, but when people literally are dying because of government corruption suddenly the U.S. is adopting a hands-off approach?

"This land and those who have governed have entered into corruption to rob of us our resources which are the minerals, the waters … foreign companies have come to exploit us. In few words they have always kept us enslaved. And we want to free ourselves already," Medense told me.

But will freedom come? Even if the International Commission against Impunity decides to try President Hernandez, who will take over? And with all the foreign involvement in Honduras, whose hands are clean enough to take the lead on an international intervention? Clearly not ours.

Havana Meets Seattle: Artists Find Common Ground, Connection

Art and revolution are often said to go hand and hand, so it was fitting that Cuba serve as the destination for the inaugural voyage of Seattle's Common Ground Music Project.

Led by Seattle playwright and musician Shontina Vernon, the independently funded project took a delegation of 12 mostly black musicians, artists, and dancers from Seattle to Havana and Viñales to collaborate, connect, and perform with their Cuban counterparts.

"I wanted these artists," says Vernon, citing each one's relationship not simply to the arts, but also to social justice. "Common Ground Music Project for me was an idea that was about investigating the intersections of music and performance art with social justice work." Her intention was to use music to promote cross cultural collaboration.

The trip's goals included creating community between U.S. and Cuban artists and centralizing the narratives of artists from the global African diaspora. Vernon also hoped to strategize how to connect and sustain the movements of social justice and freedom in both places.

Vernon says she's been thinking about "what it is to have artists who are digging around through ideas around freedom and liberation ... why it would be critical to their creative process to have an experience of those very things."

Besides Vernon, the U.S. cohort consisted of Jade Solomon Curtis, Lara Davis, Ben Hunter, Naomi Ishisaka, Christina Orbe, Chris Patin, Gabriel Teodros, Dani Tirrel, Barry Jones aka D.J. Topspin, Melissa Dow, Matt Sherrill and Adiza Ameh. In 2011 Vernon had her own first taste of Cuba. "I had this experience of a kind of safety and a kind of freedom and also an awareness of my own privilege in a different way because of the politics on the island."

Leaving the States gave her a new perspective on being a black American. "I define freedom, I think, in terms of the safety one feels in terms of being able to be fully embodied as themselves," Vernon says. Initially it surprised her to realize just how unsafe she felt in the States. "You know because I didn't really register consciously in my every day going about," she says. "We're in such a survivalist mode that it doesn't occur to you until you go somewhere and the contrast makes it obvious."

The #blacklivesmatter movement began in the wake of the 2012 murder of Trayvon Martin and the 2013 acquittal of his killer, George Zimmerman. Since then the racial politics of safety have increasingly made their way into the media and, of course, daily conversations. But Vernon would like to see these conversations broaden from the U.S. to an international context.

"What's happening there [is] what's happening here. Black people in the UK, same thing. Black people in Paris, same thing. Black people in Berlin, same thing," says Vernon.

Cuba, the island nation just 90 miles south of Florida, has defied the U.S. government for years in choosing to remain socialist and independent. While not exempt from racism, it is a country with a complex and radical relationship to blackness, from helping to end apartheid in South Africa to creating a medical program to train black people from the U.S. to be doctors. Cuba has also served as a refuge for U.S. black radicals such as Assata Shakur, a former Black Panther Party member who has been an icon for many U.S. radicals since her controversial conviction for the death of a police officer in 1973.

"Really the truth is that all around the world for people of color, for black people the story is not vastly different," said Vernon. "So I'm like, if black people from everywhere don't start talking to each other about what it is that we're experiencing in our own countries, the pie of liberation will always be minus a slice. ... So that to me is solidaridad [solidarity] and the Common Music Project."

When dancer and choreographer Jade Solomon Curtis arrived, she found, "I wasn't black in Cuba, I was American."

This claiming of citizenship brought with it both the advantage of certain privileges, but also stigma. Curtis recounts that initially the Cuban artists seemed reluctant to share their experience of blackness, but as they spent more time together they grew more open about the challenges they faced.

For Curtis, having the revelation that "feelings of exhaustion that I may experience being in this skin is something that someone else experiences as well or has experienced" became a cross-cultural bridge and made her feel less alone.

"My work prior to the work that I'm doing now was always about making sure that people saw my beauty," explains Curtis. "Making sure that people saw that, hey, there's this black girl, but guess what? She can do all these styles of dance and it's not just African and hip hop, not to diminish those, because that's my ancestors, that movement."

Somehow over the course of the group's stay in Cuba, Curtis experienced the alchemy of travel magic that sparks transformation. "Right now I am more interested in exploring what's happening deep down in me. I'm interested in exploring the conversations I'm having with people and exploring, showing work or rather creating work that reflects the current state of my existence, and that is not always pretty."

Cuban hosting organizations included the Havana Centro Cultural and Ammonite Dance, a youth ensemble. Some of the Cuban artists that participated included writer Jesus Gonzales, hip hop artist Fina, and spoken word Elier "El Brujo" Alvarez.

One of her favorite moments took place in Viñales, a town of around 30,000 that is near a U.N.-designated heritage site and has become something of a tourism center, with Madelin Azcuy, known as Mamuchi. Curtis, Mamuchi, the director of Ammonite Dance, and Seattle dancer and choreographer Dani Tirrel collaborated in the co- creation of a dance, blending steps from both cultures. "It was just really wonderful to be a part of that space or that energy. And it didn't feel contrived, just very organic," said Curtis.

For musician Ben Hunter, who describes himself as a folklorist, the experience was tremendous in many ways. "I don't know, there is something about Havana," said Hunter describing streets filled with murals depicting Cuban pride and revolution. "There's something about the place that just spilled out art and music and culture in a certain way." He compared it to New Orleans in its expressiveness.

When he wasn't with the group, Hunter spent his time wandering the streets, soaking up the music and connecting with as many people as he could. On one of his adventures he stumbled across a building dedicated to folklore and teaching Cuban youth traditional music and dance.

"That was what really turned me on," he said. "Just knowing that over my shoulder at any point in time I could see some kind of example of how the arts was a living and breathing part of their culture on a day-to-day basis which is something I think is really, really different than America."

Hunter also described time in Cuba as being on a different meter. "The culture is so different in that there is a Cuban time," he said. "And not that it was like a laziness, because there certainly was not a laziness, but it was like a swag almost, it was like a stroll, like the streets had rhythm to them."

Hunter left longing to see music more incorporated into Seattle's way of being: "Music, dance, and art is something that you only get at a museum or a concerts, but it's something you could get off the street anywhere."

A venture he's involved with could do some of that, at least in one neighborhood. Hunter is a founding partner in the Hillman City Collaboratory, known in the South End as an "incubator for social change," which hosts a variety of community events as well as housing a workspace for local non-profits. This fall, Hunter and his business partners, Chef Tariq Abdullah and Rodney Harold, will be opening a new collective in Hillman City called the Black and Tan, which will provide a café and a venue for local performers.

About the Seattle group brought together for the trip, Hunter said, "It was an interesting collection," said Hunter with regard to the Seattle cohort. "I think we had a really creative group of people from such a variety of backgrounds. It was about really meeting each other and developing relationships."

Though rich, the experience was not without its challenges. "The politics are so tense between the U.S. and Cuba that when you say you are a group of artists interested in building solidarity with Cuba and put on a performance or two, travel throughout the country, these are all things that are kind of a touchy spot," said Adiza Ameh who served as a translator for the Seattle cohort. "And   there just needs to be an understanding of exactly what you mean by solidarity."

While the trip to Viñales provided the space for both U.S. and Cuban artists to perform for and with one another in front of an audience 400 to 500 people, Havana proved to be more of a logistical challenge. Ameh says that one of the primary point people responsible for coordinating rehearsal and performance venues in Havana "totally thought we were just some more U.S. based artists here to show and tell and do a whole little performance and then leave Cuba."

"But that's not at all what we were planning to do and she [Shontina Vernon] had made it specifically very clear what our intentions were," Ameh says. "But because of this tense political situation and the history the U.S. has with Cuba ... for good reason I think, they are very skeptical of us."

Skepticism gave way to understanding, though not in time for there to be a show in Havana. Having studied abroad in Cuba in 2014, Ameh anticipated that this might be a challenge, but she took the long view of things.

"I don't think this is a one-time thing," she says. "I think this should be a two-year project where we have multiple trips to Cuba back and forth and Cubans, hopefully if there is a way to make it happen, can come back and forth, so it's not just us going there."

Vernon agrees that this trip was just the beginning. "I looked over and everybody was on stage together at the end," she says, "and it was a real moment of solidarity between North American artists and Cuban artists in a culminating events."

Global Travel Shapes Diversity in Higher Ed

"Blackness is more than melanin and skin, it's a state of mind," announced Abdul Marin Nunez at the start of his lecture on the state of black Belize.

It was the second day of the fourth annual international trip hosted by the National Association for Diversity Officers in Higher Education. This year's trip included 32 people—predominantly black and brown US born folks—who either work in building the diversity of colleges and universities or were, like myself, family members.

We were gathered in the small blue walled multipurpose room of the Muslim Center. Nunez, a community organizer, a youth worker and the center's imam, was a tall dark-skinned man dressed in blue and white African garb with a wide smile and a booming voice.

He introduced himself as a Muslim, but also as a Garifuna—the indigenous and mixed people of Belize—and asked us to join him in a call and response starting with the words:

"I love my beautiful black self!"

The affirmations he led us in felt like a call to something deeply important, particularly for a group of people whose careers have led them to shape the policies and practices of inclusion at higher education institutions around the country.

I looked about the room wondering how those who didn't identify as black felt about saying those words. Did they resonate inside them in the way they did for me?

The work of diversity officers is a part of the ongoing conversation the United States has been having about the validity and lovability and worthiness of blackness. Do we matter? Are our lives valuable in a way more profound than the commodification of our skills, labor and talents? Are we seen, heard and loved?

Many diversity jobs are predicated on numbers and the illusion of integration responding to the question: "Are there enough people of color at a given institution?"

Equally important, but not always asked, are the questions: "How are we treated? How are we protected from the psychological violence that can be perpetrated by the systems of higher education not designed for or by people of color—and especially black people?"

So it was no accident or coincidence that our first conversation on this trip would center love and blackness.

Dr. Archie Ervin, vice president and chief diversity officer of Georgia Tech, is the president of the National Association for Diversity Officers in Higher Education (NADOHE). He was instrumental, along with Dr. Benjamin D. Reese, Jr., in organizing the organization's first international trip, which was to Cuba.

He said that diversity officers needed to understand the global context of the origins of students of color in the United States.

"In the U.S. we were, at one time, shortsighted enough to think that it was about being African American or just black people," Dr. Ervin said. "But when we fully begin to understand that this was not just black people but all these other marginalizations that the Western culture had defined such as genderized roles for women and or marginalizations of those outside that paradigm, that all of these were important dimensions of inclusion that we weren't really getting or probably didn't really understand. And that we had little understanding of the complexities of international communities in the US higher education setting and the impact that that has."

The group decided first to explore the African Diaspora, said Dr. Reese, vice president for institutional equity at Duke University.

"The majority of the board feels or felt that that's the starting place when talking about difference," he said. The group has made four trips so far to Cuba, Brazil, Ghana and Belize.

Dr. Reese was trained as a psychologist and has been working on issues of race for almost 50 years.

The group, which started about 12 years ago, now has more than 800 members, a publication called Journal of Diversity in Higher Ed, a conference and formal training. A three-day institute for early career diversity officers is also in the works.

"So the organization has just grown and when I look back on my career it is one thing I'm very proud of," said Dr. Reese.

He plans to leave Duke in May after 22 years, but he's not retiring.

"In mid-July I have a fellowship in Canterbury, New Zealand talking about race and then I go right to the University of Adelaide in Australia for three weeks. Race and unconscious bias is my specialty and I'm going to work with aboriginal people for a couple of months," Dr. Reese said. "Then I'm at the University of Xando in China pushing back on some of the stereotypes about black folks… So I'm going to lecture on the history of race in America, black leadership in STEM and black leadership in business, trying to give students something other than what they see on TV."

The works he plans in China is important. Despite the increasing challenges presented by this administration's immigration policies, there is still a robust community of international students enrolled.

But, despite their numbers, Dr. Ervin said international students' often are not included in discussions of diversity.

"Because if you go to any institution of significant size today you have international presence there that we often find to be very, very segregated communities because they don't feel a part of the structure," he said. "They come there to study and get degrees and they have enclaves. They learn so little and we have to understand that that experience is not the healthiest experience for even them."

Dr. Ervin believes schools need to create inclusive spaces for all students in order to enhance everyone's ability to learn from one another.

"So the institution isn't really benefiting from their presence. You know we don't learn from that. So we're saying to understand all of that there are some global connections that are really important to understand."

Dr Reese said that U.S. programs also do a disservice to international students by not engaging with the historical context of race in the United States.

"So it's going to take some real creative thinking to sort of get us out of our boxes," he said.

The Belize trip was organized by Dr. Siri Briggs Brown, the vice chancellor of community affairs for the Peralta Community College District in Oakland. She owns Global Academics, a tour company that focuses on Africa and the Diaspora. "I really like to think it adds to their global understanding of humanity, and in this case the humanity of the African world," Dr. Briggs Brown said. "It's been helpful to them [NADOHE] in helping them immerse themselves in global diversity and what that means for their work as diversity officers back here, back in the U.S. on their home campuses with so many migrating students and all of that."

She said the officers have a better understanding of the racial politics and identity politics of the countries they visit.

This trip included lectures on black Belize and on the Guatemala- Belize conflict. We also took a Garifuna dance and drumming workshop. An hour outside of Belize City, the group chartered a boat on the New River—or the Tzulzilacob (river of foreign faces) as the Mayan named it for the Europeans they encountered there. The boat took us to Lamanai Mayan Temple ruins where we hike to the top of the Jaguar temple, saw howler monkeys and all manner of exotic birds.

We also met locals who were making an impact on Belize. Cynthia Ellis started a collective for Garifuna women to become economically empowered. Pen Cayetano is an artist and musician who was part of the band who started the genre of music known as Punta Rock. He and his wife, a German woman who is also an artist, hosted us for a traditional Belizean lunch of fish in coconut soup with pounded cassava. They walked us around the yard pointing out all of the plants and trees growing there.

We also met Cannon Jerris Valentine, an Episcopal priest and Garifuna who founded a school for the preservation of Garifuna language and culture. We hiked to the small waterfall in the Bocawina National Park, saw a crocodile way too close for my comfort, and all the while got to really know one another by sharing meals and drinks and long bus rides.

And of course we met Abdul Marin Nunez, the imam of the Muslim Center.

"The country is made of migrants," said Nunez. "We have mestizos who are creole as well, the mixture of Mayan and Aztec. We have the creoles who are a mixture of blacks and other Europeans. We have the Garinagu who are a mixture of Africans and Arawaks. We also have Americans, expatriates, Mennonites. We have all kinds of people, but what the British did strategically was to put everyone in their place."

Nunez also told the story of the Garinagu, or Garifuna. Garifuna is technically the singular tense of Garinagu, I heard it used interchangeably. Throughout the trip, we heard different versions of this story but what everyone seems to agree on is a ship full of Africans heading into slavery crashed on the coast of St. Vincent.

The survivors landed and intermarried with the Arawak people and successfully maintained their freedom, even fighting off a British invasion until they were re-kidnapped in the early 1800s. They were taken to Honduras and Belize as indentured servants or slaves— depending on who is telling the story.

"This is uniquely positioned area of the Caribbean where it really wasn't a destination for slave trade per se, but it became a stop off point for those who were trading in slaves," Dr. Ervin said. "There was a contemporary influx of people who were enslaved brought here for the express purpose of timber harvesting which was unique."

While further north, slavery was generational, in Belize, the Garinagu worked for a certain period of time and then went back to being free, become a part of the local community, Dr. Ervin said.

In the 1950s, according to Nunez, Belize was 90 percent black and Garifuna, but now it is closer to 41.6 percent. There has been an influx of Chinese immigrants who have cornered the market on grocery stores and Guatemalans who have taken over the construction industry.

Nunez says that the running joke is that the industry black folk dominates is crime. According to Nunez some of the original members of the Bloods and Crips were Belizean and living in Los Angeles. After being deported, they started up new chapters of the gang and have been contributing to the rise in violent crime ever since.

Nunez works with teen offenders to prevent recidivism, but cites lack of economic opportunity as being the top motivator for crime.

During his short lecture I learned a lot, my mind couldn't help but fixate on the ways our histories and present circumstances are inextricably linked.

"One of the things that we understand about this work of diversity, this work of inclusion and equity, the tripod of our existence is diversity, equity, and inclusion," said Dr. Ervin. "You can have it in any sort of formulation of that which you want, but your work has those three tiers and that understanding the complexity of diversity today requires you to understand the global connections that have led us to this place in time."

Kathleen Russell has been on two trips, Belize and Ghana. She has gone with her mother, Dr. Paulette Granberry Russell, who is the senior advisor to the president for diversity and director of the office for inclusion for Michigan State University. "Our ancestors came through Ghana, West Africa so it was really eye opening to be sort of in the space where we could recall our past family," Russell said.

Russell asked her mother to tell a family story about a man named Zebica who was from West Africa.

"Somewhere in the South or actually before he was brought over... how does that story go, Mom?"

Dr. Granberry Russell filled in the details of the story: "Zebica was the one brought from Ghana. Eventually he tried to fly back to his 'goodie country.' He made wings, put them on a saddle and jumped from a hill to try to fly back to what he called his goodie country, and broke most of the bones in his body. So he was no longer able to work in the fields so his responsibility was to watch over the kids in the field."

Zebica was murdered for disrupting the brutal beating of his grandson. The legend goes he took a hoe and killed the overseer and then he was killed by the plantation owners.

Dr. Granberry Russell talks about learning these stories from her grandmother and then confirming the details through various ancestry websites and property records.

"I had always said I was going to find my way to Ghana," Dr. Granberry Russell said.

While she had been to Tanzania and Senegal, her first trip to Zebica's homeland was with NADOHE.

"Last year when they said the trip was to Ghana I said I had to go," she said. "And it was, it was a moment when as soon as I landed it felt like home and I know it has a lot to do with the story. And then when I did our DNA, almost 20 percent is from Mali, Togo, and Benin, so it's all west African. So obviously somewhere within Africa is Zebica's story and that's our story."

Breaking Up with America: Black Expats Talk About Life in Costa Rica

I constantly want to break up with America. It's like he's that hot guy who every time he opens his mouth becomes dramatically less attractive and overtime you realize that not only do you have different core values, but that you just actively don't like, respect, or want to be in a relationship with this person, but you just can't seem to leave. And it turns out I am not alone in this feeling.

"To save us all I decided to leave." explained Davia Antonia about how she's spent the last 7 years living in Costa Rica where she has a thriving career as a relocation specialist particularly focused on supporting Black expats to find their freedom.

"We fled, not even in the sense of a regular refugee, but we fled because I knew if I kept up that pace of life and that level of stress and anxiety in the workplace, I knew I would either snap or I would snap on someone," said Davia.

Before taking the leap, Davia Antonia and her two children lived in Los Angeles where she worked for Advanced Data Processing which provides software sales and service used to design HR infrastructure for fortune 500 companies. But Davia's inability to advance her career and the microaggressions she experienced daily led to rheumatoid arthritis, chronic stress and anxiety.

It was her sister's birthday and they booked a trip to Costa Rica. "I was so busy with work, this is also very sad, because I was so busy I couldn't even plan a trip. I couldn't even review the hotel…I was absolutely unplugged," recounted Davia. She asked her sister to take care of the arrangements, but when she finally reviewed it, she hated the proposed trip to Tamarindo, so on a whim they went to Puerto Viejo instead.

"I fell in love, but it's two parts. There is an energy here and it's very magical and it's very powerful. This place draws whatever you want in your life good or bad and the first time I came here I actually felt that feeling, but I couldn't explain it, I didn't know what it was," said Davia. "It was just I felt powerful to manifest my own destiny or to carve my own path, but it was unidentifiable. It was just a knowing that I could, if I were to be here. That was the second part of it. Cost of living and that it is a very spiritual and magical place."

In August of 2022, my mom compiled a list of her top 5 countries to explore, not simply to vacation, but as a part of a longer conversation we've been having about living abroad. Throughout our lives we have both spent extensive time traveling or living in other countries, but our family and careers have kept us primarily based in the US. After she retired, my mom began to research more thoroughly which countries would be affordable, accessible, and feel comfortable and safe for Black Americans.

She came across Davia's website www.lifeaholiccostarica.com and booked a 30 minute consultation. Echoing Davia's story, I was too busy to plan my own vacation, so my mom booked us on a relocation tour for our birthdays in 2022. After two years of not being able to travel internationally because of the pandemic, I would have gone anywhere. We flew into San Jose then took a very long car ride to Puerto Viejo.

Puerto Viejo is a sleepy beach town set on the Caribbean Sea about 15 minutes away from the border to Panama. The landscape is dense with lush green jungles, fruit trees, and medicinal plants. There were bird of paradise plants growing taller than me and big leafy canopies and trees teaming with colorful birds and cutter ants. The weather was humid and tropical with a lot of sun then quick afternoon storms that rained warm showers. The markets were filled with fresh mangoes and pineapples. Lychee was in season and there were tons of makeshift roadside stands. The seafood specials at every restaurant were based on the catch of the day.

I didn't know much about Costa Rica, other than that it's known for ecotourism. I had bookmarked it in my head as a place where white people went to zipline and hike. I was pleasantly surprised to end up in a place that was mostly Brown and Black with a thriving pan African Diaspora in addition to a Black expat community. August in Costa Rica is Afro Descendent celebration month and it definitely felt like a party. While checking out the strip of shops in downtown Puerto Viejo, we came across an old pan African meeting house established by none other than Marcus Garvey, the Jamaican born, London educated revolutionary and businessman who started a Back to Africa movement in the 1920s. That's a reductive description so If you're not up on Garveyism and the Universal Negro Improvement Association and African Communities League you should google it. His story is complicated and at times problematic, but what felt resonant was the throughline of Black liberation and creating economic independence to escape white supremacy.

I had never been on a relocation tour before. It met my vacation needs in that there was a mix of structured and unstructured time, an opportunity to visit a chocolate farm, surf at the beach and hike to a waterfall, but we also visited a local appliance store and discussed the bureaucracy of what would be needed to apply for citizenship and buy property. We even looked at real estate and learned that for about $100,000 we could buy ¼ acre and build a two story house. Coming from Seattle where 800 sq ft shoe boxes could sell for $600,000 this blew my mind. Davia introduced us to her family, friends, and clients at a full moon party on Cocles beach.

It was there I met Levi Peterson, a Black expat residing in Puerto Viejo with his husband. "Here's the reason why I wanted to move here," he said. "Surprise. I didn't feel safe anymore. And being in an interracial relationship and living in Connecticut, seeing everything happening in the news, getting pulled over every time I drove, I stopped driving."

After 8 years of traveling back and forth and staying in a time share Levi decided the pandemic was the perfect time to apply for residency and make the move.

"Right before I came the doctors told me I had high blood pressure at 47 years old. That couldn't be my life," said Levi. "So now I don't have high blood pressure anymore because I've been checked since I've been here. There's a sense of being able to breathe and being around other people of color, which is huge for me because it was always [living in] homogenous neighborhoods which kind of sucks. And what's not to love about the beach and fresh fruit? Fresh food, never processed."

In the States Levi worked as a hairstylist and has been able to do the same in Costa Rica. When asked if he felt welcome here, he responded enthusiastically: "Yes, totally welcome. More so that anywhere I've ever lived."

But even more than welcome, Levi said he felt safe.

I tried to think back to the last time I felt either of those things. November 8, 2016, was definitely a before and after moment for our country. I woke up in my Seattle liberal bubble expecting to stand in the shattered glass ceiling of our first female president only to step into the nightmare of finding out we elected a man who is a walking toxic superlative; the most capitalist, most racist, most misogynistic, most xenophobic, most entitled, most ignorant person to ever have bought the title. Our 45 president reminds me of that scene in Ghost Busters with the Stay-Puft Marshmallow man where something innocuous from childhood becomes a huge nuisance destroying everything in its wake.

Throughout the election season my mom and I talked about our contingency plans. We decided Vancouver was like the Seattle of Canada and we could acclimate well to a universal health plan with less risk of gun violence. But we were joking. Sure, we weren't devout Hillary acolytes by any means, but looking at what my mom referred to as the "bag of mixed nuts" present in our candidate pool, like 94% of all Black women, we held our nose and voted for sanity and assumed that everyone else would too. Wow we were wrong. And things got very surreal very quickly. Just a few days after the election a white man at a fruit stand called me the N word.

He said it first as a whisper, then noticing I hadn't heard him kept increasing his volume until he got my attention. He said it like it was my name. And I looked at the 16 year old Mexican cashier behind the counter to confirm. "Is this really happening? Did he just…"

"Just ignore it," the kid said as the man slithered back to his pick-up. He said it because he could. The white hoods were off but the Klan was never more visible and there was no ignoring it. Later that week a kid came to my office crying because someone at her school had pulled her hijab. My boss and I put together an emergency self-defense workshop with Haleema Bharoocha, who flew in from the Bay area to teach our Muslim youth what to do when that happens. Even with short notice 45 girls showed up and then we hosted a subsequent 6 week series called Y-WE Fight Back because we were scared and needed to punch something.

2016 was also the year when after so much police brutality, the Bahamas issued a travel warning for Black men wishing to travel to the US imploring them to avoid demonstrations and to comply with police and to use the consulate as a negotiator in case of any challenges. But this was the land of milk and honey where refugees from other countries sought asylum. Or at least that's how we thought about it before we saw the footage from the cages where undocumented children were living after being separated from their parents. According to CNN Uruguay, Venezuela, Canada, Ireland, and New Zealand added travel warnings for their citizens traveling to the US because of our prolific gun violence and the potential of domestic terrorism. And where is the lie?

Every time I turned on the news it felt like an assault. Our voting rights were under attack, then Ruth Bader Ginsberg died and we knew it would be 5 minutes before Roe vs.Wade would be overturned. It's like somewhere someone had written down a check list with the major victories of the civil rights movement and was moment by moment doing their best to undo everything. Where do you go when the promised land doesn't live up to its promise?

Just as I was formulating my answer to that question we were hit with a global pandemic. Three days before I was supposed to get on a plane to fly to New Zealand for the Radical Self Love Life Lift Retreat with Sonya Renee Taylor and a group of Black women. My parents and besties were begging me not to get go, afraid I would get stuck in New Zealand, which in retrospect would have been the best place to be stranded. I was at the end of my domestic cycle. If I don't leave the US at least once every two years I feel like the air is going to run out and I will suffocate.

When writer James Baldwin moved to Paris he was quoted as saying "I didn't know what was going to happen to me in France, but I knew what was going to happen to me in New York." For many Black American icons— Audre Lorde, Arthur Ash, Maya Angelou, Fredrick Douglass, to name a few, living abroad has been a rite of passage. Ironically France was one of my least favorite adventures. I still hold a grudge against Paris because when I was 16 and my mom and I were flying back from Senegal to the states we stopped there for a weekend layover and were detained (as were the only other Black people on the plane) for 4 hours by a customs agent who wouldn't believe my passport was real. She berated me bilingually, alternating between French and English and referring to my picture as "that fat girl". That was my first international trip and even that awful experience couldn't diminish the beauty and freedom I experienced in Senegal. There aren't any guarantees in life or in travel. But sometimes it hurts too much to stay.

In the end the retreat and my flight were canceled and instead of 10 days of freedom, I spent the next month working my ass off to create a framework where my job could exist virtually as daily my world shrank from a robust social calendar to going to the grocery store and walking a few times a week with a friend in the park. When our governor closed the public parks, I realized there was nothing left for me here, so I did the unthinkable. I couldn't get on a plane internationally, but I wrapped myself in masks and latex gloves and flew to Arizona to quarantine with my mom. I'd never seen SEATAC airport so empty, and I had a whole row to myself because there were barely 20 people on the entire plane.

For Melinda Rhoden aka Coach Mel, a yoga instructor from Los Angeles, her before and after moment was the murder of George Floyd.

"I was living in Arizona when the pandemic hit and something just kind of snapped at me," she said. "It was shortly after that when George Floyd got murdered and I said to myself I can no longer be here, I've got to get out of this country."

Coach Mel was attending a healing arts school in Arizona. "I started my business a couple of years before that, and I made the shift to a more spiritual modality type coaching and when George Floyd hit, I was still on campus and just the response I got from a lot of the spiritual bypassing that happened on campus I was just like yeah I can't be here anymore," she explained.

She moved to Baltimore. Her hope was to be in community with more people of color, but she quickly realized what she really needed in order to find a deeper level of healing was to leave the US completely.

"The amount of people that are Black that are leaving the States... I've seen it grow just in the year and a half since I've been here. People are coming by the hundreds or dozens or whatever you want to call it because everyone is trying to get out and for whatever reason Costa Rica seems to be like one of those places, I think Mexico is another one, I think because it's still so close to the US you can just hop on a plane and be there at the end of the day, not like if you go further if you go like to Africa or somewhere in Asia," she said.

Coach Mel put her whole life into two suitcases and one backpack and got rid of everything that was tying her down and bought a one way ticket to Costa Rica. "I had absolutely no plan. None whatsoever. I just kind of showed up and was like okay I will find where I'm supposed to go."

She began her journey in San Jose where she still lives much of the time, but after discovering Puerto Viejo she found herself at home in the community. "It's been just great, the sense of relief and less stress, freedom, connection and community that I have here is like nothing I ever had in the US. Like I can't describe it. It's like I didn't even know it was missing, but now that I have it this is what I'm gonna crave all the time. It's what keeps me here."

When asked if she feels safe Coach Mel did not hesitate. "I do feel safe here. I can walk down the street and see a cop and don't get scared," she said. But more than physical safety she talked about experiencing a different level of emotional safety. Coach Mel has been able to recover from the some of the exhaustion of being Black in white spaces. "I can be myself in my community and not have people ask me dumb questions like oh how do you do your hair, can I touch it? Do you put suntan lotion on?"

The 10 days we spent in Puerto Viejo were a balm to my spirit. I slept better. I moved slower, drank more water, and felt an ease in my body. Maybe it was the yoga or the beach, the endless fresh fruit smoothies or just being on vacation. It was easy to see the appeal and hard to look at my life in Seattle without seeing the resonance in the before stories of the folks I spoke with. I have a high stress job, one that I love, but that frequently depletes me both in terms of hours and in terms of the secondary trauma from holding the stories of the youth I serve. My whole body does tense up when I glance in the rearview mirror and see the police behind me. Despite being a freelance journalist, I have to limit my news intake to keep from plummeting into rage and depression. Is this it? Am I really living my best life? Or am I settling for non-profit martyrdom?

Davia jokingly referred to herself as the Harriet Tubman of Costa Rica and implored me to get free. But the longer I stayed there the more I understood she wasn't joking at all and it's been years since I've felt free. I tried to imagine what my life would be like if I took the leap. Where would I live? What would I do for work? Would the people we met at the beach party be my real friends and not just vacation friends? It takes courage to start all over again rebuilding your social and professional network, but also having to learn a new pace and way of living. I've done it several times before but in my 20s when so many others were on the same journey. What would it be like starting over at age 43?

When I asked my mom if she wanted to move, she laughed and said this was more of a place for young people. She needed more infrastructure than Puerto Viejo could provide like hospitals closer than 30 minutes and paved roads. And that was my reality check. Though I'm sure there are some folks living in Costa Rica with wheelchairs I didn't see any and most of the place we visited including the hotel we stayed in were completely inaccessible. Could I live a sweet and peaceful life in Puerto Viejo knowing my dad could never visit me? No.

Yes, I still want to break up with America, but the ties that bind me are not easily cut. My parents still live independent lives, but as they get older I am more frequently called upon to care for them. Also, after having invested so much time in my career it feels terrifying to think about starting over in another country and building my life up from scratch. For now I'll stick to small doses of "pura vida" through the occasional vacation. Panama and Portugal are the next countries on my mom's relocation exploration list and I look forward to seeing what else is out there.

The
People

31 Days of Revolutionary Women, #19 Stanlie James

Women's History Month is not only an opportunity to remember the past, but a time to think critically on how history is created. Who tells the story has a huge impact on how the story is told. And historically, history has not always been herstory. This is especially true when it comes to lives of black women. It is also an opportunity to honor those who inspire us.

The woman I choose to honor is Dr. Stanlie James. Dr. James was born and raised in Des Moines, Iowa and was one of twelve students to integrate her high school. She went on to attend Spelman College. While pursuing her BA in Sociology and History, her calling to teach was awakened.

First she found herself interested in African American history, then African history. Through her studies she discovered a lack of information about the experiences of women in history. Particularly lacking were narratives portraying the contributions of black women to history.

Dr. James completed her MA in British Colonial West African History at the School of Oriental and African Studies at the University of London, then returned to the States to complete a second MA and PhD at the University of Denver in comparative politics and human rights.

She retired from Arizona State University as the Vice Provost of Diversity and Inclusion and is a professor emeritus of the School of Social Transformation that she helped to build. Her most recent book is *Practical Audacity: Black Women and International Human Rights* (University of Wisconsin Press (2021). She co-edited three anthologies including *Still Brave: The Evolution of Black Women's Studies* with Frances Foster and Beverly Guy Sheftall; *Genital Cutting and Transnational Sisterhood: Disputing U.S. Polemics* with Claire Robertson; and with Abena Busia, *Theorizing Black Feminisms: The Visionary Pragmatism of Black Women*. *Still Brave* is the much anticipated sequel to *All the Women Are White, All the Blacks Are Men, But Some of Us Are Brave: Black Women's Studies*. Originally published in 1982, the first "Brave" is known as the first comprehensive collection of black feminist scholarship.

In creating the sequel, Dr. James and her colleagues had the daunting task of canonizing our history and setting the tone for how our stories will be conceptualized in the years to come.

If black women do amazing things, but no one is there to remember them, how can we help the next generation of visionary pragmatists to understand their powerful legacy of forging our own path? What is unique to her scholarship is its interdisciplinary nature. Dr. James links politics, sociology, history, international studies, and human rights, putting it together to understand the work that black women have done. Her newest work, *Practical Audacity: Black Women and International Human Rights* (University of Wisconsin Press, 2021) chronicles the contributions of black women who, finding civil rights to be inadequate means of improving the lives of people, have turned to International Women's Human Rights.

When I was asked to choose a woman to honor for women's history month, so many sheros jumped to my mind from Ida B. Wells and Harriet Tubman, to Mary Elizabeth Bowser, Anna Julia Cooper, Ella Baker, and Mae Jemison. But the person who introduced me to my sheroes was Dr. James, who, in addition to being an incredible teacher, scholar, writer, and all around black feminist badass, also happens to be my mom.

She has done for me what she has done for thousands of others: given me a sound foundation of empowering role models who have helped me to know myself and the legacy of my foremothers.

Howie Echo-Hawk Confronts Native Genocide Through Comedy

When Howie Echo-Hawk takes the stage and announces that he is going to do some "genocide comedy," I am so deeply uncomfortable. It's like glancing in your rearview mirror and seeing a Hummer about to hit your car, knowing there's no space in front of you to move out of the way.

I brace for impact, afraid to laugh, because genocide is not funny and Seattle woke people etiquette is sending me conflicting messages.

There is a Native person on the stage. I must witness him. But at the same time to witness him is to acknowledge all of the ghosts standing beside him.

When he talks about the population of the Pawnee diminishing from 10,000 to 600 and compares white people to the Airbnb guests from hell— the ones that come, don't pay and never leave—it's funny and it isn't funny. And I laugh anyway.

Echo-Hawk performed in the fifth run, and final installment of Dear White People, the POC variety show produced by Boom Boom L'Roux.

Echo-Hawk pulls no punches. Every word out of his mouth illuminates an uncomfortable truth.

I laugh from shock. I laugh to keep from crying because as fucked up as black and white relations are, we are at least still here to fight about it. When he cracks another joke about how there are so few Native People that most people look at him and think he's Mexican, how even racists don't slur him correctly, I think about what it must feel like to be invisible in your own skin.

What's it like to feel that way and then say it out loud on a microphone in front of an audience? Some in the audience laugh unabashedly, some squirm in their seats with guilt or grief, and react with a mix of both? I decided to ask him.

"It's very freeing," Echo-Hawk told me. "This is the one time I can go up there and say exactly what I think in the way that I want to do it and I don't even care if I get laughs honestly."

Howie Echo-Hawk, 27, grew up in a tiny white town in Alaska called Delta Junction. Echo-Hawk's last name aptly translates in Pawnee to "The Hawk whose deeds echo silently behind him."

His mother is white, of Irish descent, his father is Pawnee and he grew up in an Athabaskan Native community that adopted them.

"Colonialism says Native identity is determined by blood quantum, but who we are is determined by so much more than that, cultural ties and stuff like that, it's always about culture, you know race doesn't exist. We were adopted and taken in so that's part of who we are."

Echo-Hawk works a consultant for a communications company and is in the American Indian Studies program at the University of Washington. His hope is to get his doctorate and contribute to the work of language revitalization and restructuring educational systems for Native people.

His foray into comedy began about a year ago at an open mic called QTPOC is Not a Rapper. The show is a "curated" ensemble of queer, trans and POC comics that takes place monthly at Scratch Deli.

"I think that for me I kind of always wanted to do comedy," he said. After leaving Alaska and seeing different parts of the world, Echo-Hawk described travel as the catalyst for gaining a new understanding of race and systemic oppression. He also became frustrated at how deeply ignorant the average "American" is about Native culture. He began doing presentations in college to address these issues.

"And I also knew that for Native People and for, I think, all oppressed people in general, a lot of our humor and art comes from some of the worst things that could possibly happen to people."

And what could be worse than genocide?

"I could just do a 5-minute set on 'Flashdance' or the different things like, 'Hey this thing is different than that thing.' That's fine, but that's not real. We're just pretending," said Echo-Hawk. "As a cynic that's really beautiful to just be able to go up there and tell it how it is, like that whole always as we're walking through the world there's the whole double consciousness thing that W.E.B. Du Bois said or like Frantz Fanon called it the colonial mentality, whatever you wanna call it, where we just accept having to have those dual identities and all these entanglements where we're questioning the way we do things in a certain space versus another space. Almost never do we just get to be us."

Echo-Hawk attended an earlier run of Dear White People and decided he had to get involved. "It's watching these people be 100 percent unapologetic and confronting with whatever it is they had to say to whiteness at the time. Funny, sad, beautiful, terrifying, whatever it is. And I just wanted to be a part of that."

And it was better than he imagined. "It's not just doing the act that's great but seeing all these other POC artists doing their act. And then we're backstage and the conversation ranges from random nonsense to talking about what it's like to be tokenized. And that's the thing I've heard so many say back there is that all the people involved have been tokenized other places. Now they're here and we all have a common thread and its really freeing and comfortable and nice and I'm bummed that it's over. I want that to be always."

Though the cast of Dear White People was POC, the audience was mixed. Echo-Hawk approached performing his material in front of white audiences with a sense of amused resignation. He confessed that he once laughed after making someone in the audience cry.

"The reactions you get from predominantly white audiences in Seattle is kind of everything you've come to expect. You get some people who are like, 'Oh should I laugh?' And some people who are laughing and some people who are laughing too hard. Some people who want to come up to me afterwards and say oh that was super funny and some people who come up and say, 'Oh thank you!' And I'm like don't touch me."

The touching happens most when Echo-Hawk wears his Native jewelry. Like most of his comedy, his joke about being mistaken for Mexican is rooted in his everyday experience. People routinely ask him where he is from or attempt to speak to him in Spanish. When he wears his Native jewelry the response is totally different.

"They want to touch you because they're like, 'Oh my God here's this thing that ... looks he's like walking and going onto a bus, he's not like a homeless person and he's not like dead,' you know all these crazy thoughts they have wrapped up in their head about what it is to be a Native person," said Echo-Hawk. "So I've had people come up and just grab my jewelry and like touch me and it's been weird."

He has had to get quick at slapping hands away. "That's a whole larger thing about Native people, I think Native people and Black people specifically that America feels like it has ownership over us and they don't even question it. Over our space and our bodies."

One thing Echo-Hawk enjoys about comedy is the distance. "There is like five to ten feet between me and the audience both physically and metaphorically where I'm just confronting them and I'm not really anticipating anything from them. I'm just there to do my thing and unburden my soul from the day."

Honesty is his resistance.

"It's absolutely an act of resistance because they tell us that we shouldn't talk about it," Echo-Hawk said. "There's always going to be oppression unfortunately and freedom does not have an end point, which is something a really great professor of mine likes to say, but it's about the struggle, right? And part of the struggle is that people will never be able to get any better if we don't confront it."

Michelle Obama Ain't the Only Fantastic Woman of Color

Alice Metropolis is throwing a conniption fit.

A disembodied yell of "No! No! No!" rings out from the gallery. I enter timidly, thinking I might be interrupting writer and artist Anastacia Reneé Tolbert in the middle of performing her one woman play 9 Ounces. But there is no one there.

Still, Tolbert's presence or rather her character, Alice Metropolis, dominates the one-room gallery known as The Alice through three TV screens and a collection of artifacts from the set of the show. On one screen, Alice buttons and unbuttons a crisp white shirt her nervous face in contrast with her playful, sing-songy voice. "Cancer are you still there?" she asks, performing a breast check. On another screen Alice paces and smokes. On the third, her rage and grief are nearly unbearable as she screams "No" again and again, before the video goes mute.

The Alice Gallery is nestled in a hipster nook of Georgetown. Four artists—Julie Alexander, Julia Freeman, Molly Mac and S. Surface—take turns curating the space. The Alice is avant-garde and immersive, an incubator for high concept art. "I am consistently interested in nonlinear storytelling and in inquiry," says Molly Mac, the artist who invited Tolbert to bring Alice to The Alice.

As I entered the stark space, all white walls and black wood floors, an altar draped in a wrinkled white cloth drew my attention. Table and floor were covered with a variety of artifacts, some ceremonial, some more mundane. A laundry basket, cowry shells, a poem inked in red, a letter to Luna (one of the three characters in the play), a pack of American spirits, half a bottle of Jack Daniels, a gold platter heavy laden with candles, a purple yoga mat, a crystal teacup and a peacock feather. Beside the altar are a pile of books, most of which also live on my shelves at home. There's poetry and essays written by iconic black feminists like Angela Davis and Andre Lorde.

Tolbert herself hadn't arrived yet, so I took in the exhibit alone. There was an honesty to it, and an uncomfortable familiarity. I felt as though I had stumbled into someone's bedroom that hadn't been tidied up for company. The videos loop like an audio-visual collage of overlapping emotions sometimes speaking over one another. "I feel unsafe," Alice told us. "It can happen to anybody." Whether she means cancer or the cancer of the violence plaguing our community is up for interpretation, but the feeling she named is palpable.

Since the elections, there has been an uptick in hate crimes in my community. I was called a nigger while grocery shopping. One of my colleagues was attacked with pepper spray. Another friend almost got in a fistfight trying to protect a woman in a hijab who was being assaulted in broad daylight downtown. Between the Black Lives Matter Movement and the advent of cell phone cameras and social media live streaming police brutality, it's been hard not to be on edge. Hearing Alice screaming "No" echoes the unvoiced dissent in my head. How many days do I wake up angry? How many nights do I run up my water bill trying to wash away the feelings of grief, powerlessness and invisibility? This is a story that goes untold, an experience of blackness that doesn't get much attention.

I was lost in my thoughts when Tolbert arrived. We left the gallery to sit in the hall beneath a rare patch of sunshine spilling through the skylight.

"I chose this space because I feel like Molly and the other gallery owners understand pushing boundaries in terms of art," explained Tolbert. "I always thought it was the perfect space for Alice because I know that it is not typical kind, it's not a usual kind of art, its not a typical kind of performance. And I know this space lends itself to experimental things."

Tolbert, who hails from Kansas City, is a font of creativity. She recently completed the year as Writer in Residence for the Richard Hugo House and has received accolades and fellowships for her writing from Cave Canem, Hedgebrook, VONA, Jack Straw, Ragdale and Artist Trust. We first met over the summer when she worked as a teaching artist for Y-WE Write, a writing and leadership camp set at the Whidbey Institute and run by Young Women Empowered. Her body of work includes poetry, fiction and performance art.

Despite being a prolific writer, Tolbert has often felt overlooked.

"There seems to be seven women of color in Seattle who get notoriety and attention and I am not one of them," she said. Tolbert convened her own show, *Leave it at the Beep*, to highlight the talent and voices of other women of color in Seattle she felt have been overlooked. She has hosted four shows so far featuring eight different women each show.

Her play, *9 Ounces*, was first shown at the Project Room in 2015. "I was the Project Room's first writer in residence and they took a risk on me," said Tolbert. "They had no idea, Jess [Van Nostrand, the founder] had no idea what I wanted to do and she was like, All right, we'll commit to it, as long is there is a larger work at the end to show what you've been doing."

After the initial debut, Tolbert took her show to the Hugo House and then the Twilight Gallery. It was there at the Twilight, in a room just slightly bigger than my living room, that I first had the opportunity to see the play. During the first act, the audience came to know three complex black women whose stories intertwined through their intergenerational friendship. "When I tried to write just a one woman show with just one person, I was extremely bored with myself. And I thought, OK, why not be totally crazy and have three characters in three different generations."

We met Saraphina, a sassy octogenarian; Luna, a vivacious spirit child with a tender heart; and Alice Metropolis, a middle-aged free spirit just trying to "keep it moving" though the difficulties of her life and emotions.

"Saraphina was born out of just matriarch women that I knew, I mean my aunt, my grandmother, an older woman in Japan that I met," said Tolbert. "She is the culmination of many older women that I respect."

Alice and Luna also have their origins in people Tolbert has known, which is perhaps why these characters have such resonance. Being in such a small venue also gave the performance an intimate, conversational feel.

The performance taught Tolbert something: "I never realized I needed to be in shape for the movements when the characters jump in my body they change Anastacia's posture, hand movements … I shifted in that, Wow, I need to be in shape, I didn't know it would get so physical."

Through snippets of their lives, watching them gossip about one another — Saraphina fretting over Alice's impending nervous breakdown, Alice being cranky about Luna's effervescence — you are gaining an insider look at the lives of black women. They are women who do yoga, ride the bus, drink shots of Jack, smile, yell and jump, normal things, not normal things. But as I watched the story unfold I thought of the opening stanzas of Ntozake Shange's choreo poem, *For Colored Girls Who Have Considered Suicide/When the Rainbow is Enuf.*

She wrote: "Somebody, Anybody sing a black girl song." This play was that, complete with the occasional Nina Simone riff. It provided an authentic representation of everyday women that I haven't seen since the TV mini-series *The Women of Brewster Place.*

"Alice has always been around," said Tolbert. In speaking with Tolbert, you get the sense that this is not just something she wrote, but rather that she has a relationship with each character beyond the page. "I sort of was looking back at writing back in 2008 where I didn't name her, but I was writing a lot of persona poems and it just sort of dawned on me like, Oh my god, actually I've been writing about her for almost eight or nine years." Then she corrected herself, "With her."

When asked how the play and these characters have evolved over the past year, she answers: "To be honest I would say many things have shifted. I have definitely had to have a stronger sense of self."

The opening chords of Nina Simone's "I Put a Spell on You" began to play as Tolbert searched for her words. "There have been nights after the show where I sit by myself in the space and I think, Did these people get it? Did they get it? Did they hear the part about this or that? Did I nail it? Did I come across the way that I envisioned it? And then I asked the characters, Alice, are you satisfied? Sarafina, is there something I didn't say that you wanted me to say. Luna sweetie, are you OK?"

Leaving the show I didn't have to wonder if I got it. It was all too real to me, the way each character talked about their fears and put words to the violence we live with daily as well as the physical and mental health disparities that plague black communities. "I thought that some people would be more engaged and enlightened at the end of shows and I thought that the Q & A would be full of social justice revelations," said Tolbert. "And I'm realizing that some people are more concerned with why does Alice wear a button down shirt and I have to be OK with that. It's not what I envisioned would happen after every show and so I have to stop being disappointed."

Tolbert said she had hope audiences would be willing to engage in a deeper discussion on what they saw. "I want them to do research. I want them to glorify and honor all women of color, not just Michelle Obama. Michelle Obama ain't the only fantastic woman of color," she said.

"I want them to stand by a woman of color at the coffee shop and say, 'Good morning.' I am tired of progressive talk not going anywhere and I was hoping the play would be a catalyst, a conduit, a bridge, a walkway, whatever analogy you want to use to making that better."

Like most artists, Tolbert hopes her work will leave a mark on audience. In 2018 she hopes to turn it over to a new actress and step into the role of director.

On a brief sunbreak in an otherwise gray day, I found myself peering through a garage door into a beautiful white space—part workshop, part gallery—

Please Touch the Art: New Exhibit Invites More Than Just Looking

filled with gorgeous oil paintings and a veritable pop up garden of stone and marble sculptures.

If you've used the on-ramp for the West Seattle Bridge at Delridge you might have seen it too. It's what Iraqi artist Sabah Al-Dhaher refers to as "the mysterious place with all the marble." Though Al- Dhaher has been at work in his West Seattle studio for the past eight years, it is only in the last year that he chose to open up the doors to the neighborhood. He's gotten a warm welcome.

"They love it when they see me in here banging on the marble and making the sound. It literally stops traffic. People waiting in line to get on the bridge see it. Some of them might see it in the morning while they are getting ready to go to work and then come back later in the afternoon," said Al-Dhaher of his studio's open doors.

A classical artist by training, Al-Dhaher's work centers on the human body.

"I see the human form as kind of my favorite subject. You can express so much emotion in it," Al-Dhaher says.

In his studio there were small white marble nudes, the smooth contours of a woman's face chiseled into a gray hunk of stone left ragged where her hair would be, and my favorite, a beautiful life sized fountain of a woman's back. The water pouring out from a jug centered on her head like a shower.

"When you think of Iraq you think war, not art," said Al-Dhaher, recalling his unlikely path to becoming an artist in Iraq. At age 15, he was accepted to a prestigious school for the arts modeled after European apprentice programs. There he learned to make his own oil paint.

"I got to study painting, sculpture, and ceramic." But he didn't find his favorite medium until he got to the U.S. "I lived in the south and we didn't have stone, so most of the sculpture I did was clay and casting. The first time

I saw stone was actually when I was here in Seattle. I saw a piece of marble and just fell in love with it. I taught myself how to carve it."

Al-Dhaher arrived in Seattle in 1983 as a political refugee after two and half years living in a tent in the desert as a prisoner of war in Saudi Arabia. "Art through my whole life has allowed me to escape."

Even as a prisoner Al-Dhaher continued to create.

"They allowed me to put a show on the fence, so on the wire I put these cardboard drawings I did," he said, describing the pieces he made using only the cardboard from food rations. "It was a very interesting show, probably my all-time favorite show, but it can never be replicated. And it was really incredible just to allow these prisoners to have a show. The pieces were just sketches on cardboard because that's the only thing that was there. We didn't have any pens. It took a month just to get access to pens."

When Al-Dhaher learned he would be allowed asylum in the United States, he did not speak any English and all he knew of his new country was Hollywood and New York. The immigration officers joked that he would not be able to survive in either place, so instead he came to Seattle. He'd received a postcard from another refugee from the same camp who had relocated to Seattle two months earlier. After his time in the desert he was ready for rain. Currently Al-Dhaher teaches at PRATT Fine Arts Center and has had his art displayed in several galleries. "I've showed a lot in schools and colleges, mostly for educational purposes to let students and people who don't usually have the time to go to galleries to bring the art to their environment."

This month, his work is part of an exhibit at Edmonds Community College that invites viewers to experience art in an unconventional way.

Please Touch, a show curated by artist Jim Ballard, dismisses the notion that fine art should only be experienced with the eyes, inviting participants to use their hands and their ears.

"I've been working with children and adults who are blind or vision disabled. Often times there are not fine arts shows where they are able to touch the pieces," explained Ballard, adding that every piece in this show is touchable.

Al-Dhaher and Ballard became friends through the Northwest Stone Sculptors Association. The exhibit also features pieces by two other sculptors: Richard Hestekind and David Varnau; paper embossments created by Ballard, and a series of seven long gray tapestries printed with ravens.

There is also a loop of three poems read by Holly J. Hughes about three extinct birds that appear in Ballard's paper embossments. The entire exhibit is narrated in braille by Caroline Meyers.

"We combine braille and tactile illustrations used by children and adults so they can learn more about the world," said Ballard.

"People think you can't enjoy art, but you really can if people let you touch things," said Camille Jassny, a woman with severe vision impairment, after a preview of the exhibit. Accompanied by Ballard, two friends and her dog Brietta, Jassny made her way from end to end experiencing each piece.

"Even if you can't see, touching is its own way to experience art."

Maru Mora-Villalpando in Her Own Words

Outspoken. Courageous. Humble. Brilliant. Unyielding. Controversial. Undocumented.

Many words have been used to describe Maru Mora-Villalpando, the 2018 Globalist of the Year, but when I ask her how she would describe herself, she said simply as a single mom and a community organizer.

Mora-Villalpando visited the U.S. several times on a tourist visa for the purpose of practicing her English. During one of her trips in 1996, President Bill Clinton signed into law the Illegal Immigration Reform and Immigrant Responsibility Act that increased the consequences for people who had overstayed their visa.

Mora-Villalpando faced a complicated choice, which became even more complicated when she got pregnant. She decided to remain in the U.S.

Eight years ago she founded a consulting business called Latino Advocacy, which focuses on racial justice and immigrant rights, and has been heralded as a modern-day freedom fighter for her tireless efforts to stand up for immigrant rights.

Last year, Immigration and Customs Enforcement began deportation proceedings against Mora-Villalpando—but she refused to back down from her advocacy.

The Seattle Globalist asked her a few questions about her life, and her activism. The following is an edited transcript.

Reagan Jackson: What was your life like before you came to the United States?

Maru Mora-Villalpando: I was really young. I was still in college when I was in Mexico. So…in a way it was much more…let's say busier because I lived in one of the biggest cities in the world so I was always busy doing stuff and traveling, but I did a lot of organizing work which we don't call that. We just survive and resist and fight back all the time.

So, since a very young age I was involved in protests and marches and supporting work stoppages or strikes. If I wasn't doing that I was going to school. And then I have a large family so I was also the babysitter in the family so I took care of all my nephews when they were little. It was a very, very busy life.

RJ: What were you studying?

MMV: I went first for computer science, but in Mexico college is free which means all classes are saturated, right? It's like hundreds of students per class. So they're very selective. If you miss one class or if you're late for that type of career then they drop you. So they dropped me. I was late to a Saturday class so I had to end up going to a different college. So I ended up going to business administration which I didn't like. So, I switched and I went to journalism.

RJ: Were you able to finish before you came?

MMV: No. No, I didn't graduate. I ended up coming to the United States and when I came here I just wanted to practice my English 'cause I had already studied some English in Mexico. When I realized that I couldn't go back and forth like I used to with my visa—my tourist visa—and I ended up staying, which was not what I wanted at all, that was not my plan. And then I got pregnant and after that I wanted to consider the possibility of going back to school, but it was really expensive. I knew it wasn't free like it is in Mexico, but I had no idea how expensive it was so I decided that I couldn't afford that, so I didn't. I decided I couldn't go back to school after that.

RJ: What made you decide to stay?

MMV: I think it was different things. I used to come back and forth with my tourist visa and I used to practice my English then go back to Mexico. I even did teach English as a second language in Mexico, but when I came back the last time in 1996, I don't remember exactly how it happened, but at some point I heard on the news that immigration laws have changed. … At that point it was new where if you had been undocumented for a certain period of time you would be barred from coming back. And at the same time I had already been aware of the situation in Mexico. Not only the economic situation, but the political situation. So it was just a combination of factors that made me think … I don't have a lot of choices, but if the choice is to stay versus going back to Mexico and not being able to come back here I'd just rather stay.

RJ: So what's it been like to be separated from your family in Mexico?

MMV: Just being here was a cultural shock because first of all it was not my intention to stay here, to live here. I always thought of this place as a transitory place for me, that from here I would go other places, to other countries. And just knowing that I would not be able to see my family for an undetermined period of time… it was really difficult. And it made me realize how difficult life is for undocumented people here in the United States.

Because it looks like we're so close to Mexico and yet so far. And you know most of the Mexican community that I've known here for years comes only for a certain period of time. There's always the hope that we're going to go back. So, once I think we're pushed to make that decision and we're pushed to leave the country you really have to become almost numb to the idea that you cannot even be nostalgic about your country. You have to be really tough. You have devote almost your entire time to thinking why are you here to meet the goals of being here so that you don't enter into depression or you'll become… let's say… emotional about it and then you end up going back knowing it will be very difficult to come back here.

So it is a very difficult decision and it is a very difficult way of living. But when your family is there, they also tell you, it's better if you don't come back because things are so bad. And there's expectation that in general families that are here end up helping the ones that are back home. So I think that's also the responsibility that many of us carry with us, to ensure that our families back home are in better shape than they were. And it makes it a little bit easier for us to be here thinking well at least I'm helping my family back there.

RJ: Looking back do you feel like you would make the same decision again or do you have any regrets?

MMV: No, I don't have regrets. I don't think I would have changed any of it. The experience of being undocumented is a very unique one because it helped me connect with other communities that I don't think I would be able to otherwise. And it made me realize also the kind of privilege that I carry because of the fact that I came with a visa, I was in college, I already spoke English when I came here, I'm light skinned. I came from a very classist city so I had to learn all these different levels of oppression that I carry with and also the level of privilege that I had and how I utilized the privilege wherever I went. So by being undocumented, it made me realize all those different levels of privilege and oppression and it made me connect with the community. I don't think I would have had, if I had been document-ed or if I had gone to a different country ... I assume if I had stayed in Mexico I would be dead by now because you know Mexico is not only a very dangerous place for political dissidents, it's also a danger-ous place for women. If you combine women plus political dissent, it's the perfect formula to be killed. So I assume it was a wise decision on my side to remain here and it had a lot of sacrifices entailed with it, but I wouldn't change anything.

RJ: Had you thought before about applying for political asylum?

MMV: No. No, because I worked so much in this environment of immigration that I know that is almost impossible. I've know people that their entire families have been killed and yet they don't get polit-ical asylum or asylum. So that's not something that I know I realis-tically I would get. I think when I became involved with all of this, I went with the wagon that we call the CIR—the comprehensive immigration reform wagon. I jumped on it. Because I kept being told by lawyers that to fix my status I just had to wait for immigration reform to happen. And the more I heard about it, the more I thought, "Well, I'm not going to wait. I have to do something for it to happen." So when I jumped on it I was like, "Give us papers, give us the green card." And the more I learned about it, the more I realized that was not the solution. So I stopped thinking about the green card years and years ago. That was not my fight anymore.

My fight was to stop the detention and deportations of all of the community. That's why political asylum or any other process never came to mind, because one, it's not realistic. And second, I wouldn't be able to apply anyway. And third, even if I gained status that still doesn't mean that my community is not going to be targeted. And myself at some point. I mean the reality is that all immigrants are being targeted right now, regardless of even having a criminal record or status.

RJ: What has it been like transitioning from the Obama administration into the Trump administration as an undocumented person?

MMV: [W]e knew that it would be more difficult, that it would be more challenging. It was not a surprise. It's still not a surprise all the things that they've done because we knew the potential of this immigration machine right? We knew that the level of power that they were acquiring and the structure of the machine, the machine was already huge, it was big.

What has been more difficult is for people who have never really believed us or that doubted us, or that thought that Democrats were the answer. And now I think it's difficult for some of them to understand that this is not a Trump issue. This is an American issue. This is not new. There are not easy solutions to it. Just like impeaching Trump is not going to end the detention and deportations or the attacks against women or against poor people or gay people. I think for one there's that, and I think the other difficulty that we've found is that we get so many people all of sudden wanting to take this on, but they haven't gone through an understanding of their own privilege that they come to us with solutions because they don't see us as leaders and they don't see us as, you know, people with expertise. They don't treat us as equals. They treat us more like victims which I refuse to be.

I don't think that people in detention are victims. People in detention are organizers to me. They are incredibly strong and in general people that migrate to this country are... they're extremely, extremely brave. They've already done so many things to get here and to remain here and survive here. It requires a lot of courage. So to treat us as victims, I think it plays the white savior mentality. And second it really is a disservice to the organizing of people who have done hunger strike after hunger strike in the detention center not only here, but throughout the nation. So that's been a challenge, to make sure that people who want to come and support our work understand that we're not victims, that we know what we're doing. We get a lot of people coming and saying have you done this, have you done that and we're like oh here we go again. But it is important for us that as people come and offer support that they don't give us more work until actually they're ready to do work with us and not for us.

RJ: What do feel like has been the most important thing you've accomplished as an activist?

MMV: I would say that I have learned that my place is not to lead, but to follow people in detention's leadership, to listen and to hold people accountable to their work. It's easy outside of detention to say you're in support of people detained, that you support immigrant rights, that you want this to stop. It's easy to say abolish ICE. It's easy to say resist. It's really hard to actually do it.

And I think that thanks to the leadership of people in detention I've learned to be… to have integrity in my work and to be accountable to them. And therefore I think I've learned how to keep others accountable to their work. And it's not an easy job and most people don't want to do it, but I've seen how people in detention, they have nothing to lose. They tell me that again and again. And I've learned that myself. We have nothing to lose.

So I think because of that our work is not about making friends or having a good image or making others like us, our work is really to dismantle an entire system. And we're very honest about our work. We don't like lying to people. We want to be really clear about what we do and what we don't do. In order to accomplish that we also hold others accountable to it. And I don't think I've ever had that opportunity to be myself held accountable to people in detention and to learn how to hold others accountable to their words when they speak of immigrant rights and immigrant justice.

RJ: In this work of dismantling the system what would you replace it with? What's the next step that you're hoping to see?

MMV: We have said again and again that people in detention, they have given us a road map. When you see their demands, when you read them, there is a road map of how to shut down the detention center and how to give people an opportunity to stay in the country. So people have said again and again that first of all people with medical illnesses should not be detained. People will small children should not be detained. And then everybody else should be released after those priorities have been released and then everybody else. Which means to us that there should be no detention of people. First of all this is a civil system and in their demands they have talked about having a fair chance to fight their cases. And I think that's really what we want to replace the entire system with. We want a system that does not rely on detention to create a business, which is what we have. We have an entire industry living off of the people detained.

But replace completely that we are actually a civil system that is fair to the people in deportation proceeding. But also that takes into consideration the root causes of migration which we have never seen in any kind of immigration reform bill.

That's what I used to do back in the day. We used to take all the different bills that were introduced from 2007 to 2013 and show to our community, read all these proposals. Do any of them match the need to end up here? People would say no it doesn't address the fact that I was forced to leave the country in the first place. And so we need to have an entire different system that is not punitive. That takes into consideration the role of the United States in creating the conditions of forced migration too. And we need to remind people that this is a civil system and it should be treated as such and not to be switched around within the criminal systems as it fits with them in order to excuse the criminalization of our people and excuses the creation of entire enterprises that benefit and profit from the criminalization of our community.

RJ: What is the one question that no one ever asks you that you would like to answer?

MMV: (Laughs.) I think people tend to forget that this is a group effort and people like to idolize one person and I always have to remind them that it would be really stupid of me to be outside of the detention center with signs saying release everybody detained. It would have no impact whatsoever. My work has been successful because it's teamwork. It took me years to get to this point where I found the right people to do this work with me.

Back in the day I was working with my undocumented community outside the detention center and it wasn't really until we did the shut down action of February 2014 when people being transported saw outside blocking the streets that they said, "OK, it's time to organize with people outside and for us to respond to their organizing inside." That took a lot of team effort for us outside to put together an action and to remain together as a group and for people inside to organize themselves and be in touch with us. And people forget all the time that our work outside is really the result of the organizing inside. And it's a whole team. There's a bunch of people around me and with me and supporting me and my daughter when ICE came after me.

People always ask me about my story. I really don't like talking about me. I like to remind people that this is a group effort. I just happen to be lucky enough to be doing this work, but there's no way that I could have done this if it wasn't because we are a whole group that believed that we could do this and that we should do this.

I hope that by the time this is published that there is no hunger strike anymore, but there's still a hunger strike happening. This is week nine of the hunger strike. Today is day 56 for one person on hunger strike. So that tells you the importance of our work outside, but also how bad things are inside that one person decided, "I'm not gonna eat and that I'd rather die in here rather than going back to my country."

We are also right now working on stopping the deportation of Saja Tankara. Saja has a lot of medical issues and ICE retaliated against him when he was featured in an article last week. It was published on Wednesday, and on Thursday he was told he was being deported.

Like, very out of the blue. So we have been organizing. And so far he is still here, and his wife is doing a lot of work. She just texted me as you and I are talking here. So I hope by the time this comes out that he is already free, but if he's not we're asking people to keep making the calls. I know sometimes people get bored when we're having our call to action everyday saying, "Make the call, call ICE, call GEO"— but [the calls] work.

And if people in detention don't stop, we shouldn't stop either. And it's really comfortable for us to make a phone call. It doesn't take much. So we're asking people to continue putting pressure on ICE. Believe it or not, it works. And if this other guy decides he wants to continue his hunger strike we should support him as well. So I hope that in your article you can reflect the need for the people outside that are not direct organizing with us that they can still be supportive of our work by just following our calls to action.

Human Rights Activist Noami Tutu finds hope in Restorative Justice, Reparations

Human rights activist Rev. Naomi Tutu is coming to the Seattle area with a message of hope.

"What I tell people is that we are unlikely in this country to experience a national program such as we're seeing in South Africa, but that communities can take the lead in making their communities more just and using a restorative justice model," said Tutu, in town to give the keynote for the YWCA Seattle King Snohomish's Inspire Luncheon.

Tutu's father, Nobel Peace Prize-winning Desmond Tutu, headed a national restorative justice campaign as the chair of South Africa's Truth and Reconciliation Commission. The commission was started in 1996, just two years after the end of the decades of apartheid that oppressed the country's black citizens.

Naomi Tutu said one example of a community taking on restorative justice is the Greensboro, North Carolina's Truth and Reconciliation Commission.

It was established in 2004, decades after a 1979 shootout between protesters, the police, the Ku Klux Klan and a neo-Nazi group after a "Death to the Klan" march. Four people were killed and several more injured.

The North Carolina commission modeled their process after the process used by her father in South Africa. It brought together all the stakeholders including the local government, the police, and people who were part of the march or lost loved ones to hear each others stories and experiences of that day.

"I think that that is the first step to restorative justice is a willingness to hear the stories, to speak, to tell your story, but to listen to the story that comes from another perspective, from those who are 'on the other side,' if you like," Tutu said. "Because if we can bring ourselves to recognize fully the humanity of our neighbor, then we can start the process of restorative justice."

Her vision of equality and equity also ties in with her support for the YWCA Seattle King Snohomish's work on the global and local level.

"I'm hoping to encourage people to support the work of the YWCA globally, but also locally," said Tutu, adding, "globally in terms of their commitment to the empowerment of women and the elimination of racism and locally especially in terms of their work around the economic empowerment of women in that community and their support for women experiencing gender based violence."

Tutu has lived in Nashville for the past 19 years. For her, growing up in South Africa was both fraught with oppression and also with a spirit of love, perseverance and transformation.

She was recently ordained in the Episcopal Church, following in the footsteps of her father, who was the first black man to serve as the Bishop of Johannesburg and the Archbishop of Cape Town during South Africa's apartheid era.

As he made his way up the ranks of the Anglican Church of South Africa in the 1960s through 1980s, he continually spoke out against the injustices faced by his fellow black South Africans.

This history has left Naomi Tutu with an important legacy. She acknowledged the blessing and the challenge of her lineage and being known not only for her own work, but for her family ties.

"I feel that I carry the legacy of both my parents, and also the legacy of my grandparents and the legacy, in fact, of the community that raised me," Tutu said.

Tutu is the divorced mother of three: Joy who lives in South Africa, Mugi who is currently working on a national campaign to combat Islamophobia, and Mpilo, a college student at Central College in Kentucky. In addition to public speaking, Tutu helped to create Nozizwe Consulting in Zaire.

But her primary work is with her church.

"I intend to continue in my responsibility to the church, one to serve the church, but also to call the church into being the church that God intended us to be, a church that works for God's kingdom, that works for justice, that works for mercy, that works to bring all of God's creation into a place of wholeness and wellness and caring."

The Episcopal church has had many conversations about its role in the transatlantic slave trade and if and how reparations can be made.

"What reparations would look like in the context of the church I'm not sure," Tutu said. "But what reparations I think would look like in the context of the nation is an acknowledgment first of all that economic ill has been suffered by black people in this country first of all through slavery and then through Jim Crow and through the cradle to prison pipeline, through continuing segregation, through education and opportunities and that I think that part of the reason that people are talking about reparations are that with reparations—as opposed to affirmative action—you are talking about justice."

Reparations right injustices, Tutu said, as opposed to affirmative action, which she compared to charity.

"The thing about charity in our context is that when the person who is giving the charity gets tired of being charitable they can stop the charity at any time or change who they are charitable towards."

It is not charity, but rather justice and sustainable transformation that Tutu hopes to encourage.

"I hope that my legacy will be the same as the legacy of those who have come before me, that I will encourage others to believe that the struggle for human rights is a worthwhile struggle, is an important struggle that holds us all to work for a more just world," she said.

Jessamyn Stanley On Being Fat, Black, and a Yoga Teacher

"Yoga is for skinny white girls," said video host Dylan Marron to his guest Jessamyn Stanley, in the opening frame of an episode of "Shutting Down Bullshit."

In response, Jessamyn Stanley, a thick black woman wearing a red sports bra and electric purple leggings, lifted herself into a headstand like a full-bodied middle finger.

Stanley then proceeded to shut down a series of bullshit statements, including "fat women should cover up their bodies when they are working out" and "fat is an offensive word."

I watched that Facebook video an embarrassing number of times, adding to its 1.8 million views. That video was the first time I had come across Jessamyn Stanley—a self-proclaimed fat, black yoga teacher and body positive activist. She spreads her message that yoga is for everybody through her frequent photos of her practice online.

After seeing that first Facebook video, anytime her pictures or videos came up on my feed, I stopped whatever I was doing and became hypnotized.

Depending on the day, my reactions to her pictures ran the gamut from "Get it girl!" to cringing and dissolving into a puddle of tears. I would cry because my discomfort with her clothing choice had nothing to do with her, but everything to do with the ways I have been taught to be ashamed of my body.

Many scantily clad women appear on TV every day, but none of them have bodies that look like Jessamyn Stanley's. Even before I switched to private lessons, the only time I ever saw a large black body doing yoga is if I caught a glimpse of myself in the mirror. And I for damn sure wasn't doing a headstand or the splits or any of the advanced poses I watched Stanley do.

I thought I had come to terms with the fact that there were certain poses I might never physically be able to do—but then I saw Stanley's videos and I felt something within me shift.

It wasn't a subtle shift. I felt like my mind exploded and all this internalized fat shaming I didn't even realize I had inside me started oozing out like a popped blister.

But what got Stanley to come to yoga was not a desire to change anything about her body. Instead, she found a different type of challenge.

"I didn't come to it thinking, 'Oh I'm going to get more flexible' or 'One day I'll be working on this headstand or handstand,'" Stanley told me in a phone interview.

In fact, she called her first experience with yoga "the worst experience of my life."

Her aunt had invited her to a Bikram Yoga class. Stanley felt awkward being the only teenager, new to the practice and insecure about her body size. The yoga room temperature of 105 degrees added to the discomfort.

"About a third of the way into the class, I became convinced that my death by heat exhaustion was imminent," Stanley wrote in her new book "Every Body Yoga." After the experience in what she called "Satan's yoga sauna," she avoided yoga for years.

When Stanley found herself going through a bout of depression a graduate school classmate encouraged her to give it a second try.

"I had come to a place where I felt like I was kind of sleepwalking through my life," said Stanley. "And yoga helped me to realize because it was so hard and because I felt like some of the postures seemed completely insurmountable and they gave me a real genuine challenge and something to strive for and I realized in my day to day life that I wasn't really doing that."

"Every Body Yoga" is part memoir, part yoga for beginners, complete with color photos of sequences to try at home. Her mission is to get everyone off the couch and onto the mat. She wants yoga to be accessible to those who need it most.

"It gave me a lot of confidence," said Stanley. In fact it helped her to gain clarity about graduate school—that she was miserable and needed to leave. She dropped out and moved to Durham, North Carolina, where she still lives.

"So I would just practice at home the 8 to 10 postures from the Bikram Yoga sequence that I felt comfortable with. And in this time it just became this medicine that I would give myself and I was always just a few breaths away from remembering who I was."

Stanley began taking pictures of her practice to track her alignment and as evidence of her progress.

"I would be thinking wow, yoga is incredible, this is amazing. I'm so strong and powerful and then I would look at the photos and I would immediately start talking shit about myself."

But the photo record forced her to confront her inner critic.

"Photos really do create a constant and you look back and you can't not remember that moment. You can't call it something that it wasn't," she said. "If you felt great and you felt strong and powerful, you are strong and powerful. It doesn't matter if what it looks like is different than what you thought it should look like."

For Stanley this was the beginning of a positive transformation.

"I feel like that kind of confrontation has really been the hallmark of me having a better relationship with myself. "

For me, yoga has been a double-edged sword. Like Stanley, I came to my practice during a low time in my life—coincidentally also while in graduate school. I was finishing up my graduate studies in Hamilton, New York, a town where I was one of ten people over 21 and under 50. It was lonely and I was bored.

When a friend invited me to yoga, I went just to fill the time. It was hard and I was surround by tiny white women who could twist their bodies into pretzels and stand on their heads. But after an hour of deep breathing, sweat and struggle, I felt a looseness in my limbs and a renewed mental clarity.

It felt powerful to be in my body in that way, but I was also confronted with my own inner critic, the voice inside me like the childhood bully that had never disappeared. It was telling me everything I was doing wrong, and worse, all the ways in which my body itself was inadequate.

Stanley's pictures became a way to have a different conversation with her body. What is beauty? What is strength? What have we been told and what do we actually believe is true and why? There is an honesty and a vulnerability to her photos. She is redefining her relationship to her body pose by pose.

That's what hypnotized me in her videos. I didn't know there could be a different conversation. Stanley made me confront the reality that the limitations I placed on my body may not actually be true.

"So I don't know that it's necessarily related to the yoga itself, but the act of photographing my body and looking back at those photos and being able to distinguish the point where self-hate originates, that has been monumental for me in terms of having a better relationship with my body," Stanley said.

When Stanley began posting photos of her yoga progress on Instagram, they went viral. Friends and strangers who saw them encouraged her to become a teacher. It launched her into another journey.

"The analogy I always use is that I found a musical instrument within myself and that musical instrument was covered in goop and blood and guts and shit and I like pulled it out and I start cleaning it off and then I start learning to play my instrument," Stanley said. "And that my whole yoga practice is me just learning how to play this instrument and become more comfortable with it."

Stanley has inspired a diverse range of people to reach within themselves to find their own instruments, to value them for what they are and to learn to play them.

This journey has not been without its challenges, Stanley said, from feeling exoticized to being overwhelmed by the sheer volume of strangers searching for connection.

"And it's this weird line of being very much in control of what pieces other people have of you or what they think they have access to and then being like a moment away from losing yourself," she said. "And I feel like that is such a huge part of my personal practice at this point."

During our hour-long interview Stanley talked about everything from her coming out story to her views on cultural appropriation, her cannabis activism, her unexpected journey into teaching and her complex relationship with social media. She also talked about her frustrations with the yoga community.

"It's all about which mat, which pants, which retreat, which coconut water, which... all these different questions about stuff that has absolutely nothing to do with the actual practice which is about breathing and looking within yourself," Stanley said. "And that conversation is much deeper. It's also more complicated and less easy to monetize and therefore less popular."

Moni Tep Explores Hardship of Queer Youth in Jamaica

Seattle musician Moni Tep's journey to explore and improve the lives of LGBTQ youth in Jamaica began in the dead of night, and in the cemetery where many of them were living.

The cemetery had no tombstones and was the site of a mass grave for those who died during an outbreak of cholera. Several dozen LGBTQ youth sought refuge there after being exiled from their families and communities in Jamaica, one of 79 countries where homosexuality has been criminalized.

"That's where these young people are staying. I saw them, at least 30 of them sitting on top of this land and we just went and talked with them and they agreed to talk with me and do interviews."

Tep, 23, a local musician and teaching artist also known as Jus Moni, traveled to Kingston, Jamaica in October to document the lives of LGBTQ youth.

"I think that it is important for us to document our own stories and to create and continue to build a network with each other to provide resources and connections," the busy artist told me in an emailed interview.

She also found that youth there had an urgent need for resources.

Tep, accompanied by a friend, drove up into the mountains to conduct the interviews in privacy. The ones who suffer most are the ones who are out of the closet. "They're not trying to pass for anything. Some of them do to get money, but for the most part they are out."

Anyone caught violating Jamaica's anti-sodomy law could face up to 10 years of jail time. There are no laws against woman to woman intercourse, but lesbians still suffer from anti-gay stigma.

Under that hostile climate, many of the youth who have chosen to come out or been outed by others, have been kicked out of their homes and rejected by their communities.

The homophobia and conservative Christianity took root during the British colonization and continues to leave its mark.

"I had articles written about me before I even landed—about how I had a gay agenda and was coming to disrupt their Christian state," said Tep with a laugh. "I guess I'm a gay evangelist coming to save everyone from the straight?"

There are some organizations that have been formed to provide support. "There is a specific collective called SO(U)L that provide so much support and love around the work I am doing," said Tep. The Jamaican Forum of Lesbians All-sexuals and Gays (JFLAG) was founded in 1998 and was the first human rights organization to advocate openly for the rights of queer Jamaicans.

"As to how effective they are, you'll hear many different stories depending on where you coming from in privilege and access," she said.

It's dangerous work. In 2004, one of JFLAGs co-founder's Brian Williamson was stabbed to death in his own home. "The community had a celebration outside of his house because the batty man was dead," said Tep. The group has since moved JFLAG to an undisclosed location.

Tep was conscious of the risks, but that was secondary to her need to help the LGBTQ youth in the country.

"Of course there were concerns, but I say this around any of the work I'm dedicated to in my life, when you believe in liberation, you give yourself selflessly to that movement."

Tep's work in Seattle includes curating safe spaces for youth through her work as a teaching artist with organizations like Youth Speak. She was a teenager herself in the leadership organization Seattle Young People's Project when she first became interested in working with youth.

"I've been a queer-identified person since before I became a teen, this was always my work," she said.

Tep's trip was made possible through JetBlue's Flying it Forward philanthropic program, which also made a video of her journey. Each awardee is selected by the previous contest winner via Twitter, and then selects the next one.

The trip was Tep's first time in the Caribbean country.

"I've always wanted to visit Jamaica," Tep said. "One because it is Black. The food, music and spirituality of that country has been something that has interested me for a long time. As I became more clear in what it was I was supposed to be doing in Jamaica, the land and opportunity presented itself to me."

Though just the beginning, her work in Jamaica has already made an impact. "The highlight of my experience was being able to look young people in the eyes who are facing some of the most adverse situations, and for them to tell me they were thankful for my existence and believe in our power to support each other."

Her next step is providing help through her GoFundMe campaign.

Tep hopes to raise $60,000 that would go toward the direct support of 10 LGBTQ youth living in Kingston.

"It's not just about personal initiative all the time, sometimes it is about circumstance and trying to navigate that," Tep said. "If you can't eat then what are you supposed to do? If you can't take a shower then you can't get a job."

The money would go directly to provide basic needs such as food and shelter and vocational training. The money would also provide help with applying for political asylum for the youth who are interested in leaving Jamaica.

"There were many unsafe moments during my trip, but so much is given much is required—had anything happened to me, the ones I love and affected would be in full understanding that it was for the liberation of us."

Pussy Riot Speaks: Russian Punk Protest Artists in Seattle For Talk, Film

The camera pans across a darkened landscape of what looks like a distant planet. Space gives way to dirt, an empty pack of cigarettes labeled in Russian, then the thick black soles of combat boots.

Drums beat like an industrial heart, metallic and brash.

A lone female voice starts to sing: "He's become his death. The spark of the riots. That's the way he's blessed to stay alive."

Lying in an open grave dressed in gray army fatigues are Nadezhda "Nadya" Tolokonnikova and Maria "Masha" Alyokhina, activists and members of Pussy Riot, a feminist collective of punk protestors based in Moscow.

Pussy Riot has been staging political interventions in the form of punk music, demonstrations, performance art and more since 2011. Similar to the style of punk performance artists the Guerrilla Girls, Pussy Riot's activism combines music and mixed media and has covered a broad spectrum of issues including feminism, LGBT rights, prison reform, and opposition to the policies of Russian President Vladimir Putin.

In 2012, Pussy Riot came to international prominence when three members of the collective, Alyokhina, Nadya Tolokonnikova and Yekaterina Samutsevich, were arrested and sentenced to two years in prison for the crime of hooliganism after performing an anti-Putin song at an Orthodox Church.

The punishment prompted outrage from groups such as Amnesty International. The women were released in 2013 shortly before the Winter Olympics in Sochi in 2014.

"In Russia now we don't have protests because the number of political prisoners are growing very fast. And since our political prison term there are twice (as many) more political prisoners," Alyokhina told me in an interview over Skype.

"Firstly conditions are really terrible," said Alyokhina when asked about her time in prison which describes as an "anti-utopian village." The prison is 3,000 km outside of Moscow in Russia's frozen tundra. "We have the post-Soviet thing where people have to work and they are working for 12 and 14 hours in day without any weekends and administration does not pay these prisoners. And it's slavery."

According to Alyokhina, prisoners spend their time sewing police uniforms while suffering through rotten food, having poor or no medical treatment and living in subzero temperatures without proper clothing.

After their release, they came to New York City during Black Lives Matter protests that followed the death of Eric Garner in New York City police custody. The protests of the decision not to indict the officer who had Garner in a chokehold inspired Pussy Riot's first song in English "I Can't Breathe," released last year.

The video is full of contradictions, army boots and camouflage with bubble gum pink nails, rich black earth overlaid with the ethereal breathy voice. It's creepy, but riveting. The song ends with the pair completely interred, and shovels laid across the earth, the disembodied voice repeating the refrain of Garner's last words, which he said as he was being put in a chokehold during his arrest. Garner's words take on new symbolism in the context of Russian oppression and the comparative narratives of what it means to live in a police state.

While public protests have been silenced, Pussy Riot's activism extends beyond music and music videos. Pussy Riot also created a news platform called Media Zona, which includes the contributions of about 20 journalists.

"Now it's really big. We have 12th place on the top of all Russian internet media now," she said. "It's covering criminal justice topics and Russian economic crisis and ... political cases."

Pussy Riot also launched a human rights organization called Zona Prava (Zone of Rights) for others who have been jailed.

"We're providing legal help for political prisoners. We have about 40 cases with lawyers and about 10 of them are in European Court now," Alyokhina said.

The cases include one of a man who nearly died after the prison administration refused to provide him his HIV medication and the case of a 19-year-old sentenced to 2 years and 3 months in prison for standing near a building that had been graffitied with political art.

Zona Prava's advocacy resulted in the release of the 19-year-old.

"We really want to show how many really good and innocent people are in prison now. I hope in our event we will show some of them," Alyokhina said.

"I think that people start to care when they see that something touch them directly. When we show that this problem is your problem, not only mine."

Alyokhina and her colleagues are aware of the potential dangers. Russian opposition leader Boris Nemtsov was assassinated last year—there is a sense that no one is safe.

"Two years of prison is really nothing. It's like candy," Alyokhina said. "So we are kind of lucky. We've seen better times." Alyokhina says she's not afraid.

"I do not have time to be afraid. But he wasn't only the leader of Russian opposition, he was also our friend." Nemtsov, a vocal critic of Putin's, visited Pussy Riot in prison and actively supported the campaign to release them. Two Chechens were arrested in Nemstov's shooting, but investigators have not released a motive. Many of Nemtsov's friends blame the Kremlin.

"I'm proud that I knew him and this is really terrible sign that they show to everyone. Not only for us who are living in Russia, but they are showing to the whole world that they can do anything and nobody will punish them for this," Alyokhina said.

Despite the difficulties and dangers, Alyokhina is not thinking of seeking asylum from Russia.

"I don't want to go. They should go. They do real crimes. They should leave Russia," she said.

"Choosing Life" Cancer Support Group Founder Continues to Enlighten, and Educate While Battling Disease

22 years ago, Bridgette Hempstead had a visit to the doctor that changed her life. What started out as a routine checkup turned into an argument.

"I called my doctor and said I wanted to get a mammogram," Hempstead recounted. "She began to give me a laundry list of reasons why I did not need to get a mammogram and the last reason, which I think is the most disturbing one, is she said I am African American and African Americans don't need to worry about breast cancer."

The doctor suggested that with no history of cancer in her family that Hempstead didn't need the test and should come back in 10 years. Hempstead insisted and was given a mammogram. She was diagnosed with breast cancer on her 35th birthday. Her doctor broke the news and apologized for being dismissive stating she had been taught in medical school that breast cancer was not a disease that impacted African Americans.

"Even during that time that was not a true assessment because even at that time black women were dying at an alarming rate," said Hempstead. "They may not have had the same amount of diagnosis, but the disparities were horrifying. And during that time younger black women were being diagnosed, but they were being late-stage diagnosis because of the symptoms that were being ignored at the time."

Hempstead described the late 90s as a time when the only visual representation associated with breast cancer was white women with pink ribbons. There was a disconnect. What about people of color or black women celebrating life after breast cancer or diagnosis?

"The numbers or the education was not there for black women," explained Hempstead. "That's how I started the Cierra Sisters...there was a huge need, and I was in the education system back then so my education skills changed from educating children to educating the women in our community: about breast cancer and about surviving the disease and educating yourself so that you can be properly diagnosed and get a proper treatment."

Cierra means knowledge. For the past 22 years Hempstead has dedicated her time and talent towards building the Cierra Sisters into a community of support, education, and advocacy with the hope that in providing better access to knowledge and support, black women could find a pathway forward into better health.

The Cierra Sisters host community meetings on the fourth Thursdays of the month from 6:15-8:15pm at Rainier Beach Community Center. The meetings often feature speakers in different medical professions, but are also an opportunity for survivor to survivor support and information sharing about how to navigate the healthcare system.

"Those meetings are really important. Very informational, very bonding because you've got women that can see other women that are going through similar things that look just like them," said Hempstead. "When you leave that meeting you're leaving empowered, encouraged and ready to deal with whatever you have to deal with when it comes to having cancer. "

These meetings are not only for women. Everyone is welcome, whether they are a survivor or the friend or family member of a survivor or simply want to educate themselves.

In addition to hosting a monthly support group for survivors, the Cierra Sisters host conferences, put on a Wellness festival in the summer, and even go door to door to make sure people in our community are getting the education they need to advocate for themselves.

"I made sure that our community would know what to do based off of my own experience and it's a very personal experiences dealing with breast cancer," said Hempstead.

Hempstead, currently a resident of Rainier Beach, grew up in South Sacramento during the era of the Black Panthers. She married young and had three daughters before getting a divorce and moving to Seattle. In addition to her work with the Cierra Sisters, she teaches in the Medical Administrative Assistant Program at Seattle Vocational Institute, is a consultant with Fred Hutch and serves on the board of the South Seattle Emerald. Several years ago she began working with renowned oncologist Dr. Julie Gralow to do breast health education in Uganda, Zambia, Rwanda, Tanzania, and soon Kenya.

"In those particular countries disparities are pretty horrifying so part of the educational piece that I do is to teach women about breast health and about their bodies and really looking at the positive in the face of such a horrifying disease that has killed so many women across the world," said Hempstead.

After 18 years of being in remission, Hempstead was diagnosed with Metastatic cancer. She had just returned from Uganda and was having some problems breathing so she went to urgent care. Her initial scans warranted further follow up, but when she tried to schedule a second appointment she was once again met with resistance. Her case had been passed onto a second physician.

"He said just take this cough medicine and you'll be fine. So the next day I get up and I call my doctor and they say there's no follow up, you just need to finish taking the cough medicine and you'll be fine."

After her previous experience, Hempstead did not take no for an answer. She advocated for herself. "Well, the nurse who is on the other end of the line says well I don't see anything and then she got very quiet and then she gasps. She says oh my goodness, the first orders were erased, but you can't totally erase the records. So then she went ahead and followed up so that I could go get a biopsy."

Cancer is scary, but even more terrifying is the realization of how life-threatening racial bias can be when it comes to accessing healthcare as a black woman. A study by the American Cancer Society reports that black women are 39 percent more likely to die from cancer than white women, not because (as some have suggested) black women are attacked with more aggressive forms of cancer, but because their medical concerns are dismissed which leads to later diagnosis.

"I think the most disturbing thing about that for me is how many other people does this happen to?" asks Hempstead. "You need to find out what's going on with you and the earlier the better because of the incredible treatments that are available out there and individuals that find themselves faced with something life threatening, I think its important to try to live a normal life and not allow the health care system that may not have respect for you dictate how you should plan your life."

Upon receiving her most recent diagnosis, Hempstead was told she only had one year left to live. "And I jumped off the table with my daughter in the room and I told that doctor I don't receive that in the name of Jesus and my daughter said let's go."

They booked tickets to Jamaica and went parasailing. When she came back, armed with the knowledge of 18 years of advocacy work, Hempstead selected another doctor to work with who specialized in metastatic cancer and has been receiving excellent treatment.

"You know the bible says tomorrow is not promised, but in that same scripture for Bridgette today is that tomorrow that wasn't promised. So each day we have an opportunity to do the best that we can not only to love ourselves, but to love others as we're dealing with health challenges, as we're dealing with family challenges, as we're dealing with issues surrounding us."

Hempstead plans to continue loving herself and her community through her steadfast commitment to health. She is also contemplating going back to school in order to develop programs for other organizations.

"Nobody is going to get out here without leaving this earth, but it's what you do while you're here," said Hempstead who has lived three and a half years longer than her doctor said she would. "It's how you live your life and what kind of quality of life you have, what kind of human being can you be to another human being. I think that's so important. Instead of contemplating or concentrating on death, how about concentrating on living your best life today."

Interview With a Death Doula

Lashanna Williams is a massage therapist with Tubman Medical Center, an art therapist, and a death care provider with A Sacred Passing. Her work in every realm is to listen deeply, align with what is needed and make meaningful impactful change on both a human to human and systemic level. She is passionate about consent and making sure everyone has agency over their circumstances. Her ability to see the joy in many situations allows her to curate spaces where her clients can experience belonging and connection.

Lashanna defines a death doula as someone who helps care for people who are dying but stipulates that what that looks like can be very different from person to person based on their relationship to death, what culture they grew up in and their current cultural context which dictates the legalities, customs and nuances of what happens when someone passes away. During her work as a massage therapist, Lashanna began working with clients in elder care facilities and noticed the deep disparities in how elders were treated based on their economic situations. She also noticed that so many of them were being deprived of touch, other than for medical reasons, so she began to volunteer to provide massages. One of her friends, suggested she had the right temperament to be a doula. While Lashanna wasn't interested in working with pregnant people, at the suggestion of her mentor, she began to research being a death doula and found a woman in Bellingham to train with.

Reagan: How do people become death doulas?

Lashanna: I think lots of different ways. I think people are really surprised to figure out that they have it in them all along, like their doula-ing is something that they've been doing for a long time. And what they what they wind up learning in courses and classes are laws, like what are the laws? How can I do this? Some of the logistical things of like how do I cool a body? How do I shroud a body?

I think people really rely on their lived experiences. A lot of people will take a course, there's so many different ways to educate yourself out there. There are a lot of ways that you have to pay for the education and there's a lot of ways that are for free. Right? So I think folks may have a little bit of an educational buffet.

I also want to say I firmly believe that the doula educational world at this moment is a pyramid scheme. It's gross. There's all these people offering certifications for shit that certification doesn't matter. You're charging someone $1,500 then they're gonna go back home and nobody's gonna pay them shit to sit bedside with someone. Like I don't know who, maybe you know, there is 1% of people who will happily fork over thousands of dollars to have someone sitting there next to their dying love, but I don't know who. But I do know a lot of students who leave trainings thinking that's what they're going to do. So I think a really good mix of reality, volunteering, and careful carefully chosen education gives people a good foundation. And then really continued learning and discovery are the components to a good, safe care caregiver. A safe deathcare provider.

Reagan: So what are some of the things that you do with your clients?

Lashanna: My mind immediately goes to people that I've had really fun things and experiences with and that feels like I'm romanticizing my work, so I'm going to start with the very boring things because they're sometimes the most important, which is paperwork. It's not romantic at all, but it is so important. It is the crux of what can protect us. Depending on where you are and what state you're in and who you are, you do not have the same rights as everyone and paperwork, completed with a health care agent, which is a human who will support everything you have in that paper, is really important. And that's something that people don't do.

People say oh, they know what I want. And then let's give them something. Let's give them something to go on. Because imagine that the roles are reversed and you're sitting there sad and your love is dying. It'd be really nice for you to have some breadcrumbs, something that you knew made them happy, some guidelines. And so I try to really express to people what an act of love that is.

So I can help folks with paperwork. I can help folks with sort of planning what type of disposition that they would like, what they want to do with their body. In Washington State.

It's a really bad word for it, but it's true—it's like a smorgasbord. We have more options in Washington state for what to do with our bodies than any other states. We have a traditional western burial, cremation, alkaline hydrolysis which is like a water burial, sometimes they call it water cremation. And we have that we have a natural burial, natural organic reduction. That might be it. But alkaline hydrolysis and natural organic reduction are only available in this State.

So really helping folks like figure out what is available, what is affordable, where are some places that are really trustworthy and treat humans with kindness and grace after death.

Sometimes I work with folks and I can make their shroud, a super super simple one as my sewing skills aren't amazing. But I make up their shroud and sometimes we'll put like pieces of special clothing in it. We do stuff like that.

We'll work on grief. We'll make a death plan. A lot of the deaths that I attend our medical aid and dying deaths. So they're very much planned and folks know what they're going into.

So we have a lot of opportunity to talk about the cadence of things and the fact that a lot of the stuff after death is very much for the people who are living and we can soften some of those edges. And so people tend to be more like, oh, okay, do they want it if they want it, okay. Having a conversation with the people with people involved is really important and part of the work, as many folks as the dying person wants to include or as few.

Reagan: How do you make a death plan?

Lashanna: I have it here. I'm just going to show it to you if that's okay. The way that I do a death plan is a series of questions. This is my death plan form. It has a little checklist of some really important legal items here that accompany this because this in and of itself isn't legal, but what it does is it fills in a lot of the holes.

We go through these portions of things that happen before someone dies. We go through this and we make three or four different plans. One plan is what is your optimum, your first choice or your second plan is for if things aren't exactly as you want, but what might be okay. A third plan is for an unexpected death and the last is if you would like to create some sort of a plan for if you die by unexpected violence, something that cares for people after your death.

So when we approach this we're thinking about the place that you would like to die. What kind of a place makes you feel safe? Where's your first option? And sometimes people say home or sometimes people say oh my parent's home and so we put that here. So if I were doing this I might say home and then I might say Kline Galland Hospice is my second choice because Kline Galland is really open and they're about as much for choice as you can be and I know that they would be accommodating. Even though I don't want to go to a hospice that's my next one. So what we do is we go through each and every one of these making up our plans so that in the eventuality that something happens in the middle of all these things right, like if nothing is exactly clear and it's not the first choice or the second choice at least your people have something to go on. They have an idea of who you are okay with having take care of you. Are there certain people that you are okay with physical care, not emotional care? It there one person that you lean on for spiritual care? Is there someone who you want absolutely not to be with you alone.

And so we get to write all of that out in here in this thing. And then it's been explained.

And we get to do an after death portion too and folks who are like, oh, I'll be dead. It doesn't matter. Well, it matters to us and for this. Let's talk about those things. And we do and we go through all of it. So I'm really surprised to find out in Washington state that that we can transport our own dead saving us thousands of dollars sometimes. All you need is a shroud and a vehicle. You don't need a casket. The person just has to be wrapped and that could be in a bedsheet or a shower curtain, your curtains, anything that you have would work.

Completing one takes like three or four good rounds of getting in there and then like each time you go through it, but think of oh, I didn't think of this aspect, look at what's in there. And so what it winds up being is we'll do this chart and I'll have the chart, but I also have a written portion. And so it's very much like a story. And it reads like a story for folks who are trying to figure out how do I help this person? Well, now we have a blueprint on shit that they like and they don't like it. As a matter of fact, we have consent to share it with you because they have given us permission for you to be a part of this care team. When you're really lucky you'll be able to talk to each part, each person in that care team before this person dies.

And that's part of what we also get to talk about in the death plan. How do we assemble this care team in a way that feels good to the person who's dying and not overwhelming, still with enough time so that care team members can get a grip, get situated and try to care for someone also maintaining their own health. Because we see that so often. Our caregivers are giving everything and exhausted. We can do better by everybody when we get to plan.

Reagan: What's been the most surprising aspect of this work for you?

Lashanna: I think maybe it's twofold. My ability to process it in a way that doesn't leave me feeling heavy. Not for everybody. Every so often I catch feelings. I just have feelings for a client, like they stayed around a really long time, and you know, sometimes I go into a client relationship thinking that we're going to be together for like three months. They have an end date and then that shit changes and it's been like two years. I'm like what happened? I know birthdays now. I've come to dinner. Shit.

But a lot of times I started that relationship understanding it ends in death and it's really fucking clear. It helps me just keep all of my everything in check.

I think also the way that death can change things when you have the chance to be slow around it, either before or after, but everyone doesn't get a before and so if you have the space for after, to be able to touch your person, talk to your person, lay next to your person if you want to lay next to them, like just be with them and process a lot of those first fresh feelings. The health that is grown from that continuously amazes me. I mean I thought it, but I get to see it and it's so real.

Reagan: How have things shifted during the pandemic?

Lashanna: I feel like people started to become complacent with folks just dying by themselves.

Like oh well this is what we have. These are the rules. We can't go in so they die by themselves and I think that shifts something for us as people when we're okay with our people dying by themselves.

I feel like it creates a disconnect in us. I've seen a lot of that so I feel like it's almost like a hardening, a hardening of people. I think our medical folks are just burnt the fuck out so the ways that they used to care for people is not present either because there's no break for them.

And grief. Through the pandemic we have one off memorials, very grassrootsy, but no full acknowledgment, no regular acknowledgement beside some number on the news which was just for shock and awe, not for care. But that numbing and this disenfranchised grief, like it's over there, I think that really shifted in the pandemic. I think it's became a way of, I don't know, self-preservation, because people were like, I can't actually have all these feelings while I'm by myself. I don't know what to do with them. Or maybe it was a product of capitalism maybe its an and, and, and. I'm resisting asking you questions back. Like what did you see?

Reagan: What did I see? I don't know. During the pandemic there were so many deaths. And some were COVID related and some were not, but I've found these last couple of years we've just been in a deep space of grief and death has been very present, but also very silent.

So what's interesting to me about your work is that you're someone who can demystify some of this process or what are the options or what can happen. I think people are so busy avoiding death that I don't know very many people who are prepared for it and that comes with its own trauma.

Lashanna: And then it can be retraumatizing right, the ways that families hit their archetype roles right? Who was the brat in the family and how that comes right back up and you know, nobody's healed. From any of it. So it all comes in. Yeah, it all comes down.

Reagan: What advice would you give to folks seeking to prepare for the inevitability either of their own death or the death of a loved one? How can you prepare for that?

Lashanna: I really think at a basic basic level an advanced directive. An advanced directive isn't for sick people, necessarily. It isn't for people who are all really old, literally an advanced directive is for anybody who is going to die, anybody who might be in a situation where they are unable to speak for themself. So what it really is and I try to explain to folks is that this is for accidents.

Yes, it certainly is for the end of your life and if the end of your life is way down the road and you are growing into it that's great, but in an accident or unexpected situation you need this. And accidents and unexpected shit, that happens to us. That happens to us in our teens and our 20s and our 30s. You know, it's the really sad situations of the people who died early. Those people who died early, like we have the ability to buffer right now with something. And it doesn't mean that we're okay with dying, it means that we recognize that we drive a car, we get on a bus, we take a flight, recognizing you introduce death into your life around every next corner. Depending on who you are your proximity to death may have never been far, but always up front and center. So your relationship with death might actually be I don't even want to fucking deal with it anymore. It is ever present.

And so a way of squashing the ever presence is saying at least I know these people got me.

These people know I want CPR right now. Because my plans change right. I am 43. I want CPR. I want an electric jump. I want you to keep me on a machine and look for my eyes to flutter. Like that's me right now. But when I'm 80 that will change. I want to say peace out. It changes and it shifts and so at 80 people don't have to resuscitate me. Don't resuscitate me.

Or you can say you want care. And it's important to say you want care, so that everybody knows you want care because there is also an assumption sometimes that folks are like oh they don't want to struggle. This isn't okay for them. When actually that might be absolutely okay with them, but nobody knew. And it's that nobody knew part … nobody wants to sit with that. I don't want to sit with that decision. I want to know because you wrote it on a piece of paper.

Maybe it was us all having dinner and none of us wanted to fuck with this stuff and Lashanna came over and we did this paperwork while we had wine and food and we each decided to be health directives or health care providers for each other. And then it starts a conversation with people. Then I think your community becomes tighter too because then you have that intimacy of understanding that I can care for you in this way and you trust me to care for you in this way.

Reagan: A lot of what you are describing around giving folks agency to choose feels liberatory. What is your relationship to death?

Lashanna: I'm an avid pro-choice human. My personal relationship to death is that when I'm ready I welcome it. When I'm ready, I'm not ready now. I'm not afraid of it. I've seen some really beautiful moments when people are transitioning that leave me with a hope that there is something really cool, I don't know what it is, but I know I'm gonna have ... oh my eyes are watering ... but I've seen people get super excited and smile. And they were not here. They were absolutely not here and their whole face shifts. They are in a place and they see something that is there, that is them, that they feel. I've had folks start to sing a song ... and that's not here. And everyone else here understands they're over there. And so I feel like it's gonna be cool. It's gotta be something ... not that we didn't expect, but something that's really tanglible.

Reagan: No fear?

Lashanna: No. Not of death. I think I fear pain or if something were to happen or if I were to have a long illness, being uncomfortable. My personal belief ... I go back to science. I feel like we're matter and that matter is going to do what it does in some other space. And so I kind of get excited that like I'll be recycled ... for lack of better words. What that means to me feelings wise is that after my death then I just get to be dispersed and then what that means to me in human language is like when I meet someone and I'm like dang I have no idea why I like you, but I really like you, I don't know what it is, but there's something in you and I feel like that's a thread of someone that I've loved before that is in that person, like somehow someway before there's the essence of someone. And so I think that I get to come back in that way and just a little bit here, a little bit there kind of way. And I think it comforts me.

And we don't know what the fuck happens so we can tell ourselves a beautiful story. And I have and I sit with them. Why would I tell myself anything else. If I get to choose? Why would I find a story that didn't make me feel like a warm womb awaited me.

There is a poem called the *Parable of Twins* and I struggle with it because I don't really see anything in the uterus as a life life until its out here and like doing the things. But this poem is from the vantage point of twin in utero and they're arguing about ... well what do you mean life after birth? Is that even possible? How are we ever gonna live away from our mother? This is our source? How are we ever gonna life any other way? And it's this fun little argument between the two and it ends in birth and having an experience that was even more magical than they could think of.

Reagan: Is there anything else you want to share?

Lashanna: I think people are stronger than they think when it comes to supporting people through death. A lot of folks are like I can't do that and I think that people can. And there's community people to help. That's the other thing is that you don't have to do it alone. And if you are doing it alone find my website, find my name because there are people who can help you. You don't have to do it alone.

Reagan: Thank you.

A Conversation With Adana Protonentis

Adana is a scholar-activist, disability doula, curator, and mama. Adana is passionate about wisdom and possibility that exists in the borders, margins, and in-between spaces. Adana's work centers the intersections of race and disability in service of uncovering liberatory wisdom and practices that create conditions for us all to give and receive the care that is our birthright. In her work, she nurtures communities of practice, by helping groups and organizations build their skills toward interdependence, liberatory hospitality, and deep care. She is the co-director of Kindred Consulting.

Reagan: Adana, how do you like to be introduced?

Adana: I usually introduce myself as Adana. My pronouns are she and her. I'm a mama. I'm a scholar and an activist. I'm a disability doula. And I'm an optimist.

Reagan: Why an optimist?

Adana: Because we're still here and we aren't "supposed" to be right? I read Audre Lorde's "A Litany for Survival", probably once a week. I'm just thinking about that. I think about my optimism as being an act of subversion in the face of a world that tells me I shouldn't be.

Reagan: That's beautiful. How do you define the term disability doula? What is that?

Adana: I think of a doula in general, as a person who holds space, extends a container, acts as a tether or an anchor for another person as they're going through a transition. And so, in the context of disability, that means a couple of different things. I think it means holding space for someone as their relationship with their sense of disability is changing. So maybe that's because they have a brand-new diagnosis. Maybe that's because they have acquired another disability in addition to what they had before. It could mean that they're coming to a place of understanding of an impairment or condition they've had for a long time as a disability. And so, it's more, it's not about the diagnosis that changed. It's about their relationship to it that changed.

The biggest part of my work as a disability doula is about being like a lighthouse. I think it's shining this beacon that helps people identify a direction to go to find community. So, thinking about people who, like a good friend of mine, who is technically and legally disabled in terms of having a psychiatric disability, and is still in this space of kind of nibbling around the edges of am I disabled enough to get to use that word? Is what I'm experiencing something that counts as disability? They're sort of negotiating their relationship with disability and with disability as an identity.

The work that I do as a doula supporting them is affirming what they're experiencing, connecting them with resources, whether that's like stories and wisdom from other disabled people who share that diagnosis or community resources or even like systems navigation stuff like here's how you get these services and here's how you use the word disability to access legal supports. Yeah, so I think of it that way as a lot of like, shining that light so, so that people out there in their boats, you can find their way to this community of folks who are like, I can show you what I know about being disabled, I can show you how I do disability. And you can use that information to figure out how you want to do disability in a way that feels authentic for you in a way that honors where you are at this particular moment and really kind of expanding your level of exposure to what's possible out there. That's it.

Reagan: During the transition of my dad losing his ability to walk and transitioning into being full time in a wheelchair, he had access to an occupational therapist, or someone theoretically, who was supposed to come in and show him how to do things in a different way. But that feels very limited compared to the way that you're describing a disability doula. No one really talked about the emotions of the experience or connected us to community where he might be able to talk to someone who had been through that. And even the occupational therapy wasn't particularly useful. He mostly just figured things out for himself. I'm wondering are there disability doulas available through hospitals or through a community? How does one access a disability doula?

Adana: Short answer is not yet to my knowledge. I found disability doulas in kind of varying degrees of formality. In some cases, it was just reaching out to another person I know who has bipolar disorder, after I got my diagnosis and being like, whoa, I just learned this thing. I don't know what it means, and I need help understanding what it means. And that was a way that someone was a disability doula for me; holding that space, educating me, orienting me, helping me just like try to wrap my head around it very much with this focus toward meaning making, I think, as opposed to some of the work that providers do, which is about skills and about a particular kind of skill too, because I also think it's a skill to learn things like how to manage your meds. And it's a skill to learn how to tell your story of disability, how to how to talk about it in a way that makes that makes you feel safe enough. And how to discern how much to share and with whom. I took to the internet to find people when I needed them. And I still do if people reach out to me needing disability doula support, and it's an area of disability where I don't have lived experience. I can help them find someone.

The Longmire Institute is a really great resource (they have a fantastic newsletter that includes really useful resources. One of their offerings is called Café Crip and it's a monthly Zoom gathering of disabled folks for discussion and support), I can email you a couple of other names like Sins Invalid, and a couple other groups of people. I highly recommend connecting to The People's Hub—they just launched a cohort dedicated to supporting folks in unpacking and healing from internalized ableism. There are a lot of collectives that have been popping up on social media, especially through COVID of people creating mutual aid networks, but also just creating spaces for people to come and just explore the idea together. I think of it kind of also like Black Twitter, like how educational it can be to come and just to be able to just watch the conversation and start noticing like, oh, I see myself here, I see myself there. I wonder what it might feel like for me to try to use this language to talk about what I'm experiencing. Starting to find the disability hashtags, so that you can watch those conversations can be like a really, really supportive way to get connected to peers and mentors. (Folks I follow on social media are

Imani Barbarin @crutches_and_spice, Dr. Sami Schalk @fierceblackfemme, Alice Wong @alicatsamurai, Catarina Rivera @blindishlatina, Dustin Gibson, TL Lewis, just to get folks started).

Reagan: What was your entry point into this work?

Adana: It started before I knew I was disabled, it started through my son's disability. So my son was identified, I say identified as being autistic rather than diagnosed with autism because I think of neurodiversity as just normal, and not something we need to pathologize. I try to interrupt that notion that it always belongs in the land of medicine or that it should only be identified by doctors. So that's why I talk about it that way. But when Langston was a month shy of his third birthday, we got the formal diagnosis from a doctor saying that he's autistic. And I remember just immediately craving wisdom from autistic adults and being really struck by the fact that not a single medical provider through a six-months long process of evaluation ever even mentioned autistic adults to us. They didn't connect us with those people. They didn't tell us how to find those voices. They only ever talked about autism as it relates to children and as something to be managed, minimized, or fixed.

And so I started looking for myself and finding blogs and Facebook groups and all these other things. This was in 2013 or so and as I just got deeper in relationship and started talking with autistic folks in particular about how I could be of service to autistic community by reaching out to non-disabled parents of newly identified autistic kids and trying to find ways to sort of support their understanding of what it means to parent an autistic child or what's possible with autistic kids, which is to say, literally, everything is possible in ways that are really affirming and respectful. So it started as kind of doula services that really centered families of kids who are disabled, especially with spectrum and spectrum adjacent impairments. And offering that kind of mentorship and support to the parents and helping them kind of navigate their relationship with disability or their relationship with being parents of a disabled person. Then later, when I identified my disability, initially it was me receiving doula services, and then transitioning into this place of also offering doula services for other people's psychiatric disabilities.

It's what we always do, right? (I mean 'we' as in marginalized folks) We learn from lived experience and we reach out to everybody, to the people around us who could benefit from those lessons so that we can maybe save people some labor and some heartache and create ease for one another. It's just living in community. That's what that is, right?

Reagan: Yeah. I mean it also seems like a pretty steep learning curve. What are some of the things that you learned through this process that you would like to share with others?

Adana: The steepest part of the learning curve, when we first learned that our son's autistic... first of all, I'd never heard the word ableism. I had no idea what it was, I think of it a lot like how white folks who are new to learning about white privilege must feel where all of a sudden all I could see was all the ways that I was ableist that I had just never thought about or all the ways that I'd experienced privilege as a not apparently disabled person. And I was like it's everywhere! Oh, my goodness, it's everywhere. How did I not see it before? I feel it's easy to go in that guilt and shame spiral and feel like a bad person for not seeing it before. And ultimately, that is not of service to literally anyone. So you know, you've got to knock it off at some point.

I think the first big piece was that awareness raising work and that looking inward work about really starting to develop a set of tools, strategies, and frameworks I could use just to examine my own attitudes, my own behavior, my own assumptions and stereotypes. And I am still doing that and will never stop doing that. I find new and different exciting ways that ableism shows up. Internalized ableism shows up in me all the time. I think that's the biggest hardest learning curve. After that, it feels like it's more about learning, like how to find the language to talk about access needs, especially because we live in this very white supremacist and ableist culture, where we're constantly taught to minimize the appearance of needing anything and to pretend to be independent all the time. And so learning how to talk about my own access needs really was kind of like a key sliding into the lock in terms of then starting to develop language to be able to ask other people their unmet needs, and help them reflect on what their needs are and how to come up with some strategies to address them. But I think that the systems navigation piece is the easiest part. I think unpacking the internal stuff is the hardest part.

Reagan: What does that mean when people say the future is disabled? That's a book title right?

Adana: Yes, I love that book by Leah Lakshmi Piepzna-Samarasinha. It is so good. I have this challenge with Leah Lakshmi's writing, which is that I find myself highlighting and underlining so much that the highlights and underlined stuff lose their meaning. To me, it means that I see it on levels, I see it on one hand, like a personal level, like with all of us. If we live long enough, we're very likely to experience disability, whether it's temporary or long term. So on an individual level, my future is disabled, I hope to one day be an elder and that means I'm probably going to have… who knows what's gonna happen? I might have arthritis, I might lose my hearing, I might lose my eyesight. That's likely going to happen for me and I don't need to be afraid of it because it's a gift to get to live long enough that we experience those things.

So I think about it that way. I think about it in terms of the trajectory of the world, like climate change keeps unfolding, pandemics are going to keep happening, those things are going to create more and more disability, systems of oppression, create disability and the longer that they persist, the more disabled folks we're going to have. I don't see that, inherently as a catastrophe. I see it as just a fact of life we need to reckon with as we do the work of dismantling oppression and of tending to climate change. I think collectively as a society, our future is more and more disabled as these things keep happening. You know, we've got a lot more disabled people now than we did before COVID, whether that's from psychiatric trauma that happened during lockdown or from the physical disabilities that came from experiencing the illness itself. You know, some people ended up with long COVID or organ damage, all sorts of things happened.

I think about wildfires, and how many people are developing respiratory related disabilities because of exposure to smoke. More and more of us are going to be disabled, I think it's entirely possible we will have a majority disability culture at some point. And that could be incredible in terms of what it unlocks in our ability to adapt and to be creative, and like I've never met a more creative group of people than oppressed folks. It's just what we do.

There's this book by Dr. Sami Schalk, called *Bodyminds Reimagined* about reimagining disabled bodies and it's all about examples of disability in sci fi, futuristic writing, especially by black women. So like

N.K. Jemison's work, Octavia Butler's work. There's a lot of disability in it. And I think that it's because as black folks, we understand disability has been part of our lives for a really long time, especially since being brought to this continent. It is part of our futures. And we're not afraid of it. We designed for it, we plan for it.

Reagan: This makes me think about my dad. He bought a wheelchair 5 years before he needed it. He often referred to it as that black spider in the corner, because he hates spiders and they are always within 6 feet of us. But being an amputee at a young age and walking with a limp for years, he always knew that at some point he might need a wheelchair and as the time got closer he bought one, partly out of practicality but partly to just wrap his mind around it.

Adana: We work with it. I've heard TL Lewis talk about how one of the reasons it's so hard to talk about disability in black community is because it's so ubiquitous, that it feels bizarre to name it. It's just something that all of us are experiencing, or so many of us are experiencing and such in ways that start to feel common. It's part of our past, present, and future. And I think I find that almost kind of comforting in a lot of ways that we've been doing this for a good long while we're finding new ways to talk about it.

I often hear a grief narrative around disability, and I don't think there's anything wrong with allowing yourself to just feel your feelings, whatever they are, wherever they are, we need to do that. And I think part of that grief narrative comes from ableism. And it would be really great if we could start to identify the times when that grief is rooted in ableism so that we can talk about how that's not really serving us and we could tell ourselves a different story about what disability means.

Reagan: What is your most liberated experience of being disabled?

Adana: Radical permission to be honest with myself about my needs. I think a lot about the concept of "too much" when it comes to access needs and how often we're made to feel like our needs are too much. It's not that our needs are too much, it's that they've been planned for too little. They've been resourced too little, they've been tended to too little. And so like in the public school system we're told your kids needs are too much. No, they're not, it's just that those making decisions about the system haven't planned for these needs enough. They didn't allocate resources to our needs enough. That's not a question of the needs being too much. It's about the system providing too little.

I reached a point with my disability where I was at the proverbial rock bottom. I was in a really, really frightening place. I was in a really dangerous place; my life was in danger. That makes you get really radically honest with yourself about, okay when I get through this, if I get through this, in order to make sure I don't end up back here or in order to have as long as possible before I ended up back here, I've got to be more honest with myself about what I need to do, or what I need to access in order to stay as well as possible.

I had to get real, real honest and unapologetic about my capacity and about identifying what my access needs were and thinking about setting boundaries with people who weren't willing to meet those access needs. And that's been really liberating, to be able to just have that clear, bright line. That's, that's been a huge gift.

Reagan: If you could make a wish for a more equitable future, what would it what would that look like? What would it be like?

Adana: Ah, I only get one.

Reagan: Okay wishes, plural.

Adana: All right, I think the biggest one, the first one would be, I wish that never again for someone's needs be regarded as too much. I want to start there. I would really love to reorient our understanding of need to a place of like, we all have needs and that's super normal. Like we talked earlier about the experience with my kids going through special ed evaluations and what you document and what you don't document. I want to lead with us honestly, candidly, openly, really, really exploring what the needs are, like almost in a vacuum, like they just the needs, they just exist and they're honored and they're validated and affirmed. The conversation about how we organize ourselves to meet the needs, that comes second. Like the needs are the needs and that we don't we don't try to repackage them or curate what gets on the list and what doesn't get on the list based on what resources we've got or what resources we're willing to devote to meeting those needs.

I think that's my wish—to really be needs centered and to really stop making people feel like their needs are too much and like they have to prove it, like they have to apologize for it, like they're asking for too much or taking too much. I want that to stop. We just have an unusual orientation for me, I'm usually oriented toward like, what do I want to see as opposed to what do I not want to see anymore? In terms of what I want to see … I want to see equity look like what Mia Mingus calls access intimacy, where we are so at ease naming what our needs are that we can work together to figure it out, that it just feels like it's just second nature, that we don't question whether it's okay to name what our needs are, that we see it as a way of being in deeper connection and in deeper community with one another. We see it as an opportunity to really get to know each other better. I think that's the other half of that wish.

Reagan: Beautiful. Any final thoughts?

Adana: My closing thought for now would be one of the most valuable things that I've learned being a disabled person, loving disabled people, supporting disabled people has been to find comfort and possibility in the messy middle. Like in those periods of transition when it's not clear what's going to happen or how or when, we can reframe that as an opportunity rich moment. Because that uncertainty means that there are a lot of possibilities. There's a lot of potential futures that are all present all at the same time. That's why it feels messy. That's why it feels murky. And so I see disability as a continuum that we're all on and that we move around on throughout our lives, and being kind of softer around the edges and full of ambiguity as an invitation for a lot more connection a lot more creativity a lot less rigidity.

The
Body

Beyoncé, Barbie, and "Posing Beauty" at the NAAM

How do you want to be seen? Distinguished, thoughtful, stylish, outrageous, proud...these are the words painted above the newest exhibit at the Northwest African American Museum (NAAM), Posing Beauty.

Curated by photographer Deborah Willis, the images form an eclectic collage of black expression shown in the faces and bodies of dolls, models, celebrities, activists, and just people you might see on the street. From the black and white of a shirtless young Huey P. Newton holding a Bob Dylan record to Lil Kim with platinum hair, her midriff bare, mic to her mouth rocking a Queen Bee belt like a badass. These images are both the expected and the unexpected.

Posed and unposed, raw, understated, and complex.

"I'm hoping it will inspire people to think about how they construct themselves both esthetically how they style themselves, but also how they pose themselves," said Serenity Wise, the Director of Community Engagement at the NAAM. "I'm a dancer so I think a lot about the pose. I think a lot about our body language and, you know, how we carry ourselves so this show is right up my alley in that sense, but I hope we're able to spark lots of conversations with the public on how they pose themselves and their body language."

As Wise and I walked through the exhibit together she pointed out her favorite piece, a man in a three-piece suit angling his body like a dancer against the backdrop of an ordinary street. "He just couldn't, he couldn't get any more posed up, fresh, I mean it looks like the photograph was taken spontaneously when they met him on the street," she laughed noting the distinctly east coast style of dress that reminded her of her own ties to Baltimore. "He's like I don't care if I have an interview to go to today, if I have a party to go to, I'm just gonna get dressed and be right outside McDonalds. And at the same time his pose is so perfect it's almost dancerly, I mean the lines that it draws."

From there we crossed the invisible line between the "pose" side of the exhibit to the "beauty". Wise introduced me to the exhibit's namesake piece. Created by Hank Willis Thomas (son of Deborah Willis) the piece takes up almost the entire wall and is filled with black pin up girls lined up in rectangles almost like the elements in a periodic table.

"I'm particularly always drawn to the really old images where they have sort of biographies of the women," said Wise. "Its fascinating to see how not only the women are posing but how the bio poses them, what seem as the most attractive or appealing way of describing each woman."

Pointing to the bio that caught her attention during the installation she said: "This is about a woman who is really into feminine things like fashion and despite her last name being Sargent she knows nothing about the military. She knows as much about the military as a man would know about frilly, feminine fashion, that's literally what the intro says."

As I walked around the exhibit I found myself staring at a portrait of a Barbie doll's face. She was the deep tan of ambiguous ethnicity, her brown hair pulled back in a ponytail, one eye brown and one blue.

The blue eyed side of her face was done up with make up, the lashes long, the cheek accentuate with blush whereas the brown eyed side was bare. The plumped up lips of the brown eyes side gives her the appearance of a crooked mouth. It was like a picture of both Saturday morning chill and Saturday night swag all in one plastic face.

My mother didn't like me playing with Barbie. In fact the only reason I had one is because my uncle gave me one and there is no diplomatic way to take a gift back from a child. Ironically he was also the uncle that also gave me what my mother feared Barbie would, a complex about my body.

Clothes shopping with my cousin, who was a year older than me, half my size and light skinned, with "good" hair that flowed down her back is the first real memory I have of beauty being comparative. My uncle cracked jokes when we couldn't find matching outfits because I had to shop in the plus size section. Until that point I hadn't made the mental leap that us looking different meant one of us (me) wasn't pretty and one of us (her) was.

What followed in the years of attending predominantly white public schools did little to interrupt or contradict the seed of a distorted self-image that had been planted. I learned to see myself the way kids on the playground did, the way my gym teacher did, and it wasn't particularly flattering. Looking at pictures from my life in Wisconsin, I almost never show my teeth. I stand up straight, but less out of confidence and more for the purpose of sucking in my stomach.

"Yes we know the exhibit is photography presenting black aesthetics of beauty, but on a really personal level something we can all tap into is that when somebody puts a camera in front of you and they say cheese you don't just look at the camera and do exactly what you were doing before. You get into position," explained Wise. "And what is it about the poses we choose to strike when we're in front of a camera?"

This year especially has brought to the forefront a myriad of images of blackness posed and unposed: from black bodies shot dead and left to litter the street like garbage, to Beyoncé grinning wickedly, dressed in a yellow ruffled dress slamming a baseball bat into a car window. Whether black is beautiful, powerful, a mark of tragedy, fear-worthy, angry, or revolutionary depends as much on who is behind the lens taking the pictures as it does on who is posed in front of it. Moreover, there are so many contributing factors to how someone will process the images before them. These are conversations taking place throughout Seattle's art community, from Donald Byrd dedicating an entire season of spectrum dance to the contemplation of race to perhaps the most high-profile example, the Kehinde Wiley exhibit at the SAM.

"It is really exciting to see all these institutions that haven't historically been linked with African American culture with African American people starting to embrace that," said Wise. "And to give them their credit, a number of them are not of the mentality that they can just do it on their own…'oh we're going to talk about black things now and not engage black people' like they are genuinely engaging in a lot of the community, working with black artists, working with us, reaching out to us and that's really heartening to see."

Beyond Seattle, Wise sees this trend of examining black aesthetic reflected nationally in the way that Beyoncé's Lemonade has been so critically acclaimed. "I'm really grateful that Lemonade came out a couple days ago because what I love about Lemonade and why I feel like it actually relates to this show is that its so contemporary," says Wise. "It's art for people in a way that usually art that comments that much on life and society and social structures and conceptions of race and what not, usually that art tends to be reserved for some kind of elite presentation, some elite presentation that people don't tend to personally relate to, but everyone relates to Beyoncé."

Wise believes that Posing Beauty does the same thing. "So it's a photography show that's all about beauty which is an immediate entry point for people because we all like I mentioned in posing we all present ourselves in a certain type of way usually in a way that is trying to convey some sense of our idea of beauty and you know doing it in photographs so its individuals presenting themselves is such an immediate thing, it's not conceptual," she said. "It's not like a Rothko on the wall, okay this color, how does this relate to me today? Posing beauty is glamorous and beautiful and very personal at the same time."

The Making of a Burlesque Dancer

I'm standing on a darkened stage in fishnets and heels with a rainbow fish windsock strapped to my ass, thinking that in 3 minutes and 12 seconds this will all be over. It's time to go big or go home.

The curtains part and the music breaks. From behind a wooden screen decoupaged with green glittering reeds and blue tulle, I wave a single elbow-length black glove stitched with spiky gold fins. The crowd goes, ooooh.

I can't believe I'm actually doing this. After an intense six weeks of Burlesque 101 with Seattle's Academy of Burlesque, I'm making my stripper debut as Cocoa La Swish, a fish diva emerging from the reeds of self-doubt into the shiny confidence of my own bedazzled body.

Six weeks earlier, I'd walked into the first night of our class at Studio Blue, a dance space on Rainier Avenue. The room resembled every other dance studio I'd ever been to. It had a hardwood floor with a wall of mirrors and an adjacent wall of cubbies separated by a curtain of pink fringe. A metal rack draped with feather boas reminded me that though I'd taken dance classes before, this would be a different experience.

After filling out some required paperwork, I took a seat at a table in the center of the room with an awkward smile and wave to my classmates.

"Hi, what's your name?" asked the chipper brunette in fishnets and hot pants.

I answered and she introduced herself as Crystal.

"She's like the Mayor of burlesque class," the man beside her explained, and I wondered in the five minutes since we arrived when elections had been held.

Looking around the table at the group of seven white women and one white man—the majority of them younger than me, and definitely in better shape—I wondered if they were mentally undressing me, too. I felt my insecurities begin to whisper.

A woman who called herself The One, The Only, Inga introduced herself as our stripper spirit guide and life coach. If there were a casting call for a naughty Tinkerbell, Inga would fit the bill: petite but well-muscled, with short, chic blond hair. She told us she trained in jazz and modern dance for 16 years before attending her first burlesque show at the Rendezvous Dance Theater downtown and getting "the call" to perform. She toured the world as a member of the Atomic Bombshells, and was Miss Viva Las Vegas 2011.

Inga announced that the goal of the class was to turn us into "magical sparkly naked people" on stage. There was a round of introductions. Like Inga, several of my classmates talked about getting "the call."

I felt my stomach fall. I had never thought of public nudity as an aspirational goal. I saw *The Burlesque Nutcracker* last Christmas. The costumes were lavish and the dance routines were so fun that when the opportunity to take the class for free arose, I thought, why not?

By the end of the first class, all the *why nots* showed up in stereo and danced in my head like hyper critical sugar plum fairies embodying the voices of every kid on the playground who ever called me fat, ugly or nappy.

"You can't have your 10th performance until you've had your first performance," Inga said, encouragingly.

There was no dancing in our first class. Instead, Inga gave us a comprehensive history of burlesque. Burlesque had its origins in Greek Theater circa 426 BC, then spread to the Romans, through the UK, and later to the U.S. What began as satire performed by men (call it ancient Saturday Night Live) gradually integrated women in the late 1800s and evolved from sociopolitical commentary into chorus lines and strip teases.

We learned about Lydia Thompson and her British Blonds, whose six-month tour of the States turned into six years and gave birth to the concept of girls in tights doing chorus lines. Little Egypt caused a stir at the Chicago World's Fair by performing the first recorded belly dancing in the United States.

For many years, strip acts were illegal in the U.S. except in New Orleans, so cunning dancers used to wear "nude" bathing suits. At one point, it became illegal to touch your own body in public, so strippers used puppets and trained birds to remove garments for them.

During the 1920s and '30s, the New Orleans jazz scene provided a soundtrack to a racier version of burlesque, with more Creole and black women performing. Many white performers drew inspiration from women of other cultures—Little Egypt, for example, who was actually Syrian, but borrowed dance moves from Moroccan belly dancers—raising questions about cultural appropriation.

Inga was all about the business. It was a more thorough introduction than I had expected, but it made me feel grounded. I've always been an activist. Stripping for stripping's sake felt overwhelming, but joining a legacy of woman who danced in ownership of their own bodies seemed like an accessible way for me to rationalize trying something new.

For homework, we had to create our stage personas. This part was easy. I named my alter ego years ago. I even wrote a children's book about her called Coco La Swish: A Fish from a Different Rainbow. Coco is a vibrant and vivacious fish who overcomes the jeering of hater fish to be her fabulous self. But how to take Coco and turn her into Cocoa?

More than just a name, I had to build my character's backstory. Where was she from? What was her favorite drink? Her crush? Her favorite pick-up line? I decided Cocoa would be like Grace Jones combined with Godzilla and rolled in glitter—fierce and unapologetically bold.

When we met for our second class, my classmates and I re- introduced ourselves by our invented personas. The others had names like Scarlett Herrington, Muffy Thyme, and Ivy Thorny. There was Lana del Spray, creator of messes, Crystal D'Cummings, who arrived in the world on a magical flying unicorn to be a sex and life coach, and Kat Trick, a submissive, perennially heartbroken, small- town waitress whose super power was stripping.

Cleopatra of the South (who in real life is a civil war re-enactor from Alabama) based her character on Isabella "Belle" Maria Boyd a confederate spy from West Virginia. Perry Von Winkle, a gender fluid immortal, was born to a family of witches and raised like Samantha from *Bewitched*.

My mind pinwheeled out into questions: What is sexy and why? Who gets to decide? We like what we like and we know it when we see it, but how much of this is personal preference and how much is determined by cultural norms?

Becoming Cocoa was an invitation to enter a world of fantasy and play, and I was excited to try it out. I went home and narrowed down my song choices and began plotting my act. But reality kept interrupting my fantasy life. When I looked in the mirror, I didn't see Cocoa, I only saw myself and the various intersecting identities that didn't match up with any image I'd ever seen of a burlesque dancer.

Growing up, I learned early on that being black and beautiful meant being thin, having light skin and hair that hung straight and long with no kinks. Basically, the standard of beauty was being the whitest version of black, with occasional exceptions for those coal-black African models who were bone-thin and "exotic."

I'm none of the above. I'm thick and tall with brown skin and an afro. It took me a long time to get over all the teasing I got as a kid and to embrace myself as beautiful. I had to work hard to undo all the negative programming.

Being big, black, and beautiful in this society is an act of courage, but I didn't want it to be. I wanted, for once, to experience the privilege of assumed beauty, to feel sexy and confident without it being a political statement. Maybe that might have felt more attainable in a situation with different demographics, but as I visualized our recital, I felt like the token. Could I really do this? Did I even want to?

Waxie Moon, a brilliant boylesque performer, was our guest instructor for week three, the bump-and-grind week. It felt good to be on my feet and out of my head. We learned the art of the shimmy, and strutting in heels with and against the beat. Then we practiced teasingly removing our gloves.

Teasing is an art—what you show and what you don't and how you invite an audience to get invested in what you're willing to give. While I still hadn't decided what I was willing to give, Waxie gave me some perspective. In sweatpants and heels with sculpted facial hair, he reminded me that outside-the-box could be a positive.

The evening culminated with each of us performing a sexy walk to a chair where we did three poses, a glove tease with a "deny" (that classic give-you-a-little-skin-then-take-it-back) and then the dance move of our choice. We wolf-whistled and cat-called as one by one we showed off our moves, and I realized I was actually having fun.

Then came week four. Inga says that everyone freaks out in week four. I freaked out. Even though I'd been keeping up on my homework and attending private lessons in addition to the regular classes, I still didn't feel ready.

It occurred to me that this wasn't some theoretical performance anymore. In two weeks I was going to go on stage and take my clothes off. Strangers were going to see and judge my body. Friends were going to see and judge my body. I was going to trip on my stripper heels, my boobs were going to come flying out of my gold beaded butterfly breast plate, my ass was going to explode out of my sequined hot pants, and I was going to literally die of embarrassment.

Inga assured me that I didn't have to get totally naked. I could strip to pasties or even to a flesh-colored bathing suit if that's what felt comfortable. Nothing about this experience was comfortable. I wanted to scream.

Over the weekend, I got sick, so I missed the optional tassel-twirling class, where all of my classmates took their tops off and became titty sisters. They were all BFFs afterwards, and though Lana del Spray invited me to come to class early to catch up on my boa work, I felt a little left out.

After the optional bump-and-grind class, Kat Trick, Cleopatra of the South, Muffy Thyme and I went on a costume shopping excursion. We had lunch first and it was nice to get to know them. Kat is a realtor. Cleo is the mother of 9 children, grandmother of 15, and has been doing burlesque back home in Alabama for a couple of years.

She's only here for a few months before she returns to the South. Muffy is a biologist and has been learning how to be an aerialist.

Though we all came from different walks of life and probably wouldn't have met any other way, the class created our common ground. "We're all nervous too," Kat told me when I confessed that I was panicking. Just like everyone had their reason for being in the class, they also had their challenges too, and there was something comforting about knowing I wasn't alone.

My heart raced as I made my grand entrance. Everyone was staring at me. I knew they would be, because that is what audiences do, (and what I had just done to six of my classmates) but I didn't realize it would be so awkward.

I'd spent an afternoon painting and gluing glitter on reeds for my backdrop, but the costume still hadn't come together. I wore black peep-toe heels, fishnets and a gold beaded backless halter shaped like a butterfly. A friend used her seam ripper to pop the hoop out of my rainbow fish windsock. Using safety pins and a length of fabric, I rigged up a tail.

On top, I wanted to wear something elegant, a two-piece ball gown with full-length, black satin gloves. I'd found a beautiful wine-colored gown with a poofy skirt layered with lace, but it was still all in one piece, so I rolled down the ill-fitted bodice and wore a T-shirt. I felt disheveled and mismatched.

When the baseline hit, I rolled my body, giving life to my shimmy, but my tail snagged the back of my fishnets and my skirt kept slipping off my waist and got tangled under my heels. I tried to keep smiling, but I could see all the faces in the audience and it was freaking me out.

I took my skirt off and crawled on the floor, then stepped on my tail trying to get up. When I ripped my top off all I could think was, everyone is looking at my stretch marks. This was a new level of vulnerability, and I didn't like it.

Winded and sweaty, I managed to sit politely through the remaining acts. Everyone seemed so much more together than I felt. Their costumes were complete, and their acts were sexy and hilarious. I kept trying not to compare myself, but when I went home, I sobbed. My performance was going to suck. After a month of working on it, I felt invested—I wanted to get on stage and kill it as Cocoa, but it felt impossible.

Two days later, I had my private lesson with Inga. I didn't talk about my full-on meltdown. I admitted to not loving my run-through and Inga assured me it was great. We went over my floor work and she made me run through the routine again, making "Bugs Bunny porno faces." It is impossible to mope and make stupid faces at the same time.

I came up with a new mantra: I'll only be on stage for 3 minutes. I'm not going to die.

Then it was time for our second dress rehearsal. First up was Cleo, dressed as Maleficent and stripping to a love letter from Walt Disney. Her act had a classic feel to it and was sultry, funny and ended in tassel twirling. Then came Kat Trick, decked head-to-toe in Seahawks swag, attempting to get the attention of a man glued to the TV. Icy London played a '50s housewife sick of cleaning. She had even bedazzled her broom. She went from Donna Reed to dominatrix.

Lana del Spray's act took place in a kiddie pool, so we went outside. The burlesque studio shares a parking lot with a plumbing company, so one confused and embarrassed plumber caught the gaggle of us cheerleading Lana in various states of dress. Though it was freezing, Lana performed like a pro. Her act involved stripping out of rain gear. (Just a year ago she was engaged and living in a yurt on a pot farm. She gave all of that up to start a new life in a new city.)

She was supposed to end in a merkin and pasties with tassles, but I think the pasties came off in the kiddie pool. She kept twirling anyway.

We went back inside and Ivy Thorny played a naughty nurse resurrecting a dying patient with the power of her pussy. Then it was my turn.

Somehow, between contributions from four friends and several trips to thrift stores and fabric shops, I'd pieced together a workable costume. With my costume complete, steps and faces refined, I got through my routine— and it didn't suck.

Muffy Thyme performed after me. She was a gender-bending rodeo cowboy/girl who stripped to the country version of "99 Problems and a Bitch Ain't One," while knife-throwing and dancing a two-step. The big finale was Perry Von Winkle, pizza stripper extraordinaire.

Perry, a bank teller by day, pranced around light-footed in denim and red dance pumps with a pizza box before stripping to a pepperoni pizza leotard studded in rhinestones and trimmed with glittery cheesy fringe.

Maybe, just maybe, we were going to pull this off.

The day of the recital, even arriving four hours early, I felt rushed. I was up late the night before spray-painting my tailored prom skirt with blue and green glitter, and then sewing, pinning and tying it with green and gold ribbons. My fish tail was fluffed, my headdress was pinned and re-pinned.

Muffy tied me into my gold beaded butterfly bikini while Perry applied my fake lashes.

Somehow, even without having much time to get to know each other, we had become a community. When Lana handed me a brush and asked if I would glitter her butt, I didn't hesitate. We zipped, tucked, snapped and strapped one another into our respective costumes, wolf whistled for each other during our dry runs, and kept each other in chocolate and bobby pins.

And then there I was, standing in the dark, listening to Indigo Blue introduce me. It was a reckoning, those final jittery moments. But in the midst of all that painting, sewing, music mapping, rehearsing and wrestling with my insecurities, I'd made a space in my life for whimsy and magic. And most importantly, I'd made a commitment to not be half-assed.

Spotlight on me, I shed my gloves, then touched my bare arms and shimmied from one side of the stage to the other. I turned around and began my skirt tease with a grin. When I dropped my skirt to reveal gold hot pants and my shiny rainbow fish tail, the audience erupted in laughter and applause. I tossed my skirt to the side, crawled center stage, struck a sexy pose, then belly-flopped and made fishy faces while I kicked my heels and swam.

I got up and darted back behind the screens of reeds for one last tease. I dangled my top on one finger before tossing it aside. Then I emerged with my worm boa, in my gold beaded butterfly breastplate, to strike my triumphant final pose. For one moment, I stood confidently in my own skin. The crowd went wild.

In that moment, as the audience cheered, I realized how much I needed this experience. I realized that I'd needed to heal the parts of me that had internalized what media, kids at school, former lovers and even my parents have said about my body. I realized that I could choose to love and approve of myself exactly as I am—at this weight, this height, this physical incarnation. I didn't have to be Cocoa to shower myself in glitter and ribbons and to feel sexy, strong and confident.

Burlesque may not have felt like a calling at first, but I'd been called—and despite all my hesitations, I'd answered. And I'd found a community of really cool people who held space for me to do what turned out to be some pretty deep personal work. Through the process of shedding my clothes, I opened myself up to shedding my fears, insecurities and self-imposed limitations.

I don't know if I'll ever do it again, but I take with me the pride of knowing I was brave enough to try.

$25 Foot Massage

We don't really talk much beyond discerning if I want the regular foot massage or the combo, which is $5 more and includes rolling over onto my stomach for a proper back massage. He disappears into the back and returns with a plastic bag filled with steamy water in a wooden bucket. I roll my jeans up and stick my feet inside and lean back on the burgundy recliner. It's not like the white places where you get naked beneath soft sheets in a private room that smells like lavender while listening to Peruvian pan flutes. The foot massage place is Chinese owned with a bamboo plant by the cash register and posters of anatomical acupressure mannequins hanging from the wall. They are open late. There are six recliners all in one room and as many massages and there are people. $25 pays for an hour long foot massage.

Sometimes there is Chinese music which is on too loud, sometimes there is a strange fusion of old 80s songs remade into muzak done on mandolins. Globalized Bryan Adams medleys that are as strange as they are distracting. If I'm lucky, there is silence. If I'm unlucky, one of the ladies isn't giving a massage but instead watching Chinese soaps on her phone or talking really loudly. For $25 I can't justify being irritated by a lack of ambience.

Sometimes I just need to be touched in a way that isn't taking from me. Not passion, not comfort, not negotiation, not absolution. And sometimes I'm just tired as fuck and need to be in my body and remember I am a human being.

I remember the first time I went three months without a single person touching me. It was in Japan. I arrived in summer and it was so hot I barely wanted to touch myself beyond cool showers and damp face clothes. I learned the words for weather first. Atsue ne. Hot ain't it? Hot ain't it? Hot ain't it? The common greeting. As though the sweat pooling at the base of my spine before 9am needed a catch phrase. I was in the process of learning many things. How to use chopsticks, how to calculate yen to dollars and dollars to yen, how to use a squat toilet without pissing on my shoes, and how to bow.

There were degrees. Deeper for Kocho sensei than regular sensei. Shallower for my own students to whom I was sensei. Angles and respect. No handshakes unless someone else initiated them. No handshakes, no hugs, no high fives, no pat on the back. There was no casual touch except perhaps on the subway where the white gloved pushers would shove everyone in, but that was more of a city thing. The trains in Kaibara were never so crowded and even when they were, I wore my blackness around me like a bubble everyone seemed afraid to burst. I became an untouchable. Touch with eyes. Fingers pointed. "Kakoi," came the hushed whispers, strangely misgendering me with the coolness that belonged to Michael Jackson and Smap. I became outside person, black person, small face, big body, stylish, American teacher, untouchably outside of language, of custom, of family, of home, caged in the hyper visibility of my too tall, too fat, always hungry, sweaty body.

Over the next two years, I would take on a series of inappropriate lovers: The Jamaican, The Brit, The Srilankan. I would fall in love with long nights of salsa in a new and suddenly necessary way surrounded by Peruvian and Columbian expats who weren't hesitant to touch my hand, to slide a hand to my waist and twirl me. And I would begin my relationship with massage.

In Japan, even people paid to massage you don't ever really touch you. Swate kudasai. Sit in the chair. Fully clothed on a chair. They would drape me with a blanket or towel and rub until my skin began to vibrate. It was more like being played like a drum than being touched, and yet it was better than the void of never being touched at all. I could close my eyes and not answer any questions or field any stares for a set amount of time. This was worth every yen.

I let a stranger plunge his hands into my fro and rub my scalp, my neck then down each arms to my hands. He unfurls my fingers that rest naturally in a half clenched fist. My body betrays these truths about me, what I'm holding onto and what is trapped within the space between my shoulder blades. Sometimes it hurts. Sometimes it's simply a relief. The language barrier is a gift. No one is expecting me to understand anything and I can give up any pretense of trying.

He pulls my feet from the bucket, towel dries them to rubs them with oil before towel drying them a second time. I usually get the same guy, older and a bit paunchy with a graying comb-over and soft hands. Sometimes I wonder what his name is and if the other people working in the room are related to him. It has the feel of a family owned business. I wonder how many massages he gives in one day and whether he is judging the size and shape of my body. Sometimes, I see the other women looking at my hair like they want to touch it.

But they don't. They are the lone Chinese business in the Vietnamese Plaza in what some consider a black neighborhood. They've seen this hair before. But for $25, I am only touched by the person I pay. The massage is solid. He doesn't know my name either. Strange that an hour of anonymity would be what I need to remember my humanity.

The Detoxing of Sugar Woman

Growing up my parents told me that I was beautiful. But there is a gap between what we are told with words and the truth we live. I grew up in Madison, Wisconsin and lived in a predominantly white community where beauty looked like Britney Spears. Nowhere in that image did I see myself, a thick, awkward black girl with braces and uncooperative hair. I learned to experience my body as unacceptable, too black in a white world, too white in a black world, too tall, too thick, dressed in nerdy mom jeans. There were some things about my appearance that will never change, but as a teenager and through my 20s I applied myself with discipline to the seemingly solvable problems of my hair, clothing, and weight.

My mother was the queen of the weight watchers cookbook. We drank skim milk and ate wheat bread. We had one egg quiche and cabbage soup. All of our food had points. I never knew what we were counting exactly, only that it was a numbers game and we were losing.

Mom attended meetings where there were weigh ins and workbooks, food logs, and accountability couches. We had a scale in the bathroom and one on the kitchen counter to measure food and to measure the results of eating that food. I didn't have to go to the meetings, but since she did the cooking I was a participant whether I liked it or not.

Of course there were cheat days, holidays like Christmas where decadence was mandatory. Grandma's homemade fudge filled the cookie jar, there were fat slabs of rum cake and the freezer was stocked with peppermint ice cream.

But most of the time it was rules, regulations, and restrictions. My mother did so much step aerobics she ended up needing a knee replacement. She treated her body like a cautionary tale. I'm sure she never said the words aloud, but after years of living with her through her perpetual diets the message was clear: don't get fat. I learned that how much you weighed was a question that had a right answer. For most of my life my answer has been wrong.

It is difficult to hold yourself with both love and loathing. There came a time of rebellion, a time of embracing my cravings, from rocking glitter boots and miniskirts, to shaving off the chemically straightened hair that hung down my back to grow an afro. My deepest desire was to stand unapologetically in my own skin, to accept myself and be accepted. And while I was at it, to hell with diets. To hell with eating cereal for breakfast when I really just wanted a brownie sundae. Yet in my pursuit of authenticity, perhaps one of the most healthy impulses I've ever had, I found myself ensnared by an unexpected addiction. Sugar.

I don't smoke or do drugs. I used to drink socially, but I don't even do that anymore. I say this because I don't think of myself as a person highly susceptible to addiction and yet my relationship to refined sugar evolved into something akin to the NRA's relationship to guns. Live free or die, consequences and reasonable constraints be damned. Sugar had become more than a mid afternoon pick me up, but an inalienable right to comfort, a reward for hard work, and a consolation for life's many heartbreaks.

Last October, I was given the opportunity to go to Washington D.C. for National Crittenton's first annual conference called In Solidarity We Rise: Healing, Opportunities, and Justice for Girls. I went for work. As part of a girl serving organization we have been really working through how to be inclusive of gender non-binary and trans youth, so I went to be in community with others doing this work and to find out some best practices. That is not at all what I got out of the conference or the trip.

The conference began with a beautiful ceremony performed by Native elders from around the country. I met a woman named Dorene Day. She is a Medawyn, a water woman from the Anishnabe Ojibwe tribe in Minnesota. She prays for the water everyday of her life. She gave a workshop about being a water woman and started talking about the origin story of her tribe and their indigenous traditions and I found myself in tears.

I cried for the earth, for the water, for the incredible disservice we are doing to the future generations, but mostly I cried for the loss of my own cultural traditions. Yes, slavery is over. White people remind me of this all the time. I am supposed to be over it too. There are many people from all sorts of backgrounds who for whatever reason have come to America and lost ties with their ancestry and been melted into whatever social identity is ascribed to them. But as a black American who can trace back my ancestry on both sides into slavery and no further, there is a hole, a missing piece. Now in this age of information I could probably do some DNA test and approximate where my people came from, but even if I were to find out and move there, I will forever be separated from that cultural heritage by the history of the diaspora and my own Americaness.

As she talked about her origin story, the story of her people, the unbroken lineage, the way she learned to pray that has been passed down for generations, I felt the strength of her resilience and also the deep well of unaddressed grief I hold within myself. Let me be clear, I do not envy the trauma that First Nations people have endured through the genocide that has and continues to decimate their population. And I don't fall into the trap of comparative oppressions and needing to measure or decide who has had it worse. America has fucked us all over. But my time with Dorene pinpointed something I've been unable to articulate. Wrapped up in that missing piece of me is the ancestral knowledge of how to heal myself, a cultural definition of what whole even feels like.

Dorene was kind to me. She gave me a big hug and told me about the African women she met. How they too were indigenous and had their own traditions. She recounted the story of performing a water ceremony with them. "We wore our jingle dresses and carried our copper bowls," she told me, "And the black women wore white and carried glass bowls." It isn't too late she assured me. I could find my own way.

Later that day I visited the African American Museum. Music, sports, innovation, the black Greeks, the history of the slave trade. Pictures, short films, letters, artifacts. The museum was incredibly rich. As I wandered through each floor, I found myself in a huge exhibit about the slave trade. When I think of slavery I tend to think about picking cotton, but there, in black and white, was the triangle between the east coast, Cuba and Ghana, where sugar beget shackles. What is it Faulkner says: "The past is never dead. It's not even past." Slavery may have ended, yet I was personally enslaved to the very substance that was the foundation of the capitalist underpinnings of the system that stole my ancestors. It was a strange moment of intolerable truth.

I don't remember what I dreamt that night, which is often the case when my spirit guides come to me. I just remember waking up with more energy and more clarity than I've had in a long time. I got the message. It was time to fast. It was time to pray and meditate regardless of whether I knew the right words or rituals. I felt an urgency. It was time to once and for all release my addiction to sugar and make friends with my body.

My fast began just before Halloween, which is literally the stupidest time ever to not eat sugar. My neighbors came by and dropped off homemade pan de muerto and the office was filled with bags and bags of Snickers, Twix, and my personal heroine Reese's peanut butter cups. It didn't bother me. Then someone donated 15 boxes of pizza for a meeting. This bothered me a lot. But I ate kale salad and it was delicious.

The first two weeks were the most challenging. I decided that in addition to breaking my addiction to refined sugar, I would detox from refined flours as well. No alcohol and limited meat (mostly fish) and dairy. I began with a four day fast intentionally to reset my palate. I entered into a conversation with my body. What do I need? What feels good? What doesn't? What is healthy? What is realistic? And everyday I continue to learn new answers.

Detoxing hasn't been the hell I thought it would be. Cheese helps. I do still dream about warm bread slathered in melted butter. I wake feeling vaguely guilty, but it's easy to avoid the obvious shit. I don't eat cake or ice cream or caramel. But to truly escape refined sugar is complicated. I have to read the labels on everything.

I have all these new questions. Why does relish have high fructose corn syrup? Can I make bread from ground almonds, eggs and honey? What tastes like chicken but isn't tofu? Why doesn't tofu taste like anything? Are lentils and nuts providing enough protein? How many deviled eggs can I eat before I start to feel sick?

These questions seem silly in the context of our political landscape. We are a sneeze away from being at war with North Korea. DACA and healthcare are being attacked. Black people continue to die in unwarranted police shootings with no semblance of justice or accountability. It snowed before Halloween in Seattle, so in case anyone had any lingering doubts, climate change is real. The DAPL leaked oil and did contaminate indigenous waters, like they said it would, and not a single major news outlet is covering the story. In short the world is going to hell in a hand basket and I'm at the PCC reading the label on a package of seaweed about to spend $6 for 5 ounces of organic pesto to eat with my quinoa noodles.

After two months of no sugar, unsurprisingly, I lost some weight, my skin is clear and I am obsessed with macadamia nuts and avocado oil potato chips (snacking has to happen). The big surprise has been how food has impacted my emotional landscape. For one thing my PMS has vanished. That two- three days a month where I literally become a crazy person with intense depression or homicidal anger just didn't happen. This is a problem I never had before my 30s. I sought medical help, even consulted a naturopath and not one person ever mentioned that there might be a correlation between sugar and hormones.

Maybe I shouldn't be surprised by the failings of a system that has been failing me all my life. Just recently I went to visit the doctor with a case a strep throat. I was miserable, congested, feverish and with a throat that felt like I'd been gargling with broken glass. Having been a sickly kid, I've had strep throat no less than a dozen times and knew that this was my problem.

The nurse practitioner who attended me did the thing that all doctors do. She asked me to hop on the scale. Then she gave me a 20 minute lecture on diabetes and vitamin D. I finally cut her off to ask for the prescription for antibiotics to address the strep I did have and not the diabetes I don't have. In the end I tested negative for type A strep, so I left with no medication and had to return to see a different doctor 3 days later. The same thing happening. This doctor gave a shorter lecture, did confirm that I had strep, but refused to give me the antibiotics saying that this strain would just go away on its own. In short I spent $250 to be fat shamed and to heal myself with homeopathic, over-the-counter remedies.

Being fat has always been a source of discomfort and embarrassment, not usually because I feel any physical discomfort. I've always been active and flexible. Being fat is uncomfortable because people are assholes. I had a black nurse put me on the scale at the doctor's office once. She looked at me and then at the number. We were both surprised to see I'd hit obese on the BMI index. I didn't feel obese. I also didn't have any of the health issues that accompany such a diagnoses.

"Don't worry," she'd said with a conspiratorial wink. "We're always a little extra."

That nurse was the only medical professional in the history of me going to the doctor to ever say that, to suggest maybe that since by every other metric I was healthy that the number on a scale might not be the only determining factor of my over all health.

My mom, my aunt, my grandma, my great grandma. We are all "a little extra". Big boned or thick, healthy as they call it in the south. At the time it didn't occur to me to question the metrics. Who makes the BMI? Who gets to decide what is allowable or proportionate? Was I "a little extra" or was that actually where my body was supposed to be? At the time I thought of my body as a problem to fix. Run longer, sweat harder, skip dessert, weigh in till I get it right. Spoiler alert: I will never get it right.

So what does it mean when the people who are paid to heal me are also missing that crucial link. The word health takes it's root from the concept of restoring oneself into wholeness. I live in a country where our history is being legally deemed 3/5 human. There is no legacy of wholeness here for me. Beyond redemption from sugar, beyond liberation from foods that are harming me, this process has summoned me to begin a healing that has nothing to do with numbers on a scale. But there is no blueprint for what I want to build, no map to where I want to go.

Something else I've had to come to the terms with through this process is the fact that sugar, like alcohol, has been a tool I've used to take the edge off. In a shitty mood? Have a cookie. When there is no cookie and no rum and coke, no big gooey plate of gluten-y mac and cheese, the shitty mood is what remains, and worse having to address the root cause of said shitty mood. With no buffers, and no substances anesthetizing me, I have had to confront the truth that I am intensely emotional. Or more to the point that there is a lot that happens in my life to elicit intensely emotional responses.

I think a lot about the wall that has surrounded me and the haze of bad habits I have built, not out of any attempt to neglect or mistreat my body, but rather out of self defense. In the fullness of clarity I am angry. I am hurt. I live in a country where my mind, spirit and body are continuously assaulted. And often there is no recourse. I never thought of sugar as a silencing agent, but when your mouth is full it muffles the scream. Now the strategies I have crafted to defend myself no longer serve me. It is time to return to health. And this is the beginning.

Reader's Guide *to* STILL TRUE

When my publisher asked me what my goals are for this book my immediate answer was for people to read it! I mean that's what every author wants right? But what I realize is that I don't just want this to be a book that is read passively then left to sit alone on a coffee table. I want my readers to get involved. I want you take what you're reading and think deeply about it. Have a conversation with your neighbor, your mom, your rabbi, your best friend, that guy at the coffee shop... whoever.

I love the idea that somewhere a group of you are gathered over a charcuterie board with a nice bottle of shiraz about to have a fist fight because of something I wrote. Feel free to disagree with me and each other. Feel free to fervently agree with me. Feel free to debate the issues I bring up without even referencing my opinions or thoughts about it at all. Tell your story. Talk about your community. Talk about your beliefs. Laugh with each other. Cry. Be vulnerable and honest. Say things you never thought you would say. Wake up the next day as hung over from your vulnerability as from that cheap wine your neighbor brought.

Then pick another book and keep going. Make a thing out of it. Create a community and then a movement. Bad and bougie book clubs for life. Get a tattoo... okay maybe not, but I would LOVE it if you want take sometime to really have the conversations this book is begging you to have. Here are some starter questions to help you on your journey. Thank you.

R.E.J.J

A book club guide for the curious, and for potential journalists and storytellers

Though this a book of articles and essays it begins with a memoir piece of the author becoming an unexpected journalist. What came up for you as you read this introduction?

What stories are told about your community? By whom?

Do you trust these stories? Do you trust these storytellers? Why or Why not?

Have you ever been tasked with telling your story, the story of your family or a story from your community? What choices did you make and why?

What are your ethics for story telling?

When do you feel comfortable telling a story and when do you not?

The Hood

Where do you live and why?

What are some of the factors that contribute to where you live and are they all in your control?

Has gentrification impacted your life or your community? In what ways?

Has gun violence impacted your life or your community? In what ways?

What is your relationship to safety?

What helps you feel connected to the people in your community?

Are there rituals or activities that you share with your community? Describe them.

If you could tell a story of your neighborhood what would it be?

Now that marijuana is legal in many states what impacts have you seen (if any) on your community?

Which piece in this section resonated the most for you and why?

Were there parts that challenged you?

The Struggle

What is your proximity to the Black Lives Matter movement? Has this evolved over time?

Have you grieved for and/or with Black people over Black deaths? What is your relationship to Black grief. Describe your experience(s).

If you are Black, how do you experience or express Black joy? If you are not Black how do you contribute to (or detract from) Black joy?

If you could make a wish for all the Black folks in your life, what would it be?

In the piece We Fight Back, Jackson talks about the prevalence of gender-based violence, toxic masculinity and rape culture. How have you been impacted by these issues?

What is your opinion of reparations?

What is your opinion of the reparations project described in Reparations ReImagined: Can online giving counteract systemic oppression?

If you lived in Seattle during the pandemic and experienced the CHOP what was your experience? If you didn't have first-hand experience, did you see CHOP on the news-how did you perceive it and did that differ from the account in Jackson's article?

What struggles are you currently noticing in your community and how are people navigating them?

What is your relationship to power, privilege, and allyship? Does this change based on different circumstances in your life?

Which piece in this section resonated the most for you and why?

Were there parts that challenged you?

The World

What role has travel played in your life?

How would define global citizenship? What roles/responsibilities does it entail?

Which piece in this section resonated the most for you and why?

Were there parts that challenged you?

The People

Name the three most influential people in your life. Who are they and why are they important to you?

If you could have a dinner party with 5 people living or dead who would they be and why? What would you serve? What would be the vibe of the party?

Which person's story did you resonate the most with and why?

Which person's story did you resonate the least with and why?

What did you learn from the stories the author shared about these people?

Where there questions you wished she had asked?

The Body

Describe your relationship to your body.

What did you learn about your body growing up—from your family, from friends at school, from the media you consumed—and how has the impacted your life?

What is your relationship to addiction?

What is your sexual orientation and how has it impacted your life? Do you have a coming out story?

Which of your social identities are most visible/obvious? Which are hidden? How has this impacted your life?

Which piece in this section resonated the most for you and why?

Were there parts that challenged you?

Still True Overall

What did you think about this book?

Which section was most resonant?

Were there parts that were difficult to read?

What did you learn about the author?

What did you learn about yourself?

Is there any subject you wished she had addressed?

Would you recommend this book to others? If so who and why?

REAGAN JACKSON is a multi genre writer, artist, facilitator, and fourth generation Black feminist. Her passions include international travel, cooking, reading, taking long walks, and creating communities of belonging for teenagers. She also hosts and produces a podcast called The Deep End Friends. Seattle is her home. You can find out more about her at www.reaganjackson.com.

Publication History

Seattle Globalist = SG; South Seattle Emerald = SSE; Crosscut = CC

Who's Afraid of Rainier Beach (SG, July 3, 2014) ✳ *Seattle Freeze Thawing in Rainier Beach* (SG, March 11, 2014) ✳ *Brad and Becky Are Coming to Rainier Beach* (SSE, December 27, 2017) ✳ *The Displacement Tax: An Update from Gentrification Ground Zero* (SSE, November 26, 2018) ✳ *What's Not to Like About Uncle Ike's* (SG, April 20, 2016) ✳ *Rainier Beach — A Beautiful, Safe Place to Live?* (SSE January 29, 2022) ✳ *Vitriol Against People of Color Yoga Shows Exactly Why It's Necessary* (SG, October 15, 2015) ✳ *Who Can We Call?* (original) ✳ *Black History Month: The Same Old Song and Dance?* (SG, February 26, 2014) ✳ *Do Black Lives Matter in Seattle as Much as Tacos Do?* (SG, May 8, 2015) ✳ *#blacklivesmatter at a Crossroads* (SG, December 26, 2014) ✳ *The Necessity of Black Joy* (SG, July 18, 2017) ✳ *Accomplices vs. Allies* (SSE, July 6, 2016) ✳ *Reparations ReImagined: Can Online Giving Counter Systemic Racism* (SG, July 20, 2016) ✳ *The Scariest Thing About Get Out is Black Trauma* (SSE, March 4, 2017) ✳ *On Fear and Anger and Fighting Back* (SSE, November 30, 2016) ✳ *Calling Out (and Calling In) White Media* (SG, September 22, 2016) ✳ *The Tea on Our Juneteenth Black Out and the Necessity of Black Healing Spaces* (original) ✳ *A Long-Awaited Cotillion* (original) ✳ *Why I Started a Study Abroad Program for People of Color* (SG, October 27, 2014) ✳ *Soup or Salad: Afro American Cultural Erasure in the US and Mexico* (SG, August 22, 2014) ✳ *Soccer Fields and Chainstores: Weighing U.S.Influence in Honduras* (SG, September 15, 2015) ✳ *Why Isn't The World Talking About The Scandal in Honduras?* (SG, September 19, 2015) ✳ *Global Travel Shapes Diversity in Higher Ed* (SG, April 9, 2019) ✳ *Breaking Up with America: Black Expats Talk About Life in Costa Rica* (original) ✳ *31 Days of Revolutionary Women, #19 Stanlie James* (SSE, March 19, 2016) ✳ *Howie Echo-Hawk Confronts Native Genocide Through Comedy* (SG, February 27, 2018) ✳ *Michelle Obama Ain't the Only Fantastic Woman of Color* (CC, December 13, 2016) ✳ *Please Touch The Art: New Exhibit Invites More Than Just Looking* (SG, January 23, 2015) ✳ Maru Mora-Villalpando In Her Own Words (SG, October 22, 2018) ✳ *Human Rights Activist Noami Tutu Finds Hope in Restorative Justice, Reparations* (SG, April 17, 2018) ✳ *Jessamyn Stanley On Being Fat, Black, and Yoga Teacher* (SG, April 20, 2017) ✳ *Moni Tep Explores Hardship of Queer Youth in Jamaica* (SG, January 19, 2016) ✳ *Pussy Riot Speaks: Russian Punk Protest Artists in Seattle For Talk, Film* (SG, February 3, 2016) ✳ *"Choosing Life" Cancer Support Group Founder Continues to Enlighten, Educate While Battling Disease* (SSE, March 26, 2018) ✳ *Interview With a Death Doula* (original) ✳ *A Conversation With Adana Protonentis* (original) ✳ *Beyoncé, Barbie, and "Posing Beauty" at the NAAM* (SG, May 10, 2016) ✳ *The Making of a Burlesque Dancer* (CC, December 29, 2016) ✳ *$25 Foot Massage* (original) ✳ *The Detoxing of Sugar Woman* (original)

Hinton

Future Hinton publications

Three Alarm Fire & Other Stories
by Juan Carlos Reyes

The Goode Within: essays
by Sean Goode

A String of Apologies: essays
by Danielle Marie Holland

Printed in the USA
CPSIA information can be obtained
at www.ICGtesting.com
JSHW082230110424
61038JS00002B/22